"Yellow Kid" Weil.

# THE CON GAME
## AND
# "YELLOW KID" WEIL

The Autobiography of the
Famous Con Artist
*as told to*
## W. T. BRANNON

*Dover Publications, Inc., New York*

Copyright © 1948 by W. T. Brannon.
All rights reserved under Pan American and International Copyright Conventions.

Published in Canada by General Publishing Company, Ltd., 30 Lesmill Road, Don Mills, Toronto, Ontario.
Published in the United Kingdom by Constable and Company, Ltd., 10 Orange Street, London WC 2.

This Dover edition, first published in 1974, is an unabridged republication of the work first published in 1948 by Ziff-Davis Publishing Company, Chicago, under the title *"Yellow Kid" Weil: The Autobiography of America's Master Swindler."*

*International Standard Book Number: 0-486-23127-5*
*Library of Congress Catalog Card Number: 74-12575*

Manufactured in the United States of America
Dover Publications, Inc.
180 Varick Street
New York, N. Y. 10014

# FOREWORD

Long before I ever met the Yellow Kid, I had heard of him. His adventures fascinated me. I had a yen to know the inside story behind those fabulous tales I heard and read in the newspapers.

When I started to dig, I learned that the Kid had been a figure in criminal circles so long, that he had become a legend. Criminologists had devoted considerable space in their books to his exploits. But all this was third person stuff, based on a mixture of fact, rumor, and hearsay.

I determined to get acquainted with the Yellow Kid. But that was something of an undertaking. I trailed him all over Chicago before I finally found him. Not that he was trying to evade me. He's just an elusive sort of fellow. I can imagine how the police of two continents must have pulled their hair when they were trying to nab him during his heyday.

Far from finding the Kid a man of superficialities, I discovered that he has many real accomplishments. One of these is his uncanny knowledge of human nature. In this respect, he may be far ahead of some of our more celebrated psychologists. He can size up a man and accurately forecast his reactions to almost any given set of circumstances.

Another trait of the Kid's which rather surprised me was his knowledge of world affairs. Not only does he keep abreast of important happenings at home and abroad, he has very strong opinions about them. He is never indifferent about anything; he is either for it, or against it.

Some of his opinions have been interwoven into the story of his career. But in the main, this has been written to entertain and inform the reader. Many of his flim-flams are still being used to

## "Yellow Kid" Weil

fleece men with money. Anyone reading this book should be able to avoid these swindles.

I have tried to present Mr. Weil as he portrayed himself to me: a very colorful gent, including his often quaint verbiage. To have changed that to please the sticklers for proper grammar would have been to alter the Yellow Kid's unique personality.

I hope you'll enjoy reading of the Yellow Kid's exploits. *Don't* try to imitate them!

CHICAGO, ILLINOIS                                                                   W. T. BRANNON
*January 1, 1948*

# CONTENTS

PAGE

1. EARLY ADVENTURES IN CHICANERY............ 1
2. CHICANERY IN CHICAGO......................... 11
3. A TIP FOR MR. MACALLISTER..................... 20
4. HOW TO BEAT THE HORSES..................... 40
5. TWO UNWARY STRANGERS..................... 47
6. FROM NAGS TO RICHES......................... 59
7. GIVING AWAY REAL ESTATE.................... 73
8. THE GET-RICH-QUICK BANK..................... 86
9. RED LETTER DAYS............................... 95
10. MILLIONAIRES AND MURDER....................105
11. I TRIED TO GO STRAIGHT........................129
12. EASY MONEY ON RAINY DAYS..................141
13. A DEAL WITH FATHER FLANAGAN..............150
14. SOME CREDIT — AND LOTS OF CASH............154
15. THE MAN WITH A BEARD........................161
16. THE FARO BANK PAY-OFF.......................173
17. MEET ME IN ST. LOUIS..........................191
18. THE LAW CATCHES UP..........................208
19. MAGIC MONEY....................................211
20. THE HOTEL MARTINIQUE........................232
21. THE LEAVENWORTH COUNTRY CLUB...........236
22. THE COMTESSE AND THE KID..................240
23. THE CASE OF THE REFUGEE....................252
24. A PROPOSITION FOR A. HITLER.................265
25. TRICKS OF THE TRADE..........................269
26. THE LITTLE THINGS COUNT....................282
27. WHERE THE MONEY WENT......................289
28. THE LAST WORD.................................293

## 1. Early Adventures in Chicanery

I WAS BORN NEAR HARRISON AND CLARK STREETS IN CHICAGO, THE SON of Mr. and Mrs. Otto Weil, who were reputable, hard-working people. They ran a grocery store which brought them a modest sustenance. I was sent to the public school at Harrison Street and Third Avenue. I can, without boasting, say that I was a bright pupil. Proficient in all my studies, I was particularly good at mathematics.

After classes, I helped Mother in the store, though there were times when I sneaked off to the racecourse. Horse racing had a strong appeal for me, especially the betting. But my folks could not afford to give me money to bet on the races.

When I was seventeen, I "quit" school and went to work. For about two years I worked as a collector. The salary was not large — by no means enough to satisfy my wants. But I soon discovered that, by the use of my wits, I could earn more on the side than my regular salary.

There were other collectors, cashiers, and bookkeepers. If there was a scrupulous one in the lot, I don't recall him. Each was entrusted with the handling of money. The bookkeepers were supposed to record everything that the collectors brought in. I quickly discovered how much skulduggery went on.

The collectors were not turning in all they collected, the cashiers were holding back a little out of each collection, and the bookkeepers were not recording all that finally reached them. By various means, they managed to cover up their peculations.

I was just a young fellow, but I had a sharp eye and a quick wit. When I quietly made it known to my fellow employees that I was aware of their peccadillos, they became ready, without further urging, to contribute small sums so that I would keep their secrets. All told, these sums amounted to considerably more than I was ever paid in salary.

During this time, I met a beautiful girl. I called on her regularly and, before long, we were engaged to be married.

One day I took her to meet my folks. My mother looked her over and approved. She called me to one side.

"Joe," Mother whispered, "she is a beautiful girl. But she is a girl for a rich man. She should not be a poor man's wife."

"And I'm not going to be a poor man!" I replied. "I will give her everything she wants."

Having seen my parents struggle for their existence — my mother got up at five in the morning to open the store — I knew that such a life was not for me. Further, I had seen how much more money was being made by skulduggery than by honest toil.

In my travels about the city as a collector, I had run into a customer who interested me very much. At other times, I saw him at the racecourses and in the saloons.

Doc Meriwether always seemed to have an inexhaustible supply of money, a large part of which he spent at the race tracks. One day we got to talking over a glass of beer.

"Joe," he said, "you're a bright young fellow. How much do you make on that collecting job?"

"Not much," I admitted and told him the amount.

"It's not enough. How would you like to go to work for me?"

"I'd like to," I replied. "But what do you have that I can do?"

"Plenty," he declared. "And I'll pay you three times what you're making now."

He explained his proposition in detail. I didn't need much time to make a decision. At the end of the month, I left my job and went to work for Doc Meriwether.

Doc Meriwether was one of the most picturesque characters in the Middle West. He was tall, broad-shouldered, and gaunt. He wore a Van Dyke beard and pince-nez glasses. He usually dressed in black — black trousers and black frock coat with extra long tails. He wore

## Early Adventures In Chicanery

a flowing black cravat that covered half his shirt front.

Out on the far west side of Chicago, Doc Meriwether had a "plant" where he manufactured "Meriwether's Elixir,"—good for the ills of man or beast. Doc particularly urged it as a sure cure for tapeworm.

Meriwether's Elixir was put up in tall, thirty-two-ounce bottles. It was a dark liquid with a pleasant taste—Doc saw to that by putting in a little of the right flavoring. He left most of the bottling and manufacturing to his wife, a buxom, pleasant-faced, industrious woman. The Doc felt that he had done his share of the work when he made up the formula.

I don't remember the exact recipe now. But the chief ingredient was rain water, caught and strained in big cisterns in the back yard of Doc's combined home and factory. This rain water was drained off a barrel at a time, and into it Mrs. Meriwether mixed the other ingredients.

One of these was cascara, just the right amount in each thirty-two-ounce bottle to get results—plus alcohol. It was an evil-looking concoction, but pleasant enough to take, thanks to the alcohol and flavoring which Doc had thoughtfully included.

I cannot truthfully say whether anyone who took the Elixir ever got rid of a tapeworm or not. But many thought they did, for the cascara worked on everybody. As matter of fact, I doubt if very many people had tapeworm, though nearly all imagined they did.

For in that period we had a tapeworm fad. Everybody who was undernourished, anemic, or suffered from some form of malnutrition, was firmly convinced that a parasitic tapeworm was eating away his substance. Consequently, Doc Meriwether's Elixir was a pushover at a dollar a bottle.

Meriwether's Elixir was not on sale at drug stores, though a few grocers and general merchants carried it. Most of it was sold by the Doc himself, during the summer months when he toured the bucolic areas. Farmers and residents of the smaller towns were easily convinced that they harbored the tapeworm.

The Doc had a medicine show which appealed to men. In addition to Indians, he had a couple of girl dancers. He made it a point to park his big wagon at a spot where the males congregated. It was a man's world — in those days. Any crowd in a public place was likely to consist largely of men.

I acted in various capacities, depending on the locality. In some instances, I was a barker and helped to attract a crowd. At other times, I remained in the background and was the "shill," posing as a customer from another community.

As soon as Doc had entertained the crowd a while, he would go into his spiel. "Some of you men are healthy," he would say. "I can tell that by looking at you. But there are many of you who are not. Why? I think I would be quite safe in saying that a tapeworm is eating your life away. A sallow complexion, hollow cheeks, lean faces, wrinkled brows — these are all symptoms of the existence of a tapeworm.

"Are you men going to let a parasite eat away your body, your very life? Or do you intend to do something about it?" Here, he put up a hand as somebody started to speak. "I know what you're going to say. You've had the family doctor in. He's given you something for it, but it didn't work.

"Well, I've got something that will work. It's absolutely guaranteed to get results. Meriwether's Elixir is the product of years of research. It has been found to be an absolute cure, through elimination, of the worst tapeworm that ever preyed on a man's life."

He exhibited the bottle with the fancy label and the black liquid. If there was good response, Doc Meriwether kept up a constant, jovial flow of patter and took in the dollars. But if business was slow, that was my cue to step in.

"I'll take two bottles," I would say.

"Two bottles, sir? But one bottle is enough to rid you of tapeworm."

"It's not for me," I would say. "It's for my two children."

"Have you used this preparation before?"

"Indeed I have, Doctor. In fact, I owe my life to it."

"Would you mind telling us about it?" Doc would invite.

"Well, all right. A year ago, I was so run down and emaciated that I was not able to walk, let alone tend my farm. Doctors had done all they could for me, but my case had been given up as hopeless.

## Early Adventures In Chicanery

The mortgage on my farm was nearly due. I thought that I would lose everything and that my poor wife and children would go hungry." I would pause here to brush a sleeve across my eyes.

"Then I heard about Meriwether's Elixir. I bought a bottle of it. I didn't think it would do me much good, but everything was lost, anyhow. So I took it. Before I had finished the bottle, my tapeworm had been eliminated. I was able to walk again. I got my strength back. Soon I began to recover. I felt so much better that I was able to do twice as much work. My crops were extra good. The mortgage was paid off.

"And I owe it all to Meriwether's Elixir. I'm going to give it to my two kids. I'd buy it, even if it was five dollars a bottle."

"Sir," would be Doc Meriwether's tremulous reply, "you have stirred me deeply. You have made me feel that I have done something worth while for humanity. As a token of my regard, let me present you with two bottles — absolutely free."

This bit of play-acting usually brought the crowd around. They almost pushed each other over in their rush to hand in their dollars for the wonderful mixture.

This may sound unbelievable, due to the naïvete of the rural people of the nineties.

It is true that the medicine man and his traveling show have nearly disappeared from the American scene. But the same old fraud is still going on. In a new and fancier dress it's being promoted by medicine men with millions at their command. Their audience is nationwide and includes more city people than farmers. I refer to the patent-medicine radio shows.

In addition to the bottles, Doc Meriwether offered a "special" treatment at his suite for those who wanted to get rid of their tapeworms in a hurry and were willing to pay extra for it.

The success of the special treatment was mainly a matter of having the right stage setting and the props. The most important of the latter was a potato. This was peeled into one long coil which, for all I know, might look like a tapeworm. In an unbroken spiral it was deposited in a basin and water was poured over it. The basin was carefully hidden in a darkened room.

## "Yellow Kid" Weil

When the patient arrived, he was treated first in an outer room. Now the mixture was more potent: the chief ingredient was epsom salts. The patient was allowed to recline on a couch while the medicine took effect. Then he was led into the darkened room.

As soon as the dose had acted, he was led into the outer room. That was my cue. I fetched the previously prepared basin with the potato peel to the outer room, and handed it to Doc Meriwether.

"There my friend," Doc would say, displaying the basin, "is your tapeworm! Evil-looking thing, isn't it?"

Every victim of this hoax was deeply impressed. Not one ever questioned it. He paid the ten-dollar fee and left with the feeling that he had been vastly benefited. Maybe he had.

For he had had a good cleansing, in more ways than one!

During my travels with Doc Meriwether, I met an itinerant merchant. He appeared to be very prosperous. He told me he lived in Chicago. When I got back the following winter, I looked him up. Over a glass of beer, he related how he was able to make enough during his summer travels to support him the year round. He invited me to join him the following spring.

He was a traveling salesman who sold various items to farmers for small profits. But I had ideas of my own, though I did not tell my partner that. It was not my intention to labor among farmers for small profits. Before we left Chicago, I bought a sizable stock of the equipment we would need, in addition to the stock items my partner carried.

Once on the road, I told him my plans. He fell in with them. As soon as we reached the farming section we began to put them into practice.

Among the items my partner sold was a magazine — *Hearth and Home*, I believe. Catering exclusively to bucolic interests, it was a great favorite with rural folks and not difficult to sell. A year's subscription was twenty-five cents; the bargain rate was six years for a dollar. My partner was allowed to keep half of the money and was generally satisfied to sell one year's subscription at each farm.

"Let me do the talking," I proposed, "until you catch on to my scheme."

## Early Adventures In Chicanery

He was willing enough. Later, we pulled in at a farmhouse.

"How do you do, sir?" I said to the farmer who answered my knock on his door. "I am representing that unexcelled journal of rural life, *Hearth and Home*. I'm sure you're acquainted with it."

I produced a copy and offered it.

"That is the magazine for the womenfolks," he replied. "My wife might want it. How much is it?"

"Only twenty-five cents a year, sir."

"Wait till I call the missus."

By the time the farmer returned with his wife, I had my "clincher" out of my bag.

"Yes, I would like to have this for a year," the farmer's wife said. "Pa, give the young man a quarter."

"Madam," I said, "I have a special offer to make. For a limited time only, with a six-year subscription at the special rate of a dollar and a half, we are giving away, absolutely free, a set of this beautiful silverware."

I unwrapped my clincher. It was a box containing six bright and shining spoons. "These silver spoons, Madam," I continued, while she gasped in admiration, "are worth the price of the subscription alone. As you can see, they are the best sterling silver."

The woman's eyes shone as she took the spoons in her hand. "They certainly are beautiful," she said. Then a flicker of suspicion crossed her face. "But if they're real silver, they're worth more than you're asking without the magazine. How — "

"Quite true, Madam," I said quickly. "But the publishers wish to put this magazine into every farm home in America. That is the reason for this extraordinary introductory offer. Of course, they will lose money on the transaction, but it will be made up by your good will, which will bring more readers and more advertising."

"That's right, Ma," said the farmer. "Them papers make their money on advertising."

The sale was quickly completed and I took down the name and address of the lady, giving her a receipt for the subscription. I also gave her the half-dozen spoons.

But my business did not end there.

## "Yellow Kid" Weil

"Incidentally," I said, reaching into my pocket and withdrawing a pair of pince-nez glasses, "when we were coming down the road, my partner and I found these spectacles. Do you happen to know anybody in the community who wears glasses like these?"

"No, can't say that I do," the farmer replied, taking the glasses from me.

"Too bad," I said regretfully. "If I could find the owner, I would return them. They look like expensive eyeglasses. I imagine the person who lost them would pay three or four dollars reward for their return."

As I was talking, the farmer tried on the spectacles. He held up the sample copy of the magazine I had given him and the print stood out clearly. Probably he'd been intending to get a pair of glasses the next time he went to town. He looked at the rims, which appeared to be solid gold. They looked costly.

"Tell you what I'll do," he proposed. "I'll give you three dollars and keep the glasses. I'll look around for the owner, as long as you won't be able to make a complete search."

"That's right," I agreed. "I can't afford to go from house to house inquiring who lost a pair of glasses."

So I took the three dollars and he took the glasses. Of course, he had no intention of looking for the owner — any more than I did. As a matter of fact, he was just as anxious to have me on my way, as I was to go. In time, he would discover that the frames were cheap and that the lenses were no more than magnifying glass. If he took the trouble to ask, he would find that he could duplicate them in the city for twenty-five cents.

His good wife would soon learn that the beautiful silver spoons I had given her were cheap metal. I had bought them before leaving Chicago for a cent each. My net profit on the deal was about $3.50, which I figured the farmer could well afford for a lesson in honesty. He had paid for the glasses because he thought he was getting something expensive at a fraction of their true value. His wife had thought she was getting something for nothing.

This desire to get something for nothing has been very costly to many people who have dealt with me and with other con men. But I

## Early Adventures In Chicanery

have found that this is the way it works. The average person, in my estimation, is ninety-nine per cent animal and one per cent human. The ninety-nine per cent that is animal causes very little trouble. But the one per cent that is human causes all our woes. When people learn — as I doubt they will — that they can't get something for nothing, crime will diminish and we shall all live in greater harmony.

My partner soon caught on, and we both worked the scheme throughout the trip. There were variations to the routine and we had to be ready to answer many questions. But each of us managed to make about ten sales a day — thirty-five dollars profit. That was more than I had made in a whole week in Chicago.

As a rule, we worked an entire community. My partner would drop me at the first farmhouse, then proceed a mile or two down the road. I would go forward while he turned back. We called at every house until we met. Then we'd be on our way again.

I realize that this may seem an old game. It is. But I am telling about it because I am the man who originated it. My partner and I worked it successfully throughout the farming sections of Illinois, Iowa, and Wisconsin.

For me, there was one drawback. While my partner rode from one farmhouse to another in his buggy, I had to trudge down the dusty road with my bag. At best, although I have enjoyed fairly good health, I am frail, and this constant walking became very tiresome.

Among the items I had brought with me from Chicago were a number of pocket watches. They were gold-plated and stamped on the back, "14 Carat." I had paid $1.98 for each, and they were fairly good timepieces. What is more, they were legitimate products. In those days — 1899 — there had been no legislation prohibiting manufacturers from stamping anything they pleased on watches and jewelry.

Of course, I sold them for as much as I could get — as high as fifty dollars. There was nothing the buyer could do about it. True, he had paid much more than the watch was worth, but at that time the law held that he had done so with his eyes open. The victim had to suffer in silence and charge off his loss to experience.

One day I came to a farmhouse whose owner was very much in need of a watch. But he was a horse trader at heart. As soon as I

## "Yellow Kid" Weil

offered to sell him the watch, he started to bicker. I finally agreed to accept a horse and sulky in exchange for the watch. The farmer thought he had put over a good one. The horse was a plug and had almost outlived his usefulness.

But the rig served my purpose. Now I could ride during the remainder of the summer. I am sure the farmer got good service from his watch as long as I did from his plug.

By the time the summer was over and we had concluded our jaunt, I was tired of the rural life. So I dissolved our partnership and, with a sizable stake, returned to Chicago.

## 2. Chicanery in Chicago

I HAD BEEN AWAY FROM JESSIE, MY FIANCE, FOR SEVERAL MONTHS AND was anxious to see her. She and her family welcomed me back, and that winter, I saw her often. She thought I was a traveling salesman for a reputable firm, but I told her that I was tired of the road and intended to set up my own business in Chicago.

In those days, a woman seldom questioned a man's work. Her place was strictly in the home. Jessie didn't ask me about the sort of salesmanship I was engaged in. It was many years, long after we were married, before she found out that I was anything but a respectable business man.

She and her mother were devout members of the Sacramento Congregational Church in Chicago. With them I attended services every Sunday. The minister had a forceful delivery, using a clever choice of words to sway his audience.

This set me to thinking. I said to myself, "Joe, you are not capable of hard physical work. You're too frail. Whatever you accomplish in life must be done through words. You have that ability. You can make words beautiful and scenic. What marble is to sculpture, what canvas is to painting, words can be to you. You can use them to influence others. You can make them earn your living for you."

As I have said, that minister made a deep impression on me. I wondered would he help me enter a good theological seminary where I could study to be a pulpiteer. I broached the subject to Jessie and her mother. They were overjoyed.

One Sunday evening we waited after services and approached the minister. His advice was realistic.

"First," he said, "you must give your soul and your whole life to God. Have you done that?"

"Not yet," I admitted.

"Are you familiar with the Scriptures?"

"Some of them. Not all."

"You've got to make up your mind that you will give yourself to the work," he urged. "Then you will have to be able to pay your way through school."

"I can pay part of it," I said. "And I imagine I can work to pay the rest of it."

"Yes, that can be done," declared the minister, "if your heart is in it. Here is what I advise you. First read some religious texts. Study religion for a while in your own way. Then if you are ready to give your life to God, come back to me and I will tell you how and where to enroll."

That minister must have been psychic. He must have realized that my heart had not been given over to God, but that I was seeking a career to further my own ends. However, he gave me a list of books to read.

First was the Bible. I read through it, then the other volumes he had recommended. I supplemented these with books of my own choice. I studied the lives of Moses, Buddha, and Mohammed. I secured a copy of the *Catholic Encyclopedia* and read that.

The net result was that I lost all desire to become a pulpiteer. There were so many inconsistencies I could not reconcile that I became an iconoclast. I arrived at these conclusions: Man has all the bestiality of the animal, but is cloaked with a thin veneer of civilization; he is inherently dishonest and selfish; the honest man is a rare specimen indeed.

However, my reading firmly convinced me of the power of words. I felt that its proper use could lead me to fortune. In that I was to be right. The use of words led me to many fortunes.

When I told Jessie that I had decided that I was not cut out to be a preacher she accepted my judgment. She continued, however, as organist at the Sacramento Church and retained her faith. Though I became an iconoclast, I attended the services because of my great

## Chicanery in Chicago

love for her. And I still have a high regard for that minister and his power with words.

In those days, the police were not like our police of today. The force was not so large, and the Detective Bureau had not yet been organized. The Municipal Court was not a big organization. Most of the courts were operated by justices of the peace. We called them "Justice Shops." Each justice had his own constables, who were the detectives of that period.

There was practically no restriction on either gambling or vice. A man could earn money by his wits without any interference from the constables or the police. There was none of this pickup business, where a man is locked up and held indefinitely in a cell without a charge being placed against him.

Both civil and criminal cases were tried in the Justice Shops. I knew one of the magistrates quite well — Judge Aldo. He used to send me out to select jurors. Juries were composed of six men. When I was assigned to get a jury, I was, first of all, told which way the case was to be decided.

Naturally I went into the saloons. I'd tap a man on the shoulder and say: "How would you like to make a couple of easy dollars?"

If he was interested, I explained to him that he would have to vote right — to earn his money. In this way, I picked up half-a-dozen men, led them into Judge Aldo's court, and saw them sworn in as jurors. The trial, of course, was a farce — the verdict had been decided before the jury had even been assembled.

I picked up money in various ways, hanging around the saloons and hotels — always by persuasive words, playing upon the gullibility of some sucker who was anxious to make easy money at someone else's expense.

But most of my time was spent at the race tracks. There was no pari-mutuel system then. Bets were accepted by bookmakers and betting commissioners who determined their own odds. I pretended to be in the confidence of owners of race horses and sold inside tips to other bettors.

I made no bets myself, because I soon learned that there is no such thing as smart money at a racecourse. I yearned to be an owner of race horses myself, but the time for that was not yet.

I had sold the plug I had acquired from the farmer, but I kept the sulky. I heard of a socially prominent young woman who owned two horses. But they were so high-spirited that she couldn't control them. I contacted her and bought them for a ridiculously low price. They were named Nicotine and Mutineer.

At this time, sulky racing was still popular. I used to race one or the other of my horses hitched to my sulky, at Billy Gilliam's racecourse at 35th and Grand Boulevard. When I could afford it, I bought a buggy and used Nicotine and Mutineer as carriage horses.

Driving up Michigan Avenue in my buggy, with these two blooded horses prancing and champing at the bit, I often attracted attention. One day a well-dressed, elderly man hailed me. I stopped.

"Young man," he said, "is that rig for sale?"

"I hadn't thought about it," I replied, "but I'll sell it for the right price."

"How much do you want?"

"A thousand dollars," I declared, after some thought.

"I'll give you five hundred."

"No," I said. "A thousand is my price."

"Well," he grumbled, "if you change your mind come to see me at my office. I'm Mr. Loomis, you know."

"Yes, sir, I know," I replied.

Mr. Loomis was the head of a large wholesale grocery firm which was then, and still is, one of the leaders in the Middle West. His proposal inspired me with an idea for a new confidence game. This one was to be an excellent money-maker — and within the law.

Two days later, I called at his office.

"Have you decided to accept my proposition?" he asked eagerly.

"No, I haven't, Mr. Loomis. But I have come to make you a counterproposal. I want you to lend me $5,000."

"What!" he exclaimed, when he had recovered from my effrontery. "That's a lot of money, young man. Do you have any collateral?"

"All I have is my rig," I replied. "But if you will make me the loan, I will put up the rig as collateral and at the same time tell you how you can make a lot of money."

## Chicanery in Chicago

"I suppose I ought to throw you out," frowned Mr. Loomis, "but you interest me. In the first place, I'd like to have that rig. Now what is your proposal?"

"Are we alone?" I asked, looking around his office. "This must be strictly confidential."

"No one can hear." To make doubly sure, he got up and closed the door. "Now, what is it?"

"You know of the big handicap race at Hawthorne three weeks from now?"

"Of course."

"I am going to tell you how to make a lot of money. I happen to know the race is fixed. The man who weighs in the horses is a friend of mine. The winning horse will carry no weight. I also know the judge. In case my horse fails to win, he will declare it no contest. In other words, Mr. Loomis, you can't lose."

"And your proposition?"

"Lend me $5,000. When the race is over, I'll not only pay you back out of my winnings, but I'll make you a present of my rig. Just to show my good faith, though, I'll pledge my two fine horses and buggy. If, by some mischance, our horse should fail to win, then you'll have my rig."

Mr. Loomis required only a few minutes to think this over. He wrote me a check for $5,000. I gave him a mortgage on my outfit. Then I told him the name of the horse — Mobina.

Actually, Mobina was a selling plater and hadn't won a race in months. There was so little chance that Mobina would win now that he was listed at 10 to 1.

Of course, the odds appealed to Mr. Loomis greatly. He got ready to make a killing. He was helped along by my enthusiastic reports from the track. Within a few days, he was figuring up the vast sum he was going to add to his already sizable fortune.

But before the race came off, I took Mr. Loomis for more money. I dashed in to say that the judge was afraid and that we needed a couple of hundred dollars to keep him quiet. On another occasion, I told him that the jockey had threatened to expose the whole thing. On one pretext or another, I took him for an additional $1,700.

## "Yellow Kid" Weil

Then came the day of the race. Mobina didn't even show. Of course, the race hadn't been fixed and nothing had been paid to the judge. The only fixing I had done was to give the jockey a couple of hundred dollars to pull the horse, just to make sure it didn't win.

Sorrowfully, I went to Mr. Loomis and gave him the rig.

"I can't understand it," I said. "Something went wrong. It has absolutely cleaned me out."

Mr. Loomis got his rig. And there is a moral to this story: if he had been willing to make an honest deal for it in the first place, he could have bought it. But he wasn't willing to pay a fair price and in the end, it cost him $6,700, in addition to whatever he lost on the race.

I tried the same deal, with variations, on other wealthy men. Almost without exception, they were eager to get in on the easy money. I didn't have my rig as bait, but I played on their natural greed. I asked for a loan and told my story of a fixed race. The amounts I got varied with the individuals. But I never found another who was as gullible as Mr. Loomis.

One day, I approached John R. Thompson, who founded the Thompson restaurant chain. I asked him for a loan of $2,500 and told him my fixed race story.

"If you are desperately in need of $2,500," offered Mr. Thompson, "and if you can prove it to me, I'll lend you the money. But I will have absolutely nothing to do with a fixed race."

I didn't take anything from Mr. Thompson. I probably could have talked him into the loan, but I didn't. In my long career, I can truthfully say that Mr. Thompson was the only man I ever met who was one hundred per cent honest.

There was, of course, a limit to the number of suckers who would take part in this con game. After my experience with Mr. Thompson, I went back to touting at the racecourses. I met a man named Frank Hogan and worked with him successfully for a number of years. For a time we operated a bucket shop on La Salle Street, and engaged in other enterprises to separate people from their money.

In the saloons and poolrooms of Chicago, we were known as a pair of young fellows with sharp wits. Our favorite hangout was the saloon of "Bathhouse John" Coughlin, located on Madison Street near La

## Chicanery in Chicago

Salle. The Bath was then Alderman of the First Ward. He was a swell fellow, as many another will tell you.

One evening the Bath saw me glancing at a newspaper, *The New York Journal,* to which he subscribed. A comic sheet had caught my eye. It was called "Hogan's Alley and the Yellow Kid."

"I'm through with that paper, if you want it," said Coughlin.

"I like that comic sheet," I told him.

"Then I'll save it for you every day," said Coughlin.

He did. And I read the comic regularly. The Yellow Kid depicted was malformed, as far as body structure and facial equipment were concerned. He had large ears, an enormous mouth, and protruding teeth with much space between them.

One night a race-horse tout named Jack Mack entered Coughlin's saloon. It was after midnight, but the saloon never closed. Downstairs was the bathhouse and above was a hotel. Tommy Chamale, who was later to become a millionaire banker and the owner of the Green Mill, the Riviera, and Tivoli theatres, was night porter and bar boy.

Jack Mack had an egg in his hand and he was attempting to stand it up on the bar. That attracted Chamale, who asked what Mack was trying to do.

"I'm trying to stand this egg on end," replied Mack.

Chamale tried it, but without success.

"I can make it stand up and I can do it without injuring the shell," said Mack. "How much have you got in the cash register?"

"Twenty-eight dollars," Chamale returned, after counting his money.

"I'll wager that twenty-eight dollars that I can do it!" snapped Mack.

Chamale took him up.

Mack had some salt in the palm of his hand. He dampened the end of the egg and pretended to cleanse it in his hand. The salt adhered to the end of the egg, giving it a foundation the same as the legs on a table. The egg stood erect.

Mack collected the twenty-eight dollars and left. A few minutes afterward I retired to the bathhouse to spend the night. When Bathhouse John came in Chamale told him about the wager.

"Where was Weil?" asked Coughlin.

"He was standing at the bar, reading the comic paper."

## "Yellow Kid" Weil

"You've been tricked, my boy," said the Bath. "Weil is probably in league with Mack. They worked a con game on you."

The next morning, when I went upstairs to the saloon, Coughlin said: "Were you here when Chamale made that wager?"

"Yes."

"Did you and Hogan have anything to do with it?"

I denied this.

"Maybe," said the Alderman, shaking his head, "but I don't believe it. I think you and Hogan got part of that money." His eye fell upon the comic sheet lying on the bar where I had left it. "Hogan's Alley and the Yellow Kid," he read aloud. "Hogan and Weil. From now on, you're the Yellow Kid."

That was in 1903. And from that time on, I was invariably known as the Yellow Kid. There have been many erroneous stories published about how I acquired this cognomen. It was said that it was due to my having worn yellow chamois gloves, yellow vests, yellow spats, and a yellow beard. All this was untrue. I had never affected such wearing apparel and I had no beard.

Bathhouse John was my friend until his death a few years ago. He began as a rubber in the bathhouse of the old Brevoort Hotel. Later he became the owner of this bathhouse and a protégé of "Hinky Dink" Kenna. He was a politician all his life, though he dabbled in horses and opened an insurance brokerage house on LaSalle Street. He was a big, hearty fellow, loved by all his friends, as well as by the voters who regularly returned him to the city council.

An impressive figure, he had a flair for brocaded vests, which made him even more a person to attract the eye. He gained a reputation as a poet and composer, but it was common knowledge that his stuff was ghost written. Perhaps the most famous of his songs was "Dear Midnight of Love." This was composed by May de Sousa, the daughter of a detective at the headquarters of Mayor Carter Harrison.

The Bath befriended many underworld characters, but I don't believe that he ever received a cent from any of their enterprises. He was the sort who would help anybody in need.

Frank Hogan and I dissolved partnership, and he went on to become a prominent investment broker, though the methods he used were

*Chicanery in Chicago*

shady. When the law was at his heels in 1907 he went to France, where he bought a villa outside of Paris. He never returned to the United States.

## 3. A Tip for Mr. Macallister

ONE HOT SUMMER NIGHT I STOOD AT THE BAR OF BATHHOUSE JOHN Coughlin's Randolph Street saloon in Chicago, quaffing a glass of beer. I had spent a strenuous day at the racecourse.

The saloon was crowded with men engaged in drinking and in animated conversation. It probably was as mixed a group as any ever assembled under one roof outside of a penal institution. Pickpockets, thieves, safecrackers, and thugs of every degree mingled with cardsharps, swindlers, gamblers, policemen, and politicians.

At the other end of the bar stood Alderman Coughlin, resplendent in a two-gallon silk hat, a mountain-green dress suit and a red vest with white buttons. He was talking to a blue-coated policeman named Fred Buckminster.

I had only a casual acquaintance with Buckminster. He was technically on the side of the law, although his chief duty was to collect tribute from the crooks on his beat and turn it over to the politicians. I doubt that Fred got much of the graft, because the politicians had a very good idea of who was paying off and how much.

However, I was operating pretty well within the law at that time and I had no reason to pay tribute. Not for several years did I really become acquainted with Buckminster, whose cherubic, extremely honest-looking face and portly bearing had earned him the sobriquet of "The Deacon."

As I stood there a well-dressed man, several years older than I, approached the bar.

"Good evening," he said. "Won't you join me in a glass of beer?"

"Thank you," I replied.

## A Tip for Mr. Macallister

The bartender drew two glasses of beer, and we began to quench our thirst.

"My name," offered my companion, "is William Wall."

"Glad to know you, Mr. Wall," I returned. "My name is Weil — Joe Weil."

"The Yellow Kid!" he exclaimed. "I've heard about you. They say you're a pretty sharp young fellow."

Of course, I had heard of Billy Wall. He was known as one of Chicago's leading confidence men. We conversed for some time, taking turns buying the drinks.

"There are many things to learn in this — ah — profession," said Wall. "Besides having a sharp wit, you must be a smooth, polished actor. Maybe I can help you some time."

I was flattered. But I was not yet ready to enter into an alliance. Our meeting broke up with my promise that I would think it over and get in touch with him.

One thing is very important to the successful con man: honor. That may sound strange, but it's true. I don't know how much truth there is to the old saying about honor among thieves, but it is an absolute necessity among con men.

Though a con man may conspire to fleece others, he must always be on the level with his associates. The victim's cash is usually taken by one man, who disappears. And it would be a sorry day indeed if this man, who had taken the money, didn't meet later with his associates to divide the spoils.

During the next few days, I made careful inquiries about Billy Wall. Everyone had the highest praise for him: he could be trusted. So I contacted Billy and we formed a partnership.

For a while we worked the old con games that were, even then, growing whiskers. Billy Wall was an accomplished actor, and I learned a great deal from him. But he lacked imagination. He never thought of anything new.

I was not satisfied. My mind was alert and full of fresh schemes. One day I proposed one to Bill, and he readily agreed to follow my lead.

My first step was to insert a blind ad in an evening newspaper:

## "Yellow Kid" Weil

WANTED — Man to invest $2,500. Opportunity to participate in very profitable venture. Must be reliable. Confidential, Box W-62, care this paper.

That brought several replies, each of which was tucked away for future reference. The one that intrigued me most was from a man whom I will call Marcus Macallister, owner of the "Macallister" Theatre, one of Chicago's leading playhouses, which offered the best in legitimate stage productions.

I knew also that Macallister was one of the principal backers of a new amusement project then in the planning stage. It later became White City, which included an arena for boxing and wrestling, bowling alleys, a dance hall, a roller-skating rink, and other recreational features. Macallister was our man. He not only had money, he was a plunger.

The day after I received his letter I called at his office. In those days I traveled under my own name.

"What is your proposition, Mr. Weil?" Macallister asked.

"My brother-in-law," I confided, "is in desperate need of $2,500. If you will lend it to him, I will show you how to make a fortune."

"What does he need $2,500 for?" he inquired.

"Well, he's hopelessly addicted to betting on the horses. He began borrowing money to make bets. Now, he's in the clutches of the loan sharks. He owes them $2,500, but his wife — my sister — doesn't know about it. The loan sharks have demanded their money. If it isn't paid by tomorrow night, they are going to my sister and expose him."

"How can a man like that help me make a fortune?"

"By giving you absolutely reliable information on the races. He works for Western Union. He will tip you off on a horse after it has won. You can make a bet on the nose and you can't lose."

There is something about a "sure thing" on a race that a horse player can't resist. A gleam of anticipation appeared in Macallister's eyes. He tried to cover it up.

"I never bet on the horses," he said. "How does it work?"

I knew he was lying, but I led him to the Redpath Saloon at State and Jackson. In the rear was a poolroom.

## A Tip for Mr. Macallister

In those days, most handbooks — which were legal — operated in poolrooms. Their equipment included a cashier's cage for taking bets and paying off winners, wall sheets where the odds on various horses were posted, and the telegraph desk.

Western Union furnished racing information by wire. Most of the poolrooms subscribed to this service and had direct wires from the Western Union building. Of course every bookmaker had to employ an operator who jotted down the messages. The results were called out by a clerk.

In present-day handbooks all betting is closed at post-time. In those days bets were accepted until the telegraph operator received the flash, "They're off!" He received a running account of the race which was called out by the clerk. At the finish the winners were announced.

Mr. Macallister seemed fascinated by the amount of money that was changing hands.

"You could make a fortune," he agreed, "if you had the right horse."

"If you know the winning horse beforehand you can't lose."

"But how is that possible?"

"Come over to the Western Union building with me."

On the way over I explained that my brother-in-law knew nothing of my plan.

"He's too honest," I said. "If he wasn't he could have cleaned up himself."

The Western Union building was an eight-story edifice, but the elevator ran only to the seventh floor. We took the stairway to the top floor, which was one big room, where about a hundred operators sat at their desks. We could see them through a glass partition. They were coatless and wore green eyeshades.

I threw up a hand, and an operator waved back. He probably thought I was someone he knew.

"My brother-in-law just signaled," I told Macallister. "He wants us to meet him on the fifth floor."

We went down to the fifth floor and waited in the corridor. I knew that Billy Wall had been waiting in the washroom on the sixth floor. In a few minutes, he came down the stairs. He wore a green

23

eyeshade, was hatless, and his sleeves were rolled up. He was my mythical brother-in-law.

"What's the meaning of this?" he demanded, with a fine display of indignation. "Haven't I told you not to come around here when I'm working? Suppose the boss finds out I'm away from my instrument —"

"No worse than if he finds out about the loan sharks," I retorted. "This gentleman is here to help you."

I introduced them and they shook hands.

"Are you really willing to help me?" Billy asked.

"He will," I promised, "if you give him a winner."

"How can I do that?" he asked innocently.

"You're on the gold wire, aren't you?"

"Yes, but —"

"What is the gold wire?" Macallister asked.

"That's the wire from New York that we get the race results on," my "brother-in-law" explained. "I get them here and flash them to the poolrooms."

"Then here is what you can do," I said, lowering my voice. "Hold back the results for a couple of minutes and give Mr. Macallister a chance to make a bet before the poolrooms get the flash that they're off. You can send through some sort of signal so he'll know which horse won."

"But that's dishonest!" Billy protested. "And my job —" He hesitated. Then he shoved his hands in his pockets and paced up and down the hall. "No! I can't do it."

I shot him a scornful look.

"You love your wife and family, don't you?" I goaded.

"More than anything else in the world," he replied.

"And you know what will happen if my sister finds out about those loan sharks, don't you?"

"Yes," he said, wearily. "She'll leave me. My home will be wrecked."

"In that case," said Mr. Macallister, "it seems to me that you haven't anything to lose by going along with us."

That was the tipoff. It meant that Macallister was sunk.

24

## A Tip for Mr. Macallister

"All right," Billy returned reluctantly, "I'll do it this once. But only once."

"That's all right," said Macallister. "We can make plenty of money on just one sure thing."

"I'll have to pay off the New York operator," Billy grumbled, "He wouldn't go in a deal like that for less than a 50-50 split."

We turned questioning eyes on Macallister.

"That's all right with me," he said. "I can afford to pay him if I get a winner."

We then arranged the details. We would take the sixth race at Saratoga on the following day. As soon as the winner had come through, Billy would flash a signal. Mr. Macallister would place his bet and two minutes later Billy would send details of the race to the poolrooms.

"As long as this is a sure thing," Billy proposed, "you might as well bet the $2,500 you're going to loan me. Then I can repay the loan out of what I win."

Macallister agreed to that. We parted after I had arranged to meet him the next day.

The poolroom I led Macallister to the next day had been arranged for his special benefit. We had rented the banquet hall of the old Briggs House, and outfitted it fully with equipment which also had been rented for the occasion. Of course, the telegraph instrument was not connected with Western Union, as Macallister believed. It received messages from another instrument which we had installed in a room of the Briggs House.

To be our innocent props we had hired a hundred actors. We had told them that Mr. Schubert Henderson, the producer, was casting for his new play and wanted some actors for a poolroom scene. They looked real enough to Mr. Macallister. The cashier's cage, wall sheets, and telegraph operator all looked authentic too. We had stooges at the cashier's cage and other stooges went to the windows and placed bets. Among those who helped were a number of minor con men.

The big wall clock had been set back a few minutes. This was done because we wanted time for our operator in the other room to find out the actual result of the sixth at Saratoga before he began sending his message. Our scheme required that we have the actual winner because it would be easy enough for Macallister to check up.

Came the time for the sixth race to start, according to our clock — actually the race was already over. The telegraph began to click. The clerk called out:

"Colorado is delaying the start."

That was the signal we had agreed upon. It meant that Colorado actually was the winner. The odds were 4 to 1.

It had been agreed that Mr. Macallister would bet the $2,500 that he was to lend Billy Wall. Besides the $2,500 to pay Billy's loan and the cut to the New York operator, Macallister could keep the profit. He hurried to the window, but it was completely blocked by several men in a violent argument.

"We wish to place a bet," I said, pushing toward the window.

One of the stooges gave me a shove that sent me reeling backward. The argument continued and Mr. Macallister tried frantically to get to the window, while the clock ticked away the precious seconds. He was no more successful than I and the altercation was still in progress when the flash came: "They're off!"

That meant all betting on that race was closed. Mr. Macallister and I stepped back and listened as the account of the race was called out. Of course, Colorado won.

If Macallister had been able to bet, he would have won $10,000.

Of course, we had no intention of letting him do that. That was why the argument had been staged in front of the cashier's window.

"Look here!" I said to the cashier. "My friend had $2,500 to bet on that last race, but he couldn't get to the window. Those fellows cost him $10,000."

The cashier shrugged. "I'm sorry, but what can I do? I didn't start the argument."

"Hereafter," I said, truthfully enough, "we'll go elsewhere to make our bets."

With that, we left. We had previously arranged to meet my supposed brother-in-law in the Western Union building for the payoff. As before, we went to the eighth floor where the operators were at

## A Tip for Mr. Macallister

work and I pretended to signal. Of course, Mr. Macallister had no way of knowing that I was not acquainted with any of the operators. And in such a large room with so many men busily at work, he could not distinguish anyone's features well enough to identify him.

Nor could he know that the closest Billy Wall had been to the operator's room was the washroom on the sixth floor. It seemed natural enough when Billy came down the stairs, wearing a green eyeshade and dressed like the operators we had seen. Even to tenants of the building he appeared to be a bonafide operator.

Billy came toward us, his face beaming. He grabbed Macallister's hand and shook it heartily.

"Mr. Macallister, you don't know how grateful I am to you," he said happily. "You have saved the day for me. Now, I can pay those loan sharks and go home to my family without fear —"

At the dejected look on my face he broke off.

"What's the matter, Joe?" he asked. "Did something go wrong?"

"We got your signal all right," I said, "but Mr. Macallister wasn't able to make the bet."

"But you had two minutes to get it down. I don't understand —"

"You tell him, Mr. Macallister."

He told Billy how he had been prevented from making the bet.

"This is awful," Billy quavered. "What will I tell that New York operator? He's expecting $5,000 out of this deal. And my wife —"

"I don't know about you, Bill," I said, "but I'm going to pack my grip and get out of town. I don't want to be around when my sister discovers you're in the clutches of the loan sharks."

"I'll go with you," muttered Billy. "No use for me to try to hang onto my job. And I can't face the humiliation —"

"Just a minute," declared Macallister. "I told you I'd lend you the $2,500 and I will. It wasn't your fault the scheme failed."

"That will be wonderful," Billy said gratefully. But the elation quickly went out of his voice. "But what am I going to do about that New York operator? He thinks I won $10,000 and he's expecting half. He'll expose me."

"I'll pay that, too," Macallister offered. "Can you come over to the bank with me?"

"Not now," said Billy. "I'm on duty, you know." He looked at me. "But Joe can go with you. He'll bring me the money."

I accompanied Macallister to the First National Bank, where he withdrew $7,500 and gave it to me. I told him I would deliver it to my brother-in-law when he got off duty.

But he was not to be disposed of so easily. He wanted to know when we were going to make the killing. So I arranged a meeting with him the following day at the Western Union building.

Then I met Billy Wall and we divided the profit, which exceeded $7,000, since expenses had been less than $500.

"Macallister is a good bet for another deal," I told Billy. "But not right now. We've got to hold him off."

We devised a method of doing this and put it into practice the next day when I met Macallister. We went through the usual routine, eventually meeting my supposed brother-in-law on the fifth floor.

Billy Wall was a good actor. He wore an uneasy expression and glanced furtively about as he came down the stairs. He was the picture of dejection. Before either of us could speak, he said:

"I can't stay long. I think the boss is suspicious. He has taken me off the gold wire and put me on straight messages."

It was Macallister's turn to look dejected now. He probably had visions of his $7,500 flying out the window.

"Do you mean to say," I demanded, "that we can't help Mr. Macallister win his money back?"

"Maybe," said Billy. "But not now. We'll have to wait until this blows over. If the boss makes an investigation and finds out everything is on the square, he'll put me back on the gold wire. Then we can do something."

"How long do you think that will be?" Macallister asked, obviously disappointed.

"I don't know," Billy said sorrowfully. "You have no idea how bad I feel about this, Mr. Macallister, after you were so good as to help me out of my trouble. It may be two weeks — it may be longer. But I will get in touch with you."

Billy went back up the stairs, presumably to return to his instrument. Macallister and I left together.

## A Tip for Mr. Macallister

"I'll let you know, never fear," I told him. "After all, I got you into this, and I want to see you get your money back — and a lot more besides."

He was none too happy, but there wasn't much he could do except wait. He might have called the Western Union to check up on Billy, but to do so would be to expose his own part in the conspiracy. So he impatiently bided his time.

Meanwhile, we contacted other suckers and worked the same game on them, though none was so gullible as Mr. Macallister. We kept a baited hook dangling just out of his reach. Our dilatory tactics served only to whet his appetite and to ripen him for a bigger killing.

On one pretext or another we put him off. In due course we told him that Billy was back on the gold wire. We made preparations to get a winner, delay the results, flash a signal to a poolroom, and let Macallister clean up. But before we could go through with it, the Western Union inspectors appeared for a general checkup — or so we told him. This meant any phony business was out until the inspectors had completed their work — and we had them hanging around for weeks.

Before I decided to take him again I strung Macallister along for several months. This time, I had an entirely different plan. I made no mention of my brother in-law. Macallister, too, seemed to have forgotten him. He went with me to Willow Springs, a suburb of Chicago, and I showed him the layout.

John Condon had a poolroom in Willow Springs, and received the Western Union wire service direct from Chicago. Condon had several telegraph operators. Willie de Long was the chief operator and got the results on most of the big races. I took Macallister to the poolroom where he could see for himself that big money was bet there.

Then I led him to a secluded spot near Archer Avenue and Joliet Road, where the telegraph line ran. It was not far from the depot. I explained that, with the right equipment, we could tap the wires, get the messages intended for the poolroom, and send our own messages. We could control everything that went into the poolroom.

Macallister had heard of wire-tapping and the idea intrigued him. Back in Chicago, I took him to Moffatt's Electrical Shop at 268 South

## "Yellow Kid" Weil

Clark, just back of the Western Union building. We asked to see the device for stopping messages.

Joe Moffatt showed us into a room filled with expensive-looking gadgets. He pointed out a "special transformer" — a box about three feet square and eighteen inches deep.

"This is one of the most intricate mechanisms ever constructed," he said. "Just lift it once."

Both Macallister and I tried lifting the box. But all we could do was to get one end of it off the floor. It was extremely heavy.

Moffatt launched into a detailed and highly technical account of the device inside the box. Then he raised the cover and showed us the intricately strung wires and switches, including a telegraph sending and receiving instrument. Attached to each end of the box was a long cable, on the end of which was a special attachment.

"How does it work?" Macallister wanted to know.

"It allows you to control messages," Moffatt explained. "One cable sidetracks the message into the box. It comes over your instrument. The other cable allows you to send any message you want to. Of course, you need a telegraph operator."

Simple enough, as Moffatt explained it. Actually there was no such device for stopping messages. Wires could be tapped, but even then Western Union had perfected a method for determining when their wires had been tapped. Of course Mr. Macallister didn't know all this. Nor did he know that the box was so heavy because it had been filled with porcelain tubes.

He made a deal with Moffatt to buy the mechanism, including the cables and a set of pole climbers, for $12,000. It was to be delivered to me.

Moffatt's was a unique place. Though it apparently was a shop selling electrical equipment, there was hardly a workable device on the premises. Moffatt's entire business was with con men. He rigged up inexpensive but fancy-looking gadgets to be sold to wealthy suckers. Moffatt collected the money, kept a ten per cent commission for himself, and turned the balance over to the con man.

A couple of days later, with a stooge, I called at Moffatt's and picked up the equipment which Macallister had bought for his $12,000.

## A Tip for Mr. Macallister

The only person who knew that we had made the deal, besides the principals, was a man I'd seen around the tracks and the saloons. His name was Bull Finley.

It was dark when we arrived at Archer Avenue and Joliet Road. We planned to hook up the cables and bury the box. As soon as we had unloaded the stuff from the rig we were confronted by a dark figure.

"Up with your hands!" he commanded.

We raised our hands because the other man had drawn a gun. As I became accustomed to the darkness I recognized Constable Herzog of Willow Springs.

"You didn't just find us here," I said. "Somebody told you."

"Could be," Herzog admitted.

"The only other person who knew about this was Bull Finley. Did he tell you?"

"I ain't sayin' he didn't," said Herzog. "You fellers gonna come along with me quietly?"

"Why do you want to take us in?" I asked.

"You'd freeze to death if you stayed out here. And besides, it's against the law to tap telegraph wires."

"We haven't tapped any wires."

"No, but you were going to."

"Just the same, no crime has been committed," I reminded him. "You might get $20 for taking us in, but you'd have a hard time proving anything. How would you like to make $250?"

That was big money to Constable Herzog. He readily agreed to forget the whole matter. I gave him $50 on the spot and $200 the following day. To me, it was a worth-while investment: I had learned the identity of a stool pigeon. I was now reasonably certain of no interference from the law. And, as it later developed, I was probably saved from freezing.

"If you're goin' to stay here," said Herzog, "you'd better build a fire. It's ten below zero."

He departed, and we acted on his suggestion. The ground was frozen and we had to work hard to bury the box. Of course we didn't hook the attachments to the telegraph wire. But we did wrap ends of

31

the two cables to insulators on top of the pole so that it appeared we had attached them.

The next day I went to Condon's poolroom and talked to Willie de Long. I asked him what horse he would pick in the fourth race at New Orleans.

"Jerry Hunt," he replied without hesitation.

"Do me a favor," I said, handing him fifty dollars.

"Sure. What?"

"I've got a man who is coming in here to place a bet. About two minutes before post time, you hand the clerk a message. That will be a signal for my friend as to what horse to bet on."

"Sure," said Willie. "I'll do it."

I met Macallister at the depot and led him to the spot where we had installed the equipment. My stooge, posing as a telegraph operator, was there. But one glance was enough for Macallister. He didn't wait for me to give detailed instructions to the "operator." He was afraid of being seen and hurried back to the depot to wait for me.

I waited for a few minutes, presumably giving instructions to my operator. Then I joined Mr. Macallister at the depot and we went over to the poolroom.

I told him that I had decided on the fourth at New Orleans. Macallister did not question this. In fact, no sucker ever asked me why I always picked a late race. There was a very good reason why I never picked the first three. For those races, there was an established post time, and, generally speaking, the first two races went off on time or nearly on time. But, as the day progressed, circumstances often made the other races start later than scheduled. The later the race, the more chance there was that it would be delayed a few minutes. This made it impossible for the suckers to know exactly the time that any race would start.

Another thing Macallister never questioned me about was my brother-in-law. Although he had been the key man in the original scheme, the theatre manager never mentioned him again. That is one of the basic points of many swindles. The con man starts off on one deal, builds it up to a certain point. Then something intervenes and the victim's interest is sidetracked to another scheme,

## A Tip for Mr. Macallister

where he is to be fleeced. The strange thing is that the victim forgets all about the original deal.

Macallister was one of the most excitable gamblers I ever knew. When Willie de Long handed the message to the clerk and the latter called out, "Jerry Hunt is acting up," I whispered to Macallister that that was the signal. He almost stumbled over himself hustling to the window. He bet $10,000 and came back with the ticket trembling in his hands.

Avariciously, he listened to the account of the race. As the clerk called out: "Jerry Hunt won," he collapsed completely.

I revived him. He went to the window and cashed his ticket. Jerry Hunt paid $18,000 for his $10,000 bet. He was so elated that he insisted on cutting me in, and gave me $2,900 as my part of the winnings. I had taken a long chance. Had Jerry Hunt not won I was prepared to blame the operator who had supposedly cut in on the wire.

But now that was unnecessary. Macallister was convinced that I really could tap wires and control the messages going into the poolroom. He was eager to repeat the performance.

I stalled him.

"You can't go in there every day and make a killing," I told him. "They'll become suspicious. Better wait awhile."

He agreed that this was logical. Of course, I had no intention of going through it again at Willow Springs. It was hardly likely that I would be able to get a winner the next time. And there was no more money to be gained from selling Macallister equipment for the Willow Springs setup.

Meanwhile, news of what we were doing had got back to the Western Union detectives and they were lying in wait for us. Neither Billy nor I dared to go into the Western Union building.

Billy continued to pose as the gold-wire operator. One day I met a man whom I shall call Fetterman in Thebolt's Buffet. After getting him interested in a "sure thing," we arranged a meeting with my supposed brother-in-law in the buffet. Our reason for having him come to meet us instead of our going to the Western Union building was logical enough: it was a strict rule that any Western

## "Yellow Kid" Weil

Union employee caught playing the races was subject to instant dismissal.

However, Fetterman was so anxious to make a killing that he didn't question my brother-in-law's authenticity. It was arranged that Billy would hold back the result of the fifth race. He would write the name of the winner on a slip of paper, which he would put inside a slit in a rubber ball. The ball would be dropped into the court adjacent to the Western Union building. Mr. Fetterman would get the ball and hurry to the poolroom where I would be waiting. I couldn't be there because I might be recognized and get my brother-in-law in trouble.

Every time we took a sucker like Mr. Fetterman we had to have a new location. Mobility was a necessity if we were to avoid detection. We rented various places on one pretext or another, sometimes resorting to lodge halls, moved in our equipment, used it for the benefit of one sucker, then moved to a new location. However we always set up our poolroom as near the Western Union building as possible.

Since neither Bill nor I could appear in the Western Union building, we had to hire a stooge. I would get the race results, write them on slips of paper, and insert them in the rubber ball. My stooge would then hurry to the washroom on the sixth floor and throw out the ball.

Mr. Fetterman was a most amusing sight as he went chasing after the high-bouncing rubber ball. He caught it, extracted the slip, and hurried to the poolroom where I was waiting. We had told him that my brother-in-law would hold up the results for about two minutes on each race, so that when the fifth was run he would have a reserve of ten minutes. This gave him ample time to get to the poolroom and place the bet. I was supposed to be betting a large amount, too.

Fetterman was breathless when he arrived. He showed me the slip. On one side was "Lightning" and on the other side a big figure "3."

"What does the "3" mean?" he asked.

"I don't know. I suppose it means the odds were 3 to 1. Are you sure that's the slip?"

## A Tip for Mr. Macallister

"Of course," said Fetterman, anxious to get his bet down. "I took it out of the slit in the rubber ball."

"Okay, let's make our bets."

We went to the window of our fake poolroom and made our wagers, then waited for the results. The flash came, "They're off!" An account of the race was called out. Lightning ran third.

"There goes $10,000 of my money," I muttered disgustedly. "I wonder how my brother-in-law happened to slip up."

We had previously arranged to meet Billy at the Buffet after he quit work. We were there when he walked in, all smiles. As in many other similar schemes, he was expecting $2,500 to pay off the loan sharks. He grabbed Fetterman's hand and went into his usual routine of thanking him.

"Just a minute," I said. "We didn't win anything. What was the idea of giving us the wrong horse?"

"But I didn't," Billy protested.

"Look at this," I said angrily, displaying the slip.

"What's wrong with it?" Billy asked, obviously puzzled. "Lightning ran third. That's the reason for 3 on the back. Didn't you take the other slips out of the ball?"

"What other slips?"

"There were three slips in the ball," said Billy. "I wrote down the win, place, and show horses and numbered them 1, 2, 3."

I turned a stony gaze on Mr. Fetterman, who was now squirming. "Where is that ball?"

He removed the ball from his pocket. I opened up the slit and inside, of course, were the two other slips, with the first and second place winners.

"Of all the stupid people I ever saw," I cried, apparently in a rage, "you take the cake. Why didn't you make sure before you told me that horse was the winner?"

"I'm sorry," was all Fetterman could say. "I guess I was too excited to look any further."

"That doesn't get my $10,000 back," I said acidly.

"Nor the $2,500 I owe the loan sharks," complained Billy. "If I don't pay that by tomorrow night, I'll lose my job."

## "Yellow Kid" Weil

"I'll get your $2,500 for you tomorrow," Fetterman promised. Then to me: "I'll give you the $10,000 you lost out of my earnings tomorrow."

"I don't want any more to do with you," I replied.

He pleaded for another chance, and I finally relented. This is a con man's best psychological touch. As long as he can keep the sucker on the defensive, he can maneuver him any way he wants to. We always tried to place the blame for any failure to clean up on some mistake by the sucker. In every case the victim thought that only he was to blame.

"Just so there won't be another mistake," I said, "we'll make a different arrangement." I turned to my brother-in-law. "Billy, can you get to a phone?"

"Yes."

"Then call me up." I gave him the number of the booth phone in the drug store that occupied the ground floor of the building our poolroom was in.

The next day Fetterman and I were waiting when the phone rang. I answered. "What?" I asked. Then, after an interval: "I can't understand you." Finally, I turned to Fetterman: "I can't make out what he says. See if you can get it."

He took the receiver and had no difficulty hearing what Billy Wall said: "The odds were short on the winner. Place your money on Humming Bird." Then, for emphasis (and to confuse the sucker) he repeated: "Place your money on Humming Bird."

Fetterman hung up. "Humming Bird," he repeated excitedly. "Let's go."

"Wait a minute," I said. "Are you sure you heard right?"

"Certainly, I am. Humming Bird is the horse."

We hurried upstairs to the poolroom.

"Don't you think we'd better spread our bets?" I suggested. "Maybe if we played it across the board — "

"Not me," said he. "I'm going to put my money on the nose."

He did and of course he lost. Humming Bird came in second.

"You've made another mistake," I accused. "I asked you if you were sure. I'm beginning to think you're a jinx."

Fetterman and I met Billy Wall at the Buffet that evening. Billy

## A Tip for Mr. Macallister

was eager, as usual. When he saw how dejected we both looked his smile vanished.

"What's the matter?" he gasped. "Did you make another mistake?"

"Yes," I replied. "Our friend did. Just what did you tell him over the phone?"

"Why, I told him the odds on the winner were short, but to place his money on Humming Bird. Didn't he do that?"

"No, he bet it on the nose. Look here," I said to Fetterman, "don't you know what 'place' means?"

"Of course. It means to run second."

"Then why did you insist that we put our money on the nose?" I demanded icily.

Fetterman was full of excuses, but they all sounded lame, even to himself. We heaped ridicule upon him, and he took it. I really felt sorry for the fellow because he was so firmly convinced that it was all his fault. He asked for another chance.

"I won't be able to help you," said Billy. "The loan sharks will go to the boss tomorrow and I won't have a job."

So on condition that Mr. Fetterman would give Billy $2,500 to get him free of the loan sharks and save his job, we relented and agreed to go along with him again.

But this time there would be no slip-up. Each horse would have a number.

"You just give us the number of the winning horse," I told Billy. "Forget about the others. Just the winner. Is that clear?"

"Yes. Just the winner."

When the call came the following day, I let Fetterman answer it. "Twenty won," said Billy. "Have you got that? Twenty won."

Again, we hurried up the stairs. Again, Fetterman assured me that he had heard correctly. We went to the cashier's window and put our money on No. 21. Of course No. 20 was the winner.

Again Fetterman was the goat. Billy insisted that he had said "Twenty won."

We took Fetterman for a total profit of $28,000, after deducting the expenses of operating our fake setup, which included wages for the con men who acted as our stooges.

## "Yellow Kid" Weil

Several months had elapsed since Marcus Macallister had made his killing at Willow Springs. I decided the time was ripe to take him again. He had been busy with the White City construction project and now had a partner. Bill Porter was not averse to making a few thousand dollars at the expense of the bookmakers.

"The elements have damaged our equipment," I told them. "The cables have been stolen. I'll salvage what I can, but I think we'll have to buy additional wiring."

I did salvage the box, but threw away the cables. Macallister and Porter accompanied me to Joe Moffatt's shop, and we negotiated with him to repair the box and furnish new cables. The bill for this was $7,800.

There had been some publicity about wire-tapping around Chicago, so I suggested to Porter and Macallister that we set up our equipment near the Kingston poolroom, outside Indianapolis. I went ahead with a "lineman" and did the installation. I also hired an "operator" and made a date to meet them at the poolroom.

But I didn't go near the poolroom after that. The "operator" was not on hand and Porter and Macallister were doomed to disappointment. The expected signal did not come through. Naturally, two men so prominent couldn't be seen near the telegraph line where the apparatus had been put up. They returned to Chicago.

Meanwhile I had severed my connection with Billy Wall. He was a swell fellow to work with as long as he played the same role. But it was difficult to find enough for him to do, and he never had a new idea. Our parting was friendly. I went to Louisville and lost track of him.

I was in the South a couple of weeks before returning to Chicago. As luck would have it, one of the first men I met on my return was Macallister.

"Just a minute," he said. "Where did you disappear to?"

I put my finger to my lips in a gesture to indicate silence and drew him to a corner.

"We were almost caught," I told him in a whisper. "We had to get out of town fast. I'm certainly glad I bumped into you. I'm broke and I'd like to borrow $500."

# A Tip for Mr. Macallister

He laughed. "What do you think I am?"

"Listen," I said, "I've shown you how you can make a fortune. And yet you refuse me a small loan like $500."

"Oh, all right," he smiled. "Come up to the office."

He lent me the $500 and I gave him a note. That was the last I saw of Mr. Macallister for many years.

One evening, years later, I was seated at a table in the College Inn with a red-haired young woman. I noticed a group near by having some kind of celebration, but I thought little of it until a man arose and came over to my table.

The man was Marcus Macallister.

We shook hands and I invited him to sit down.

"I just wanted to tell you," he said, "that we know you swindled us on those wire deals, but I haven't said anything about it."

"Why not?" I asked.

"I went into it with my eyes open," he replied. "I've only myself to blame."

We chatted for awhile, and he told me they were celebrating the success of White City. Then he shook hands again and returned to his party.

After I had parted from Billy Wall, I bought a couple of race horses. Mobina, an old plater, was one of them. I had a fair-sized fortune and had resolved to race my own horses.

## 4. How to Beat the Horses

THERE IS A WIDELY ACCEPTED THEORY THAT CRIME DOES NOT PAY. This may be true in many cases, but it was not always true in Chicago. Numerous forms of amusement and so-called vice that are now illegal once operated wide open and with the full blessing of the law.

For example, anybody could make book on the races, whether he operated at the tracks or a thousand miles away. Today bookmaking is unlawful even at the racecourse, the only legal wagering being at the pari-mutuel windows.

Betting on the races always fascinated me. Not that I ever believed for a moment that there was any such thing as "smart money" on a horse. As long as I can remember I've known that you can't beat them by any orthodox method. But the very fact that there are so many people who think they can beat the horses is the chief reason for my interest.

On every hand people clamored to bet their money. They sought "inside tips" and "sure things." Perhaps a few have actually tried to win by a study of past performances and careful analysis of the facts. I have never met anyone who did. True, there are more or less expert handicappers; but they sell their advice to others and bet very little of their own money on their selections.

The impression among horse players has been that some races are fixed. Even today many are eager to put their money on a race they think has been fixed.

Up to now the major part of my activities had been concerned with schemes to make money on the horses. My fake wire-tapping scheme

## *How to Beat the Horses*

was extremely profitable and I was quite happy to continue it.

However, Joe Moffatt, who operated the electrical shop where the suckers parted with their money for expensive-appearing gadgets for tapping telegraph wires, dealt with only a few of us. There were not more than a dozen top con men who had entree to Moffatt's shop. I might add that his business was legitimate. The laws relating to confidence games were different in those days.

Today almost any sort of conspiracy to separate a man from his money is illegal under the confidence laws. But in those days a confidence game was defined under the law as taking "unfair advantage of an unwary stranger." This was generally interpreted as a person from the bucolic areas. Any Chicago business man, presumably acquainted with city life and its pitfalls, was presumed to have entered a deal such as a wire-tapping scheme with his eyes open, and the courts refused to recognize him as an "unwary stranger."

Every profitable idea I ever originated for trimming wealthy men was sooner or later copied by others. This was the case with wire-tapping to get race information. At one time hundreds of small-time con men were working it in one form or another. They advertised openly for victims. I recall one day when a leading Chicago paper ran more than two hundred of these ads in its classified section.

These men did not have access to Joe Moffatt's place. The equipment they put together was crude and makeshift. Some of them actually believed that they could stop messages by attaching a wire to a telegraph line. Their suckers were barbers, waiters, bartenders, and others who could raise only a few hundred dollars at most.

The effect of all this was to arouse both the Western Union and the police. I had accumulated a tidy sum and decided to change my modus operandi, though I had no particular desire to change my clientele. Horse-race suckers were — or so I thought at the time — the most gullible of all. Without exception, everyone was interested in making a killing, though each knew that the big profit he hoped for would be strictly dishonest.

After purchasing a couple of horses, I arranged to enter them in competition at the Chicago racecourses: Hawthorne, Harlem, Washington Park, and Robey.

## "Yellow Kid" Weil

I stabled my horses at Jackson Boulevard and Homan Avenue, not far from the Garfield Park course. This was a five-eighths track for trotters, but owners who wished to pay the fee could exercise their horses there. The five-eighths track served my purpose admirably.

From the start I did not become a horse owner because of a notion that I might win purses. I had already learned that it could be more profitable to lose. That is the system I devised for "beating the horses."

I always maintained the finest tack-room at any racecourse where my horses were running. A tack-room is a place where an owner keeps his saddles, weights, jockey uniforms, etc. Mine was outfitted solely for show purposes. Anybody who saw it immediately concluded that the owner certainly must have fine horses.

As a matter of fact my horses seldom ran in the money. One of them, Mobina, was an old plater that would never even show. But I put fine saddles and a well-dressed jockey on him and to the uninitiated, he looked like a good bet.

There was a man whom I shall call Epping who lived on Jackson Boulevard and was a frequent visitor to the Garfield Park race track. He saw my boy exercising Mobina and became interested.

Knowing Epping's background, I was interested in him, too. He was wealthy and had a prosperous business on Chicago Avenue. In those days a man could keep all his money. There was no income tax and he did not have to account for where he got his money or how he disposed of it.

Epping's employees were often hard pressed for ready cash. They had a habit of going to the paymaster for an advance until payday. This gave Epping an idea. Why not set up a place where anybody who was regularly employed could obtain a small loan?

Until then the only people who made loans were the banks and the "loan sharks." This latter group not only made you mortgage your life but charged unbelievable rates. Epping altered this by making regular employment the chief qualification. And he charged rates that were considered reasonable — six per cent a month. His lending business was the beginning of the present-day small loan concern.

I already knew of Epping's wealth, and it did not take me long to discover that his chief aim in life was to accumulate more. He was

## How to Beat the Horses

interested in my horses because he had heard that there was considerable money to be made in winning purses. I soon learned that he knew very little about race horses. I told Epping that the five-eighths course at Garfield Park was a three-quarter track, and he didn't know the difference. But what a difference it made in the running time of a horse like Mobina!

"That horse will make me a lot of money," I told Epping, "if I can raise the money to get him in shape."

"How much money do you need?" he asked.

"I'd have to do some figuring," I replied. "Why?"

"Would you be interested in a partner?"

"I hadn't thought of that. What do you suggest?"

He proposed that he make me a loan, to be repaid out of the profits. He would get a cut of the winnings. We discussed this at some length and decided that 20 per cent would be a fair split for Epping. I did some figuring, and explained that it was an expensive proposition to stable a horse and to pay a trainer and jockey. I finally arrived at a figure — $3,700.

Epping was a hard-headed business man and insisted that we draw up a contract. He agreed that it could be done by my own lawyer, who was in on the deal and knew the kind of contract that I would need. It was duly signed and witnessed, and Epping advanced the money. Then he waited for Mobina to start winning purses.

But there was no chance that Mobina would win. I didn't even enter him in a race. After about thirty days, Epping began to get impatient and asked for an accounting.

I told him that it takes time to get a horse in shape to race and reminded him that I was waiting for a good purse. This stall did not satisfy him. A few days later he demanded that I repay the loan.

I pointed to the contract. It provided that "When Mobina shall have raced and won, then the monies advanced by Party of the First Part (Epping) shall be paid by Party of the Second Part (Weil), plus 20 per cent of the gross winnings."

Epping saw the joker in the contract and knew that he couldn't get anything by bringing suit. But he did swear out a warrant charging me with operating a confidence game.

## "Yellow Kid" Weil

The judge threw the case out, holding that "the contract was based on a future event and that no crime had been committed or could be committed until the event had taken place."

Epping didn't bother me any more, and I don't recall that I ever saw him again. As a matter of fact, I never saw most of my victims again, once I had taken their money. This is strange, too, considering that I have been around Chicago for all these years. I probably have passed them on the street many times.

Meanwhile I met a man named A. B. Watts, who was a breeder of blooded horses. I made a deal with him to increase my stable, and thereafter all the horses I bought came from Watts. These included Title, Black Fonso, Thanksgiving, St. Durango, Sir Christopher, Dan Joe, Meddlesome, and Zibia.

These were fine-looking horses and made an excellent showing when I had exercised them for the benefit of suckers. The latter fell into several categories. Those like Epping advanced money to help train the horses and win purses. Others were led to believe that we were training a "ringer" which would later win and make it possible for them to clean up on wagering. The most gullible were those at the tracks who went for "inside tips" on betting.

At the track, I frequently posed as a jockey. I had to employ a stooge, and on many occasions was helped by William J. Winterbill. He was tall, broad-shouldered, and well-built, with fine features. He dressed conservatively.

Here is an example of the way we worked:

Winterbill and I selected a victim from the crowd of men standing near the betting ring. Program in hand, Winterbill approached the sucker and struck up an acquaintance while talking about the day's entries.

"My name is Winterbill," he introduced himself. "William J. Winterbill." He stuck out his hand.

"Mine is Harper," responded the other man. "Glad to know you, Mr. Winterbill."

Winterbill was an impressive-looking fellow. He had little trouble getting the victim to believe that he was a business man, taking a day off at the races.

## How to Beat the Horses

"What horse are you betting on?" Winterbill asked.

"Haven't made up my mind," Harper replied. "Have you any suggestions?"

"No, I haven't decided either." Then his eye wandered away from the betting ring. "Say! Do you see that fellow standing there?"

He pointed to me. I had a pad of paper in my hand and was busily jotting down figures. "Yes, I see him," said Harper. "What about him?"

"Don't you know who he is?"

"Can't say that I do."

"Why, that's Willie Caywood, the jockey. He rides for Sam Hildreth, the famous trainer."

Of course, Harper had heard of Sam Hildreth. We always picked the name of a famous trainer. (Hildreth later raced Zev, one of the greatest horses of all time.) I was slight and young and could pass for a jockey.

"Wonder what he's figuring up?" Harper mused.

"I wonder, too," said Winterbill. "If there was only some way we could get to know him."

Just then, I dropped my pencil. It rolled some distance from where I was standing.

"Quick!" hissed Winterbill. "Now's your chance. Pick up his pencil. That's your chance to meet him. Maybe he will give you a tip."

Harper hurriedly retrieved my pencil. I was properly grateful.

"Thank you, Mr. — "

"Harper. Don't mention it."

"My name is Willie Caywood."

"Not the jockey?" asked Harper.

"Yes," I admitted.

Winterbill came up. Harper introduced us.

"We were just wondering what you were figuring," Harper ventured.

"Why — ah — I was just figuring up how much I would win today."

"What makes you so sure you'll win anything?" Harper asked.

I glanced about furtively, and lowered my voice. "I know I'm going to win. You gentlemen look like you can be trusted. I'll tell you the truth, but it must be strictly confidential. The boss is going to make a killing today. So he let me in on it."

"I don't suppose you'd be willing to tell us the name of the horse?" said Winterbill.

"No," I replied. "I couldn't do that. I promised the boss that I wouldn't. And if it got around, the odds would go down on the horse. My boss is going to spread his bets. He'll wire them around the country just before post time, so that nobody will get suspicious."

"Too bad," grunted Harper, obviously disappointed. "We hoped you might give us a tip."

"I'll tell you what," offered Winterbill, as if an idea had suddenly struck him. "If you won't give us a tip, maybe you'll make our bets for us."

I considered this a moment. "Yes, I guess I could do that. But I still can't tell you the name of the horse."

"I don't care," said Winterbill, "just so I clean up. Here's $2,500. Put it on the nose for me."

Harper had already dug into his pocket. "Here's $1,500 for me."

"All right," I agreed, taking their money. "I'll meet you gentlemen right here after the fifth race."

Winterbill was enthusiastic and Harper seemed well pleased. They left me and went into the grandstand, chatting and speculating on what horse in the fifth race was to make the killing. Winterbill later excused himself from Harper on some pretext. He met me a short time later and we worked the same game on as many suckers as we could find.

But by the time the fifth race had been run, we were far away from the track. Mr. Harper and the others who kept the rendezvous were doomed to a long wait and to a sad disappointment.

## 5. Two Unwary Strangers

BOB COLLINS WAS A TOUT WHO WORKED WITH ME ON SEVERAL occasions. He helped in the case of Mr. Kahn, which was amusing, profitable, and in some ways pathetic.

Mr. Kahn was a tall, thick-set German, as industrious a man as I ever met. He had a delicatessen and food shop on LaSalle Street. Old Man Kahn took great pride in the fact that his shop had the finest food in town. He carried only the best imported cheese and frankfurters, as well as other meats and fish.

When I first went into his shop I had no designs on the old fellow. I went there because I liked his food. I had made three or four visits before the old man's curiosity got the best of him.

In those days, I dressed flashily. I wore a five-carat diamond ring, a big diamond pin in my ascot tie, and a vest chain locket with a diamond horseshoe.

Every time I was in his shop Old Man Kahn eyed the diamonds. Finally, one day, he said: "Young man, I see you like fine food. And I see you're rich, too. I know most of my customers, but I don't know who you are. What business are you in?"

I knew he had been thinking about the diamonds. "Why, I own stock in the racecourses," I told him, giving him one of my favorite stories. I still had no designs on him.

"Where they race horses?" he asked.

"Yes. Haven't you ever been to the races?"

"No," he replied. "I have been too busy. But I would like to go sometime."

"Then come as my guest," I said. "Would you like a complimentary ticket for next Saturday?"

## "Yellow Kid" Weil

"No. Saturday is my busy day. But I could go next Tuesday."

"Fine. Here's your ticket. I'll drop in and you can go with me." The old man beamed and said he would be ready.

The following Tuesday I escorted him to the track. He asked endless questions. I took him to the betting ring and showed him how bets were made.

He was especially intrigued by the concession where red hots were sold. His eyes shone in amazement as he watched people coming up to pay ten cents for a hot dog.

"That fellow over there," he said. "He sure does a good business."

"Sure," I replied, and a vague scheme began to form in my mind. "You know, people at a racecourse don't watch their money — they spend it freely."

"I can see that," said Kahn. "How much do you suppose he takes in every day?"

"I don't know. But it ought to be easy to find out. Why don't you watch for a while? I've got to see a fellow on some business. I'll leave you here and meet you again in fifteen minutes."

"Yah, sure," said Kahn. He was so fascinated that he hardly noticed that I was gone.

I looked for Bob Collins. I found him, stated my proposition, and got him to work with me on the deal. Then I returned to where the old fellow was still standing in front of the red-hot stand, counting the dimes that poured in.

"Well," I asked, "have you estimated how much he takes in?"

"Yah. It must be a hundred dollars a day."

"Oh, I think it's more than that. I believe he takes in around two hundred dollars a day."

"Two hundred dollars a day!" Kahn repeated. "Why, on that he must make a big profit. How much does he have to pay for the lease?"

"Oh, he doesn't have a lease," I replied. "It's what we call a concession. He doesn't have to pay us anything, as long as he satisfies the patrons."

"My, I would like to have a business like that. The customers would like my fine imported frankfurters."

## Two Unwary Strangers

"They certainly would," I agreed. "And you could get more for them, too. Maybe twenty-five cents. Money means nothing to people at a race track."

"No," said Kahn, "I wouldn't charge a quarter. I could put up a fine frankfurter sandwich and make a good profit for fifteen cents."

"And you could sell roast beef sandwiches, too. Would you be interested in having the concession?"

"Do you think I could get it?"

"With my help, you can," I replied. "Remember I own stock in this track."

"Yah, I remember," said Kahn.

"Come into the office with me," I invited him. "We'll talk to the secretary. He has charge of the concessions."

I led him into the office of Sheridan Clark, who was secretary of the Association that operated the track. Clark, of course, did have charge of the concessions. But there was one thing about his office that Kahn did not know. It was always open. Jockeys, trainers, and owners were constantly going in and out on routine matters. And I happened to know that, at that particular time, Clark was not in the office.

When we walked in, a man was seated behind Clark's desk. It was Bob Collins, my confederate.

"Mr. Clark," I called, "this is Mr. Kahn. I'd like you to see what you can do about getting the red-hot concession for him."

Collins stood up and shook hands. "Glad to know you, Mr. Kahn," he said. "Any friend of Joe's is a friend of mine." He walked out from behind the desk. "Let's go have a glass of beer and discuss this further." That was a pretext to get us out of the office. We didn't know when Sheridan Clark might return.

Kahn had not the slightest suspicion — only a warm glow in his heart — as we strolled to the bar.

Collins asked for more details, and Kahn told him what wonderful meats he prepared and how certain he was that he could satisfy the customers. At the right moment I added words of praise for both Kahn's products and his character. Finally Collins was convinced that the concession should be turned over to Kahn.

## "Yellow Kid" Weil

"But I'll have to give the other man a few days' notice," he said. "Suppose you begin next Monday, Mr. Kahn."

"Yah," replied the German. "That will be good."

"Fine." Collins ordered another round of beer. Then as if the concession matter had been settled and was of no further concern: "Joe, isn't it about time to make the killing?"

"Yes," I returned. "We've decided on next Saturday."

"What's a killing?" asked Kahn.

Collins hesitated.

"It's all right to tell him, Sheridan," I nodded. "He's one of us now, you know."

So Collins told him. "We have bad days, when attendance isn't very high. If it's raining or we have other bad weather, people don't come to the track. At the end of the season, we'd be in the hole if we didn't do something to make up for our losses. So we have a fixed race once every season. We take some of the Association's money and bet it on this race. That way we even up the losses."

"You mean it costs so much to run a race track?"

"It wouldn't except for the purses we give. The purses, combined with the expenses, exceed the receipts, and we have to do something to make up for it."

"I understand," said Kahn brightly.

After we had left Collins and were driving back to Chicago, I suggested to Kahn that it was a good opportunity for him to clean up. I explained that it was arranged for the winner to be a horse on which the odds would be long. But to prevent the bookmakers from getting suspicious, the money was spread around the country in various cities, including Milwaukee.

He seemed interested. The following day I dropped in at his shop.

"I'm going to Milwaukee on Friday," I told him, "to place $10,000 for the Association. Would you like to come along and get in on the killing?"

Kahn was cautious. He was eager to make money but at the same time he didn't want to take any risk.

"How much would I make?" he asked.

"The horse will probably pay about 5 to 1."

50

## Two Unwary Strangers

"I could bet maybe $500," he muttered.

"Don't be foolish!" I scoffed. "This is your chance to make a fortune. Why, $500 is only a drop in the bucket."

After some additional persuading he decided he might as well make it worth while, since it was a sure thing anyway. He went to the National Bank of the Republic and withdrew $5,000. The following Friday, we were in Milwaukee.

I had arranged a poolroom setup to take his money. I bet my $10,000 and he put down his $5,000. Then I asked him to wait for me at the poolroom.

"I have some business downtown. I won't be long. I'm expecting a phone call from Sheridan Clark in Chicago and if it comes while I'm gone, take the message, will you, Mr. Kahn?"

My only purpose in leaving was to permit Bob Collins to make the call. He called and told Kahn to tell me to "Bet as much as possible!"

When I returned and he gave me the message, I said: "I'm going to bet a marker for $10,000. Why don't you bet some more?"

"I haven't got any more money."

"You can bet a marker as I did."

"What is a marker?"

"You tell 'em how much you want to bet. They give you a ticket and they'll hold your bet until noon tomorrow. That's to give you time to wire the money."

As usual he was cautious. But he finally decided to bet a marker for $2,500, the money to be wired from Chicago the following morning.

We returned to Chicago and the next day, Saturday, the day of the supposedly fixed race, I was at Kahn's place. He gave me the $2,500 and I went over to the Western Union office. I wired $25.00 and got a receipt. It was no trick at all to alter this to $2,500. I took the receipt back to Kahn, and that's the last I ever saw of him.

I later learned the sequel, which I had intended to prevent. I had arranged to have Bob Collins call him on Monday and tell him the concession deal was off. But I had not reckoned with his German thoroughness. When Collins called Mr. Kahn had left for the track.

He had a wagon loaded with frankfurters, roast beef, and the trimmings. He arrived at the track just after dawn and began to move his stuff in. When the Superintendent of the grounds questioned him, he told of having made the deal with Sheridan Clark. The Superintendent did not question his story.

Rather he pitched in and helped Kahn unload and set up his stand. The old fellow had bought a new sign: "Now UNDER NEW MANAGEMENT. BETTER FOOD WILL BE SERVED." It was put up and he was ready to do business. Then the regular concession man came in.

Seeing the sign and the excellent food Kahn had brought, this man too thought the deal was on the level and that the concession had really been taken from him. He was about to depart when Sheridan Clark appeared.

Eventually, the old man got the drift. He packed up his things and sadly returned to Chicago. He made no complaint, and as far as I know never told the story to anyone. He has passed on, but the fine food shop that bears his name has continued to prosper.

A somewhat similar deal was made with a man named Bolton, a Dutchman with a beard, who owned a business block known as Bolton's Opera House, where public dances were held twice a week.

Patsy King, who controlled the policy game in Chicago and owned a string of poolrooms, had set Billy Skidmore up in business in Bolton's building. Skid had a cigar store, with a little gambling in the back room. A lot of us used to hang out at his place.

Mr. Bolton had a paint store in the same building. He also was a contractor and employed a crew of painters. He had seen me around.

One day he asked me what my business was. I told him that I worked for the Racing Association. I arranged for him to visit the track with me.

He too had a great curiosity. But his particular interest was focused on the grandstand, which was badly in need of paint. I contacted Collins. We went through the routine, and ended with a promise to Bolton that he could have the contract to paint the grandstand and stable the following week.

Meanwhile, I worked the "killing" game on him, and he wagered $2,500 — or thought he did. The following Monday morning, bright and early, his painters were at the track with their materials. They set up their scaffolds and were busy at work on the front of the grand-

## Two Unwary Strangers

stand when the track manager came to work and discovered them.

"What are you doing up there?" he demanded.

"We're painting the grandstand," replied the painters' foreman. "And when we finish that, we're going to paint the stables."

"Is that so?" The track manager had a vicious temper. "Well, nobody told me about it. You get those scaffolds down and get out of here."

"Not until we've finished this job."

"You're not going to finish the job," the other retorted hotly. "Come down!"

"Suppose you come up and get me!" growled the painter.

"I'll be glad to accommodate you." The manager started to ascend the scaffold.

The foreman had been mixing a huge bucket of paint. He took careful aim, slowly overturned it, and dropped it. The track manager was soaked with paint from head to foot. The painters roared.

The man yanked the bucket off his head and dug the paint out of his eyes. Then he let out a bellow of rage that was heard all over the grounds. The entire track staff came to his assistance and the painters were forcibly ejected after a wild melee amid splashing paint.

Bolton immediately contacted the track officials and learned that he had been duped. However, it was a fact that they were considering a paint job for the grandstand and stables. I later learned that Bolton very likely would have had the job since his men had already started, had not the track manager interfered.

Bolton soon learned that the race he had supposedly bet on was not fixed. But what irked him even more was that he had been misled about the grandstand contract.

He went to Skid. "Where is that little slicker?" he demanded.

Skid pretended ignorance, and Bolton poured out the whole story. "He took advantage of me, he led me on and then swindled me."

Nor did Bolton let the matter drop. He swore out a warrant charging me with operating a confidence game. I was arrested and the case came before Judge Shott in his Justice Shop. As it happened, Skid knew Judge Shott and had a private talk with him.

Over Bolton's protests, Judge Shott ruled that he was not "an un-

53

wary stranger," that he had entered the betting deal, believing he would make money on a dishonest race, and that, as a businessman, he should have obtained a written contract before he started painting the grandstand. The case was dismissed and I was released.

I saw Bolton many times after that, at Skidmore's cigar store. His rancor eventually disappeared and we became friends, though I never tried to take him again.

"You're a slick duck," he used to say, and there was grudging admiration in his voice.

The odium of the confidence-game charge did not help my standing at the track, and I decided to take a short rest until the affair had blown over. I went to the lake-resort region of Illinois, northwest of Chicago.

I soon learned of a man I shall call Van Essen, who was by far the wealthiest man in those parts. He had an estate on Gray's Lake and was a heavy investor in the bank. I had heard there was to be a big Fourth of July picnic at Gray's Lake, and decided to attend. But first I returned to Chicago to prepare my "props."

Dan Canary ran a livery service on Wabash Avenue. From him I hired a car and liveried chauffeur. All cars in those days were one-cylinder affairs and were rarities even in a big city like Chicago.

With my chauffeur, I motored to Gray's Lake and attended the picnic. During the height of the festivities there was a plea for contributions to some charitable institution. The justice of the peace, a one-armed man, made a strong exhortation for funds; then the hat was passed. I contributed twenty-five dollars.

Of course, everybody wanted to see the man who had given twenty-five dollars — a considerable sum in the rural areas. Word got around that I was the man who had driven the car to Gray's Lake. The car alone aroused considerable excitement.

My main object was to meet Mr. Van Essen, and that was no trick at all. He came forward to see the man with the philanthropic streak.

He was very cordial. I could see that he was deeply impressed by my display of affluence.

"Mr. Van Essen," I said, "perhaps you can help me. I'm looking for a farm. I want to breed horses."

## Two Unwary Strangers

"I'll certainly be happy to help you, Mr. Weil," he replied. "It must be fascinating to be a breeder of blooded horses and see them race and win and have your own colors."

"It is," I replied. "You seem to have a great interest in horse racing yourself, Mr. Van Essen."

"Yes," he declared, with a show of modesty. "I happen to own the poolroom here in Gray's Lake, and we do some wagering."

"Is that so?" This was shaping up better than I had hoped. "Now, about that farm — "

Mr. Van Essen owned a great deal of the land around Gray's Lake. He showed me the property and I chose 350 acres, with a few buildings.

Van Essen was very happy because of the prospective deal.

"Of course, I'll have to go over this with my architect," I pointed out. "Meanwhile, why don't you come up to Chicago with me and be my guest at the races?"

He accepted eagerly, and we motored back to Chicago. The Harlem season had opened and we went to that track. First, I took Mr. Van Essen to my fine tack room. He was greatly impressed by this window dressing — another display of affluence.

"How about a tip, Mr. Weil?" he asked. "As long as I'm free and in the city, I might as well take a flyer."

"I'm sorry," I replied, "but I have no tips. I bet only on certainties. I have to be certain a horse is going to win before I lay out my money." Then to throw him off his guard: "Mr. Van Essen, when we have become better acquainted — that is, when I have purchased the farm and remodeled it — I'll take you into my confidence."

"That's perfectly all right, Mr. Weil," he returned. His voice fairly sang with elation. "I can't tell you how pleased I am to have met you."

I showed him around the track. We watched a few races, and then I took him to the station. I promised to see him soon.

A week later I motored again to Gray's Lake, accompanied by a supposed architect who was, in fact, my stooge Winterbill. Guided by Mr. Van Essen, we went over the ground. Winterbill, as I have said, was very impressive looking. He carried a sketch book and pencil and from time to time made notes and drew diagrams of proposed buildings.

## "Yellow Kid" Weil

When we had completed our preliminary survey of the property, Winterbill returned to Chicago. I stayed on as Mr. Van Essen's guest.

The following morning a telegram came for me. I had arranged for it beforehand.

"I came away and forgot my glasses," I said. (As a matter of fact, I didn't even wear glasses at the time.) "Would you be good enough to read this message for me?"

Mr. Van Essen was only too happy to do so. He read it aloud:

**EVENTS HAVE SHAPED UP ALL IS SATISFACTORY RETURN IMMEDIATELY.**

"That means we can close the deal very shortly," I said, smiling.

I then unfolded to Van Essen the story of a race that was fixed for my horse to win.

"Inasmuch as you have been so gracious to me," I added, "even neglecting your own affairs to aid mine, I'd like to do something for you. I will, provided you don't tell anyone about it nor how much you win — not even your wife."

Mr. Van Essen was so delighted that he vowed eternal secrecy. He obtained a draft on the First National Bank of Chicago and we left for the city. He stopped at the bank and cashed his draft. When he came out he displayed a big wad of bills.

I said, "You'll have to get those small bills changed into $1,000 bills. When we make the bet, it will be just before post time and speed will be essential. The bookmaker wouldn't have time to count so many bills. And if we go too much ahead of time, the odds on the horse will come down when they see the vast sums that are being wagered on it."

My purpose in telling him to change the bills was that I thought he'd hand me the money and ask me to go back into the bank. But it didn't work out that way. Van Essen went himself, returning with ten $1,000 bills. I had told him that I was wagering $100,000 on the race.

On the way to the track, we stopped at several roadhouses for drinks. When we arrived at The Gardens — a popular roadhouse of that day — it was nearly time for the race to begin. The Harlem

56

## Two Unwary Strangers

racecourse was located not much more than about six blocks away.

"Perhaps it would be a better plan," I told Mr. Van Essen, "if I handled the whole thing through my betting commissioners. You might get confused."

But Van Essen was reluctant to part with his money. So I had to use a psychological touch. I was wearing a light English-whipcord topcoat.

"It's almost time," I muttered, looking at my watch. "I'll have to hurry to make it." I took off my topcoat and handed it to him. "Here, hold my coat and give me the money. I can make better time without the coat."

He took the coat and handed over the money. For some reason, he seemed to feel that, as long as he had my coat, he was holding security for his money. Actually he was holding the bag. I did not return for my coat. Eventually Van Essen went to look for me. While he was gone my chauffeur disappeared. Mr. Van Essen returned to Gray's Lake a sadder but a much wiser man.

At the track I had taken one precaution. Alderman John A. Rogers was then making book at the Harlem course. He was a good friend of mine, so I went to him.

"Johnny," I said, "do me a favor. I have a deal on with a man. I'd like you to enter $10,000 in your book on Black Fonso."

"Sure, Joe." Rogers made the entry, though no actual money was wagered.

I felt rather good about the Van Essen deal, but I hadn't heard the last of it. A former Chicago policeman had a summer home in Gray's Lake. My victim told him the story. On the advice of the policeman, Van Essen had me arrested and charged me with swindling him. But the case didn't get very far. Alderman Rogers brought his books into court and the $10,000 entry sufficed as proof that Van Essen's money had been wagered.

The case was dropped because he could hardly do anything to me for failing to fix a race!

Why did I get away with all these deals — why didn't the racing authorities do something? As a matter of fact Sheridan Clark was reluctant to press a charge against me. For one day when police had raided Hawthorne for some alleged illegal activities, I was on hand, and helped Clark to escape in my carriage. He never forgot the favor.

Most of the people connected with racing in those days — jockeys, trainers, stable boys, even owners — were touts. Many of them had no hesitation about selling a tip to a stranger.

Indeed, some of them made quite a business of it.

The only people who had any grounds for complaint were the bookmakers. If the "inside tips" had really been on the level, the bookmakers would have been heavy losers. However, they knew that when money was turned over to me to be bet on a race they had nothing to worry about.

I was a member of the American Turf Association in good standing. Because of this one fact the track officials would have hesitated to make a complaint. They had no sympathy for men like Van Essen, whose only objective was to clean up on a supposedly fixed race.

The fact that the race hadn't been fixed helped rather than hindered the reputation of the track.

But I was not yet finished with Van Essen. Little did I suspect that, as a result of that episode, I would soon be accused of murder.

## 6. From Nags to Riches

HARDLY A WEEK HAD PASSED AFTER THE VAN ESSEN EPISODE WHEN the automobile I had hired from Dan Canary's livery stable on Wabash Avenue was found on a side road near the outskirts of Joliet. Slumped over the wheel was the chauffeur who had driven me to Gray's Lake. He was dead. He had been murdered.

Detectives who investigated learned that a man using the name of Dove had entered the Congress Hotel. Approaching the switchboard operator, he asked her where he could hire a motor car. She suggested Dan Canary's establishment. Dove requested her to phone and have the car call for him at the hotel's Michigan Avenue entrance. This was done, and when the car arrived the doorman helped Dove into it.

Detective De Roche went to see Dan Canary, who knew no one named Dove. But he did recall that I had rented the same car with the same chauffeur for the trip to Gray's Lake. De Roche obtained a picture of me and showed it to the switchboard girl. She said that I was the man who had ordered the car.

The first I heard about it was when the papers came out with big headlines: "WEIL IS DOVE."

Of course, the charge was absurd. I have never carried a gun or lethal weapon of any kind. It is well known, even to my bitterest enemies, that I have never resorted to violence.

I called a good criminal lawyer named Howard Sprokel. He said that he would surrender me, but first, I must come to his office. I did, and convinced him that I knew nothing of the murder of the chauffeur.

"All right, Joe," he said. "I believe you. We'll go over to the

Detective Bureau and give you up. But first, we're going to the Congress Hotel."

He explained his plan, and we went to the Congress. Going up to the switchboard girl, he asked her to put in a call to his office. Then he took the phone and began a lengthy conversation with his secretary.

While he was on the phone, I engaged the switchboard girl in small talk.

She was a friendly sort, and I had a glib tongue. We discussed trivial matters and got along well. We conversed until Sprokel hung up and turned from the phone.

"You two seem to be well acquainted," he said to the girl. "Been friends a long time?"

"Why, no," the girl replied. "To tell you the truth, I never saw him until today."

"Are you sure of that?" Sprokel asked.

"Certainly I am."

I tipped my hat to the young woman, thanked her for a pleasant interlude, and accompanied Sprokel out the Michigan Avenue entrance. Sprokel pretended to have some business down the street and I waited in front, engaging the doorman in conversation. We discussed the man who had ordered the motor car from Dan Canary. He gave me the same details I had read in the papers.

Sprokel returned. He repeated the questions he had asked the girl. The doorman assured him that I was a stranger, that he had never before laid eyes on me.

"It worked, Joe," said Sprokel, as we went over to the police station.

We asked for Chief-of-Police Collins. He listened to Sprokel's story, then summoned Detective Johnny Halpin.

"Go over to the Congress Hotel with these gentlemen and verify their statements," he instructed Halpin.

Both the girl and the doorman told him that I was not the man named Dove who had ordered the motor car. We went back to Headquarters and Halpin reported to Chief Collins.

The chief was apologetic. The newspapers were apologetic. My wife fainted.

In subsequent years, I became better acquainted with John Halpin.

## From Nags to Riches

He rose to the post of chief of detectives. I know that he was a square fellow. I never offered him a bribe, because I knew that he would not have taken it. He was chief during the days of the infamous Barney Bertsch, the fixer. Halpin would have nothing to do with Bertsch, but was accused of accepting bribes, was convicted, and sent to the penitentiary. It was as foul a deal as I ever saw.

When Halpin got out of prison, I was in the money. I tried to set him up in business in a billiard hall. But everywhere he applied, he was refused a lease — as soon as my identity became known.

Just the same, Johnny Halpin remained square. He is an old man now, an armed guard at an industrial plant and gets along well with his fellow employees.

One day, shortly after I had been cleared of the Dove murder, I entered an establishment near the Loop — a wrecking and salvage place. I talked to the president, whom I shall call Ernest Rappe, and the vice-president of the company, Lester Bruno.

"I want to build a small race track," I explained. "I thought you might have the equipment."

"I doubt it," said Rappe, a big fellow. "But you can look around. What are you planning to do — start a new track in Chicago?"

"Oh, no," I replied. "But my partner and I want some place where we can train a horse in secrecy."

I looked around, but of course the equipment I was looking for wasn't there. But Rappe was interested and that satisfied my purpose.

"If we haven't got what you need, we'll get it for you," he offered. "Suppose you come out to dinner tonight and we'll discuss it further."

That night, I dined at Rappe's home. Afterward, while we were having coffee and cigars, he began:

"You know, my partner and I have been wondering why you want to train a horse in secrecy."

I hesitated, as if doubtful whether to take him into my confidence. Finally, I murmured:

"We have a plan to clean up on wagers. We have an exceptionally fast horse named Black Fonso. He can beat anything on the turf today. Here's what we plan to do. We've bought an inferior horse that resembles Black Fonso. We have entered him at the racecourses under that name. He will race for several weeks, but won't win anything.

"Of course, the odds on him will be long. Meanwhile, we plan to keep Black Fonso in shape. And then, after our horse has lost enough races to make the odds on him very long, we will substitute Black Fonso. The authorities will have become familiar with a horse by that name. They won't know the switch has been made — nor will the bookmakers. We expect to collect a tremendous sum in wagers at long odds."

Rappe was interested. "And you need to build a race track where Black Fonso can be kept in shape?"

"That's correct."

"Why don't you use the course at one of the tracks where the horses are not running?" he asked — a natural question.

"We could do that," I replied, "but some tout would be certain to get onto it. If we're to clean up, the training must be done in absolute secrecy."

"I can understand that now," said Rappe, as he mulled the matter over. While I lay no claim to telepathic powers, it was easy to read his thoughts: he was wondering how he could get in on this deal.

I have made proposals to numerous people for crooked bets on the races. If these bets had been made as I proposed them, the bookmakers would have lost thousands of dollars. Everyone who was ever approached on a deal of this sort was interested, but not one of them ever gave any thought to the fact that it was basically dishonest. Rappe was no exception.

"Mr. Rappe," I confided, "I am not a wealthy man. I can't afford to buy the equipment we need. That is why I was looking at your salvage material. Perhaps you would be interested in helping to defray the expenses of training Black Fonso."

He jumped at the bait without bothering to see if there was a hook attached. "I would! Provided, of course, that I could share in the profits when you clean up."

"Naturally," I replied. "Mr. Rappe, I'll make you a proposal. Tomorrow, if you will meet me, I'll take you to see Black Fonso. If you're still interested, we can make some sort of deal. If you will

## From Nags to Riches

furnish certain sums to purchase equipment and further the project, we'll let you in on the betting."

"Both Mr. Bruno and I would be interested," said Rappe. "We will go with you."

I had Black Fonso out at Palatine at old Jim Wilson's farm. When Black Fonso came prancing out of the stall they were visibly impressed. He stood sixteen hands high and had a satiny black coat, with not a spot on him. He was really a beauty — black as night and with a spirited gleam in his eye. They were very enthusiastic.

The next day I called at their place of business to discuss terms. Bruno seemed the more impressionable of the two, and I had learned that he wrote the checks for the firm. This made him doubly valuable in my eyes, and I addressed most of my talk to him.

I explained why Black Fonso must be trained in the utmost secrecy if our plan was to succeed. I was quite frank about the inevitable expense.

It was agreed that Rappe and Bruno would pay certain costs to be passed on by me from time to time. In return, on the day that I selected to run Black Fonso as a ringer, they would be given an opportunity to wager as much as they liked.

A few days later we brought in Black Fonso from the country and stabled him near the Harlem track. We clocked him one morning at the Harlem seven-eighths course. The season had closed and we had the track to ourselves.

Rappe and Bruno held a stop watch and I used a timing device then used in harness racing. It was a mechanical clock, which was started or stopped by blowing into a rubber tube attachment. It gave us a double check on Black Fonso, who ran the course in one minute, twenty-seven and a fraction seconds.

At that time, this was considered very fast, although present-day horses have been speeded up so that 1:27 for a seven-eighths course now would tag a horse as a hopeless plug. Rappe and Bruno were extremely gratified. Of course, in this case, there was no faking on the distance.

"When do we make the killing?" Bruno wanted to know.

"At the right time," I replied. "First, we must race an inferior

## "Yellow Kid" Weil

horse under the name of Black Fonso so that authorities at the course will become familiar with him. I have a suitable horse for this purpose.

"Also," I pointed out, "we must get Black Fonso in tiptop shape. We must have a place where he can be exercised secretly. I have located some equipment suitable for the purpose. In a few weeks, the odds should be long enough so that we can run him in and make a real cleanup."

While I knew that it was not good policy to touch a potentially rich sucker for insignificant sums, I did get a few hundred from Rappe and Bruno to pay Black Fonso's training expenses. I told them that I considered it better to train him in the country, away from prying eyes. They could see the logic of this.

What I didn't tell them was that Black Fonso was a "Morning Glory" — a type of horse that is not uncommon, even today. He makes a sensational showing and looks like a world-beater in the morning; but in the afternoon's competition, he folds up completely. Black Fonso was — a whiz in a morning work-out but a washout in an afternoon race.

Another thing I didn't tell them was that the horse entered at the track as Black Fonso was Black Fonso himself — he was the one and only horse I had. He didn't need another horse anyway to make a poor showing — he was quite capable of doing it himself. And of course we helped him along this path to obscurity.

It is the custom, on the day that a horse is entered in a race, to withhold all feed, giving him only a small amount of water. This helps to put him on edge by the time he goes to the post. We always saw to it that Black Fonso had even more than his usual daily intake of hay and water — a precaution to keep him from winning, if by some freak of luck, he might come near it.

He was never in the money, however, and every time he raced and finished back of the field, the odds on him became longer. In three weeks the odds against him were 10 to 1. I went to Rappe and Bruno and told them I had decided on a date when the horse running as Black Fonso would be withdrawn and the real Black Fonso would be substituted.

"Put us down for about $300," said Bruno.

## From Nags to Riches

"Don't be foolish!" I scoffed. "Here you have an opportunity to clean up and you talk of a paltry $300. I thought I was dealing with men who knew how to bet."

We discussed the betting at some length. Finally, I had them jockeyed up to $16,000.

But Bruno was skeptical. "If we bet so much, the bookmakers will become suspicious and the odds will go down."

"Certainly," I returned calmly. "Did you think I hadn't thought of that? I've arranged with my betting commissioner to spread the bets all over the country. No large amount will be placed with any one bookmaker and all the bets will be made just before post time. In that manner no suspicion will be created. But we will make a killing."

This seemed satisfactory, and the next day I brought in William J. Winterbill, who had no difficulty at all with the usual suckers; but he jarred Bruno the wrong way. The latter was cool when I told him that Winterbill was my betting commissioner and would arrange to make our wagers. He motioned that he wished to talk to me in private.

"You know, Mr. Weil," he began, "first impressions are lasting impressions. You impressed us from the moment we saw you and we trust you. But we don't trust that fellow out there. He looks too tricky."

"But he's one of my steady betting commissioners," I frowned. "I don't want to hurt the fellow's feelings."

"How much are you going to give him?"

"About $5,000."

"Well, let him place your bets. But you'd better find somebody else to take ours."

I agreed to this, although it would have been less trouble to let Winterbill take the whole thing. But I didn't want Rappe and Bruno to back down. So I dismissed Winterbill and found other stooges. They were acceptable to the two, who gave them a total of $16,000 to be spread around the country on Black Fonso.

As soon as the money was safely out of their hands and into mine I departed. And that's the last I ever saw of either Rappe or Bruno.

65

## "Yellow Kid" Weil

If they looked at the results on the day the money was supposedly wagered, they saw that Black Fonso lost.

There wasn't anything they could do. They could not go to the law and say: "We paid out money to train a ringer and clean up on crooked betting. We were going to cheat the bookmakers, but this man cheated us instead." Even if there had been a legal basis for complaint, they wouldn't have wanted their friends to know they had been taken.

An interesting sequel to the Rappe-Bruno deal was related to me by Barney Berman, who owned a large fish market and delivered fish to Bruno's home.

"Barney," Bruno said to him one day, "do you play the horses?"

"Yes," Barney replied. "I own a couple of platers."

Bruno then accused Barney of "steering" me to him. Barney vigorously denied this.

"How much did you lose?" he asked.

Bruno reflected a moment. "Well, I'll tell you, Barney," he replied, "if you had every fish in Lake Michigan on your counters and sold them at the highest prices, that would just about cover the amount I lost."

Rappe and Bruno were just two of many who participated in my "fixed" racing deals. Most of them were picked with care. The first requisite was that the prospect have money. Another was that he know as little as possible about horse racing.

There was one man I strung along for sixteen months. I never got large sums from him, but on various pretexts, I took $200 or $300 at a time. Occasionally, I took him to the track to watch my horses run and see how races were operated.

"See how dry and dusty the course is today?"

"Yes."

"That's what we call a fast track. My horses don't run as well on a fast track, so I usually sprinkle water on it to settle the dust."

When the water sprinkler came around I pointed it out to him. "It costs me a lot of money, but it's worth it."

He never questioned that I had to pay the expenses of maintaining the water wagon. He later gave me $300 to help keep the track

## From Nags to Riches

watered! This was one of my favorite "expense" items, and several others came across with cash to water the track.

On another occasion I showed him how my electric battery arrangement speeded up a horse. There had to be a special saddle so that the batteries could be concealed. I had the jockey mount a horse and press his foot against the apron across the animals flank where the switch was concealed. The horse always jumped. I never used the batteries in the races, but the sucker didn't know that. He paid for an "expensive" battery device, as well as for a special saddle. Later he contributed $200 toward the purchase of an electric whip, another potent device for goading a horse on to greater speed.

In all these deals the victims were led to believe that I was paying off the jockeys, the judge of the scales, and the presiding judge. Even a few pounds deducted from the weight a horse is carrying makes a tremendous difference in his speed. The judge of the scales was supposed to let my horses pass without weight handicaps.

The presiding judge had the power to declare a race no contest. I always told those who gave me money to pay off the presiding judge that if my horse failed to win, he would declare "no contest."

In some cases I told the suckers that I was paying off the other jockeys in the race to give my horse "clearance." The sums received for any one of these phony reasons were not large, but there were many of them and they flowed in regularly and gave me a nice income.

Training a ringer was the scheme that was particularly attractive to the wealthier suckers. I met a man who had a lucrative linotype business. He fell in readily with my plan, but worried a great deal about the possibility of the horse losing the race in spite of our precautions.

"Why, man," I said, "this horse has no more chance of losing the race than you have of losing your eyesight!"

This reassured him, and he gave me $5,000 to bet on the ringer. I disappeared and closed the books on this deal.

One of my favorite haunts in those days was the buffet of the Palmer House, which served delicious sliced chicken. One night some months later I was standing at the buffet, enjoying a chicken sandwich, when I felt a tap on my shoulder.

## "Yellow Kid" Weil

I turned. There stood my linotype friend, looking me over.

"I still have my eyesight," he declared dryly. And with that he walked away. That was the last I ever saw or heard of that affair.

During the early days of the Mayor Carter Harrison administration, there was a police chief I shall call "Boylan." He had a son who was a lawyer, with an office in a Loop building. Young Boylan had become interested in a ringer deal. The horse in this case was a two-year-old filly named Zibia which I had just secured from A. B. Watts. She was a beautiful filly and quite fast. She made an impressive showing when Boylan clocked her, but I thought she was another Morning Glory.

On the day of the "fixed" race, Boylan gave me $5,000 to put on Zibia's nose. The odds against her winning were at post time 100 to 1. But once she left the post, there was no controlling her. She walked away with the race, causing any bookmaker who had accepted wagers on her to tear his hair. No bookmaker could pay off any large bet at such long odds.

I was in a quandary. I had supposedly bet $5,000 on the nose. Boylan was looking for his winnings: $500,000! If I didn't do something, he could go to the law and, without saying a word about a fixed race, charge me with failure to bet his money.

I found Winterbill and sent him to Milwaukee, with specific instructions. The following morning I called at Boylan's office.

"That was some race," he said gleefully. "We really made a killing, didn't we?"

"Yes," I replied. "I bet $10,000 of my own money. Why, I'll collect a million dollars!"

I thought this over for a moment, as if the very thought stunned me. (I *would* have been stunned, if there had been any prospect of collecting any such amount.) Then I added: "My betting commissioner, Winterbill, has gone to Milwaukee to collect our winnings. I told him to get in touch with me here."

Boylan knew that I had planned to place the money out of town so that the local bookmakers wouldn't become suspicious at large sums being wagered on a horse at such long odds. He thought nothing of my reference to Milwaukee.

## From Nags to Riches

We were building air castles, discussing what we would do with our huge winnings, when the telephone rang. It was a long-distance call from Milwaukee. Winterbill was on the other end.

I took the phone and listened to Winterbill's story. It was what I had told him to say.

"What?" I exclaimed. "Surely, you're joking." Then: "I can't believe it. A million dollars flying out the window! Will you tell Mr. Boylan what happened?"

Boylan took the phone.

"I'm sorry, Mr. Boylan," Winterbill said. "But those bookmakers I placed your bets with have disappeared. They've left town and I doubt if we'll find them. They couldn't make good on such large amounts."

Dejectedly, Boylan hung up. He put down the phone and dropped in his chair. I paced the floor, muttering to myself: "A million dollars. A few minutes ago I was a millionaire. And now I'm broke!"

I commiserated with Boylan for a while. Then we began to reason things out. It was only natural that a bookmaker should abscond rather than pay off a million and a half dollars. I left as soon as I could without arousing his suspicions. As far as I know Boylan accepted the story and thought the money actually had been wagered in Milwaukee.

Zibia became a very troublesome filly. I soon learned that she might win, regardless of what I did to hold her back. Since I couldn't depend on her, I eventually got rid of her. She went on to become one of the country's top winners.

The regular racing season in Chicago came to an end. Robey opened up as a winter course, and I entered a few of my horses there. But most of them were stabled and only taken out for exercise. I continued to line up victims for my ringer scheme. The plan was altered only slightly. I trained the ringers here and shipped them to the South. The suckers believed that as readily as they did when the horses were running in Chicago. Winterbill continued to help me, and the money flowed in to us in a steady stream.

The following New Year's Eve Winterbill and I were killing time in Davis' Saloon. This famous place had a policy wheel, as well as other gambling devices. Upstairs was a lavish bar, a favorite with the sporting and theatre crowd. Most of the actors from McVickers Theatre — the great legitimate showhouse of that day — came in between shows. Chauncey Alcott and other famous stars were frequent visitors.

"Joe," Winterbill proposed suddenly, "why don't we get our wives and celebrate this New Year right?"

"That suits me fine," I replied. "Where shall we go?"

"Pabst Gardens in Garfield Park is a good place."

"Excellent," I said. "Let's go."

We took the Garfield Park elevated to a station near our homes. There was a saloon on the corner.

"Let's stop and have just one more before we go home," Winterbill urged.

We entered the saloon. Not a customer was there — a very surprising fact, considering that it was New Year's Eve. The only person in sight was the bartender who paced back and forth in front of the bar like a caged beast.

"Well, whatta you want?" he asked savagely.

"Why, we just want a little New Year's drink," I returned. Winterbill was too surprised to say anything.

"Mix 'em yourself," the bartender replied. "I'm through with the saloon business."

"If you feel that way about it," I said, "why don't you sell out?"

"Well, the first guy who offers me $300 can have the works."

Somewhat amused and thinking he must be joking, I retorted, "I'll give you $300 — provided it includes all your stock, the cash register, and other equipment."

"Mister, you've bought yourself a saloon!" he snapped. "I'll not only include all the stock and equipment — I'll throw in a full barrel of whiskey I've got in the basement."

Winterbill now joined in the fun and began to take an inventory.

The owner took off his apron and handed it to me. "Gimme the three hundred bucks."

I gave him the money, still believing it was a joke. He put the money into his pocket, got his hat and coat and departed. To our complete bewilderment, we found ourselves in the saloon business.

## From Nags to Riches

A few minutes later, our first customer came in. He evidently had not made our place his first stop. I hurriedly put the apron over my evening clothes and asked for his order.

"Martini," he said in a thick voice.

"Martini," I repeated to Winterbill.

"Stall him!" Winterbill whispered.

"Coming right up," I told the customer. He didn't mind waiting. He was at the stage where he wanted to talk and so proceeded to do.

Meanwhile Winterbill racked his brain, for he had only the vaguest idea how to mix a Martini. He finally settled upon a recipe. He put a dash of everything from the numerous bottles behind the bar into one drink. I stirred it up and handed it to the customer. We watched anxiously while he drank it down.

"That was good!" he exclaimed. "Best Martini I ever tasted. Mix me another."

Again Winterbill started to mix.

"How do you feel?" I inquired, none too sure of the consequences.

"Me?" asked the customer. "Fine. Never felt better in my life."

He didn't show any bad results after the second drink, and we both were relieved. As time went on more customers came in. They ordered whiskey sours, Manhattans, and Martinis. Winterbill had just one formula and that's what he gave them all. Nobody complained.

We called up Mamie and Jess (our wives) and told them to meet us in the saloon. They expected some sort of celebration, but were in for a surprise. They spent the evening watching us serve drinks to an increasing number of customers. By the time we closed that night we had taken in more than the whole outfit cost us!

Actually, we had the time of our lives. What had started out as a joke ended as a legitimate enterprise. Naturally, the receipts on other days did not equal the first, but that was to be expected.

We had been in business about ten days when a policeman from the Warren Avenue station visited us. He said we'd have to take out a license and it would cost us $1,000. We decided that it wasn't worth it. We were ready to abandon the venture, when a representative of the Atlas Brewing Company walked in.

When we told him our plans, he said: "You are a couple of wide-

71

awake fellows. You don't want a little place like this. Our brewery has an option on a corner at California and Harrison. The brewery will take out the license, outfit the place, and give you one of the finest corners in town."

We accepted his proposition and a few days later moved into the new location, a lavishly outfitted buffet saloon. Business was good. But I didn't like the idea of being tied down, so we hired bartenders and other personnel to help. Incidentally, we learned that the man who had sold out to us was a former safecracker who had found the saloon business too dull.

## 7. Giving Away Real Estate

COLONEL JIM PORTER WAS A FORMER MISSISSIPPI STEAMBOAT gambler. He was heavy-set and impressive with a ruddy complexion and a walrus mustache.

He told fabulous tales of adventures on the Mississippi and his listeners ribbed him. But he did not realize that he was being ribbed, and his tales grew taller. Nobody took him seriously, for we all thought he had delusions of grandeur. I ran across him in Skidmore's saloon.

A bunch of us got together and bought him a ten-gallon sombrero, and presented it to him with the proper ceremony. He wore it proudly and, indeed, looked like an old plainsman who had made a fortune as a cattle rancher.

One of the favorite hangouts for the sporting crowd of those days was Carberry's saloon in the Alhambra Theatre building. Besides being a rendezvous for con men, it was frequented by prominent fighters. Jim Jeffries, Bob Fitzsimmons, Kid Levine, Danny Needham and other top-ranking boxers were often there.

The women from the bawdy houses — the madams — came there in the evening. These included such well-known figures as Georgia Spencer, the Everleigh Sisters, Belle Deming, and Madame Cleo.

When the colonel began to come around to Carberry's place, we bought him a complete outfit, including a Stetson hat and a cutaway coat. We introduced him as "Colonel Porter, who owns an island in Florida."

It was done as a joke at Colonel Porter's expense, but he took it seriously. Pretty soon he was convinced that he actually did own an island in Florida. Furthermore, he looked like an immensely wealthy

## "Yellow Kid" Weil

old yachtsman, and those who were not in on the joke believed every word he uttered.

One night I was walking down State Street near 22nd with Colonel Porter. We decided to go into Frank Wing's for something to eat. Wing's specialty was Southern hash, which he produced in tremendous quantities. He sold it in bulk to the brothel keepers, who took it away in wash boilers to keep it warm. It was served both to the girls and to their men callers.

The fame of Wing's hash spread and he always had a crowd in his place. When the Colonel and I walked in we found a number of women there in the company of prominent men. A party was being given by Patsy King, who had an office in Customs House Place. King was a liberal fellow. He made a lot of money, and spent most of it on his friends. Everybody liked him.

It did not take the Colonel long to become the life of the party. When I introduced him, I dropped a hint that he was one of the Porters who had made a fortune as meat packers and merchants. The Colonel fell right in and began to relate stories of his days as a plainsman. (The wealthy Porters had been plainsmen in the early days.)

The women were intrigued by the Colonel. He had a gallant way and an eye for a pretty face, and the belief that he was one of the wealthy Porters added to his glamor. They flocked around and he basked in their adulation.

He ordered the best of everything Frank Wing had to serve and said magnanimously: "Put it on my bill."

The party grew and so did his bill. What had started as a joke on the Colonel was now becoming serious. I drew him aside and asked: "Where do you expect to get the money to pay for this?"

"Don't need money right now," returned the Colonel. "Frank's going to charge it. And if I don't have the cash when I have to pay the bill, I'll sell some of my property in Michigan."

"Or maybe your island in Florida," I said and turned away.

But the crowd was having a big time. The Colonel's tales of his adventures as a western plainsman grew bolder and more fantastic. Finally I went to Patsy King.

## Giving Away Real Estate

"This is your party," I said, "but it looks like the Colonel has taken over."

"That's all right with me," smiled Patsy, always a good fellow. "The main thing is that everybody is having a fine time."

"Do you know Colonel Porter?" I asked.

"I've seen him around Bill Carberry's place," King replied. "I thought he was a wealthy yachtsman who owned an island in Florida."

"That was all a joke," I told Patsy. Then I unfolded the whole story. "As a matter of fact Colonel Porter is broke. He can't pay for all this stuff he's been ordering."

Patsy laughed. "Don't let that worry you," he said. "Let's humor the old fellow. I expected to pay for everything anyhow. Let him have his fun."

Colonel Porter was in his glory. He was the center of attraction all during the bountiful spread. When everybody had had his fill the Colonel said to the proprietor: "Send the bill to my office, will you Frank?" He said it in a convincing, offhand manner that nobody could ever doubt.

"Of course, Colonel Porter," Wing replied. He had already been tipped off by Patsy King.

"Now, what do you say we all go over to Bill Carberry's?" the Colonel proposed.

There was not a dissenting voice. The Colonel went to the telephone and called a livery service. "Send over some Victorias right away!" he ordered.

When the carriages arrived, we all got in and were driven to Carberry's. Patsy King paid off the drivers — a detail the Colonel was too busy to bother with.

The party continued at Carberry's. The men went downstairs and gambled, but the Colonel continued to hold the rapt attention of the women, to whom he now was serving champagne.

There was such a big demand for champagne at Carberry's that behind the bar he always kept four washtubs filled with ice, in which the champagne bottles were doused. He had four excellent brands ready to serve.

## "Yellow Kid" Weil

The Colonel had a big evening, and I began to look upon him with increasing respect. If he wasn't a natural-born con man, I had never seen one. And I was beginning to get an idea. Colonel Porter might be a valuable man. I was getting tired of the saloon business.

One day soon after the party I asked the Colonel: "What were you telling me about some property in Michigan?"

"I said I could sell some of it if I needed cash."

"Do you really own property in Michigan?"

"Well, not exactly," Colonel Porter admitted. "It really belongs to my cousin. But it's in the family."

"Are you sure this cousin isn't a myth?"

"Certainly not."

"Where does he live and what does he do?"

"He lives in Hart, Michigan. It's the county seat of Oceana County and he's the county recorder."

The Colonel came out with that so quickly that I was convinced he was telling the truth. When a man tells the truth he can give you a straightforward answer immediately. I've found that when a person has to stop and think you can expect part of what he tells you to be false.

"How much property does he own?"

"Several thousand acres."

"Good land?"

"No, it's not," the Colonel admitted frankly. "You can buy all you want for a dollar an acre."

"That's interesting," I said, "very, very interesting."

The idea was beginning to take shape. But I needed more time to think it over. I didn't tell the Colonel what I had in mind.

Meanwhile I divided my time between the saloon and my racing interests. One night I made a deal that I was later to regret very much indeed.

A house of ill fame known as "The House of All Nations" was operated by Madame Cleo. It was common knowledge that she was the mistress of a famous detective chief. I should have known better than to deal with her.

Madame Cleo was like all the other horse players. She wanted an

## Giving Away Real Estate

"inside tip" so that she could make a killing. That was my business, so I told her about a race that had been fixed. She gave me $2,500 to bet for her on one of my own horses.

The horse didn't run in the money of course, and Madame Cleo's $2,500 was added to my bankroll. She was greatly incensed and immediately told the story to her boy friend. There wasn't anything he could do to recover her money, since the horse had lost.

But he had other methods of getting vengeance. He put his detectives on my trail and they were a constant thorn in my side every time I appeared at the races thereafter.

I had been thinking over the Michigan proposition and Colonel Jim Porter. Finally the idea jelled and I sought out the Colonel.

"Jim," I asked, "do you think we could buy some of that land from your cousin in Michigan?"

"Of course," he replied. "A lot of it is submarginal and he'd be glad to get rid of it."

"Could you imagine a fine estate, with a luxurious home, a lake for fishing, a private golf course, and a hunting preserve on this land?"

"I could imagine anything," the Colonel said. In this he was correct. He was a true visionary. "But anybody who would put anything like that on that Michigan land would be crazy."

"Perhaps," I replied. "But you know that northern Michigan is a favorite summer resort for Chicago people. Suppose you saw a picture of this beautiful estate — could you tell convincing stories about it?"

"My good fellow," said the Colonel, "I can tell convincing stories without a picture about any locale."

"Fine. You have just become the President of the Elysium Development Company of Michigan."

"I have?" The Colonel was startled for a moment. Then: "Mmm. It's a fine, high-sounding name."

"And it will be very profitable, I think. How would you like to make a trip to Michigan?"

"What for?"

"To see your cousin."

"All right with me. What do you want me to see him about?"

"I'll give you the details."

77

## "Yellow Kid" Weil

That was the beginning of one of the most unusual land deals ever conceived. Not a lot was sold, but thousands of Chicagoans became property owners. Thousands of dollars rolled into the treasury of the Elysium Development Company. It was the beginning of a new line of endeavor for me and the start of a brilliant career for Colonel Jim Porter.

He who pretends to be fabulously wealthy, although he may be in need, may in the course of time convince himself that he is rich. Such was Colonel Jim Porter's obsession.

He was sane enough, yet it was easy for him to delude himself that he was a tycoon. He lived the part of the retired millionaire so well that he came to believe it. Only on rare occasions did he leave his fairy wonderland to come down to earth and remember that he was a penniless old man.

I have always felt that the Colonel's dreamland was largely responsible for the success of our scheme to foist almost worthless Michigan swampland upon unsuspecting people. I think that he honestly believed that a real Garden of Eden would burgeon from the Michigan swamps.

For more than half a century, Michigan has meant just one thing to the people of Chicago — summer vacation land. Lodges and camps in the north woods have long been favorite retreats for hunters and fishermen and lovers of the outdoors. Resorts on the lake shore annually draw thousands of vacationists.

Oceana County lies on Lake Michigan, and for all I know there may be some good resort spots along the shore. But the land owned by Colonel Porter's cousin near the county seat could hardly be called ideal for vacations or for any other purpose. Most of it was undesirable acreage; some of it was submarginal.

I sent Colonel Porter to Michigan to buy some of this land and to make his cousin a proposition. While he was gone I went to see a furniture agency and arranged for them to furnish a suite of offices I had rented in a Loop building.

This suite consisted of a general outer office and two private offices, one small and the other quite large. I took the smaller room and set up the larger one for Colonel Porter who was, after all, the head of the project.

## Giving Away Real Estate

I was acquainted with a photographer who had in stock the pictures I needed. These included photographs of a golf course, tennis court, swimming pool, and hunting lodge or clubhouse. In addition, he had pictures of several luxurious yachts lying at anchor in Lake Michigan. From all these he made a panorama showing the clubhouse in the center flanked by the other scenes. The whole thing was blown up so that it stretched across one wall of Colonel Porter's office.

This panorama made it possible not only for Colonel Porter, but for any sucker who might drop in, to visualize the physical setup of the Elysium Development Company.

When Porter returned, his news was even better than I had expected. His cousin not only was recorder but county clerk as well. He set his own fees for recording deeds and for drawing up abstracts. His usual fee for recording a transaction was two dollars. But this was raised to thirty dollars, with the understanding that Colonel Porter and I would get fifteen dollars out of every transaction.

He readily sold us a large tract at a dollar an acre. I had a map drawn of the acreage we had bought, reserving a large space in the center for the clubhouse and other features in the picture. The balance was divided into lots, 125 feet deep. There were thousands of these lots.

My next step was to make up a brochure painting Michigan as a veritable paradise for vacationists. The expensive-looking brochure was liberally sprinkled with pictures of the Elysium Development project. The reader was bound to come to just one conclusion — the vacation land described and the Elysium project were one and the same.

But the brochure was descriptive — nothing more. No lots were offered for sale; no prices were quoted. Colonel Porter noted this and pointed out the omission.

"Surely," he grumbled, "you're not planning to give these lots away?"

"That, my dear Colonel," I replied, "is exactly what I am planning to do."

"But why? Why don't we sell them? With this fine booklet we could get a good price."

"Perhaps," I said. "But for only a few. As soon as the owners went up there to look at their new property and found they'd bought worthless acreage we'd be out of business. But if we give the lots away, who can say that he has been swindled?"

The Colonel still wasn't satisfied, but I went ahead. At a stationery store I bought a large quantity of blank deeds. These were filled out with the numbers of the lots on the map and were signed by the Colonel as owner. The name of the person to whom the deed was made out was left blank.

"All you have to do," I told Colonel Porter, "is to use that fine imagination of yours. Get a good picture of our development in your mind. Talk about it. Tell stories about it. If anybody comes in the office to see where his lot is located, show him the map. Tell him what a wonderful development we have. I'll do the rest."

Thereafter wherever I went I carried a supply of the blank deeds with me. Winterbill and I still had our saloon. I had to spend considerable time there in the evening. Outside of helping to manage the place I had none of the work. My main job was acting as host.

We had a fine establishment and the free lunch counter was always piled high with sandwiches. I have always been pretty good at striking up acquaintances and the lunch counter was a good place for it. I never bothered with anyone who was obviously without money.

When I ascertained that a man had a little money I became friendly enough. Eventually I called him off to the side for a confidential talk.

"You look like the sort of fellow I'd like to have for a neighbor," I would say. Then I would give him one of the brochures describing the Elysium Development.

"Do you live up there?" he would ask.

"I'm one of the owners. This is a private club and membership is only by invitation. Of course the only members are those who own property in the Development."

"Oh, you want me to buy some of the property?"

"My dear fellow, this property is not for sale. But I should like to have you for my neighbor. And that does require that you own property in the Development."

"If I can't buy it, how am I going to own it?"

## Giving Away Real Estate

"Very simple. I shall make you a gift of a desirable lot."

"Do you mean that?"

"Certainly I do."

"There must be a catch in it."

"No catch in it."

And to prove my good faith, right then and there, I would make out a deed to my new friend.

"You mean I don't have to pay you anything for it?" my unbelieving friend would say.

"Not one penny."

As soon as the man had got through thanking me, I would mention that it would be a good idea to have his lot recorded. There was nothing strange about that, for everybody who has ever had any dealing in real estate knows that every transaction must be recorded at the county seat before it is legal.

In the course of an evening I made many new friends. I even gave lots to some of my old acquaintances. From all of them I extracted a promise that the gift be confidential.

"If some of my friends heard that I had given you this lot," I explained, "they would all be after me for similar gifts."

Anybody who was interested had the privilege of going to Colonel Porter's office and locating his lot. A few did this, but not many. Most of them were satisfied not to ask questions. In time they all wrote to the county recorder.

His reply was the first blow. The fee for recording — thirty dollars — was exorbitant and everybody knew it. But they all remitted it. After all, the lot was a gift.

Colonel Porter's cousin followed up every recording with a letter suggesting that the new owner would need an abstract if he was to be able to appraise his new property. Many of the owners decided they could get along without an abstract, but a large number remitted the $25 fee asked for this.

Drawing up an abstract on one of those lots was no task at all. The property hadn't changed hands very many times since the original owner had disposed of it. With the exception of the legal description

## "Yellow Kid" Weil

of each individual lot, the abstracts were the same on all of them.

Colonel Porter and I got half of all the fees his cousin collected for abstracts. Soon the mail at the Elysium Development Company was blooming with remittances. For the sake of appearances and to help Colonel Porter with what correspondence there was, two young women were engaged and installed in the general office.

Some of the people to whom I had given deeds learned that they had been duped. But most of them were happy in the knowledge that they possessed Michigan property and didn't take the trouble to investigate until years later.

For two months I carpeted Chicago with deeds to lots in the Elysium Development Company. I even gave lots to two detectives who later rose to prominence in the police department. Both men paid the recording fee before they discovered that the land was practically valueless. Both were furious and if there had been anything they could have done about it, I would have found free lodging promptly. But I had not taken money from them: they had not been compelled to have the lots recorded. So far as the law was concerned, I was clean.

But both knew that they had been played for chumps. And they knew too that I was not being altruistic in giving the lots away. Both were bigger than I was, and they did threaten to thrash me. As much as possible I kept out of their way. When they saw me they usually gave chase. But I was fast on my feet and they never caught me.

But they never let up. After I had been in the project for two months I decided to withdraw. My net profit from the venture was about $8,000.

When I told Colonel Porter we were going out of business, he said: "Maybe you are, Joe, but I'm not. I know when I have a good thing. Some day this project will make me quite wealthy."

So I turned the whole business over to him. He stuck with it and did indeed become wealthy. I don't know whether he continued to operate on the same basis, but the law was never able to touch him.

Years later Colonel Porter, then quite an old man but still a dreamer, invested his money in one of the Florida subdivisions. He helped to promote it from an expensive suite in the Morrison Hotel.

I went to the Morrison to call on him, but he was surrounded by

## Giving Away Real Estate

assistants and secretaries. I never got farther than the reception room. I imagine the Colonel told some wonderful stories about his subdivision. At last his dreams had come true.

I worked a variation of the real estate deal in later years. I relate it as a warning to anyone who owns real estate that has greatly decreased in value. The racket is as good today as it ever was.

One day in New York City I ran into a confidence man named Bert Griffin who was down on his luck and broke. He had just one asset — a list of some 2,000 owners of lots in various subdivisions around New York. Most of them had bought the lots as investments, but they had turned out to be almost worthless. At least, the market value had dropped to about ten per cent of the purchase price.

"Joe," said Bert, "these people are all suckers. Why don't we contact some of them and sell 'em some stock?"

"Don't be silly!" I scoffed. "People don't have money to buy stocks these days. I can think of something better than that."

My first act was to get in touch with an old acquaintance, an elderly lawyer who had been disbarred because of dealings with confidence men. I showed him the list of the owners of the subdivision lots.

"You can draw up abstracts on these lots, can't you?"

"Of course."

"If I give you plenty of work, will you do it for five dollars per abstract?"

"It's dirt cheap, but I need the money. Yes."

Next, I rented two offices — on different floors — in a building at 62nd and Broadway. On one door I had a sign painted: "Great Metropolitan Development Company." On the other was: "Search Title and Abstract Company." Bert Griffin was installed in the development office and the lawyer in the abstract office.

My next step was to insert an advertisement in the classified section of one of the New York papers. The development company offered to buy lots in certain subdivisions at good prices. The ad was inconspicuous and it was not intended that many people should answer it. Very few did.

Next I began a systematic round of all those on our list. A call I made on a man in Philadelphia will illustrate how I worked.

83

## "Yellow Kid" Weil

I knew that this man had six lots in a Long Island subdivision and had paid $3,000 for them. Their value had dropped to a fraction of that figure. I represented myself to him as a real estate broker.

"I understand you own six lots in a subdivision on Long Island," I said.

"That is correct."

"Would you be interested in selling them?"

"Sure. But who would buy 'em?"

I unfolded the newspaper and showed him the advertisement.

"How much did you pay for the lots?" I asked.

"$3,000."

"I think I can sell them to this company for $500 profit if you'll let me handle the deal."

He brightened immediately. "Go ahead and try."

"How much is it worth to you?" I asked.

"I'll give you the usual ten per cent commission."

"That's not enough," I replied. "I want all the profit as my commission."

"If I give you all of it, what profit do I make?"

"You get your money back. That's more than you ever expected to do, isn't it?"

He admitted this was true, but now that the market appeared to be improving he was reluctant to go above the regular commission.

So I haggled about what I would get. I made a point of haggling over my commission, because this, more than anything else, convinced him that I was on the level. If I had come to his terms at once there might have been grounds for suspicion.

Finally he agreed to let me keep all I could get over $3,000. I asked him for his title and he produced the deeds.

"How about the abstract?" I asked.

"I don't have one."

"Well, I can't sell your property without one."

"Where can I get an abstract?"

"The Search Title and Abstract Company is a good place." I told him. "Send your deed in there and they'll draw up the abstract."

"How much does it cost?"

"Sixty-five dollars."

## Giving Away Real Estate

I gave him the address of the Abstract Company and told him I would call in about two weeks. That was the last I ever saw of my Philadelphia client. He sent in his money and the old lawyer drew up the abstract and mailed it to him. It was a bona fide abstract and the lawyer really had to work hard to draw it up, as well as all the others I brought in.

If a client ever called at the office of the Development company, he was informed by Bert Griffin that no deal could be made until an abstract had been provided. Not one of those owners had an abstract and all were steered to the other office.

The price we charged for drawing the abstract varied according to our estimate of the client's ability to pay — ranging from $65 to $300. If a client turned over his complete title to us with the expectation of selling his property, we stalled him on one pretext or another. Our only object was to collect fees for the abstracts.

Our business was one that had to be completed in a short time. It was a whirlwind campaign. I covered the entire list of 2,000 in three weeks and within a month we had collected fees from all who were willing to do business with us. The enterprise took thirty days and my profit was $7,200.

This is a racket that is as good today as it was then. I don't know of any place where it is being worked, but there are possibilities everywhere — Chicago, for example. Here there are a number of subdivisions where the lots are worth far less than the purchase price.

I am pointing this out — and digressing from my story — for one reason. Some racketeer might read of how my deal was worked and get an idea he can do it in Chicago. I'd like this to be a warning to anyone who owns lots in a subdivision. If you're approached by a stranger who makes you a good offer for your lots — but insists that you buy an abstract — investigate him thoroughly before you go ahead. He may be just another con man who is selling abstracts.

## 8. The Get-Rich-Quick Bank

WITH THE OPENING OF THE RACING SEASON, I TIRED OF MY saloon business and disposed of my interest. I expected to return to the tracks and continue as before. But I had forgotten about Madame Cleo and her bitterness toward me. She was not one to forget. To her, $2,500 was not a trifling sum.

The men put on my trail by her police-official friend caused me considerable difficulty in trying to sell "inside tips." My operations at the track were considerably restricted.

Meanwhile the detectives had been contacting some of my victims. It was not long before they had enough evidence to take the case before the racing authorities. On the testimony of Madame Cleo and others, I was ruled off the turf for life.

This meant that I had to dispose of my horses. That was not difficult to do since several of them had developed into winners. However, the ruling didn't prevent me from making wagers at the tracks.

I had met a fellow of my own age named Romeo Simpson. His father was a wealthy Chicagoan who owned considerable income property in the Loop. Romeo was a playboy and had no more scruples than I had. After I was ruled off the track I thought up a scheme for making money and suggested that he go in with me. My main reason for asking him was that I needed his father's reputation and references behind our enterprise.

I held nothing back from Romeo. I told him the whole scheme and he knew from the start that it was not exactly honest. But to him it was a lark and he readily consented to go in with me.

## The Get-Rich-Quick Bank

I wanted to rent a suite of offices in the Woman's Temple, one of the most exclusive buildings in Chicago at that time. (A good address is an asset to any business venture.) Diblee and Manierre, who managed the Woman's Temple, had made it almost inaccessible to the average business man.

At the start, Romeo and I pooled our resources. We opened a substantial account at the Standard Trust and Savings Bank. We engaged temporary offices in the Flatiron Building and set up our business: SIMPSON AND WEIL, Bankers and Brokers.

Then we made application to Diblee and Manierre for space in the Woman's Temple. Romeo's father was delighted at the thought that his wayward son was going into business and let us use his references without stint. All the references were good because of the father's position and reputation.

Diblee and Manierre made a thorough investigation and finally advised us that the application had been approved. We took a suite occupying half of a floor and moved in. It was like having a desk in the Bank of England — being on intimate terms with the old Lady of Threadneedle Street.

We engaged an advertising agency to place advertisements for us in periodicals and newspapers. We covered every section of the country except the immediate vicinity of Chicago. We didn't want any business from the Chicago area. The ads read:

> A LITTLE STORY OF A BIG SUCCESS
> How $100 Makes $1,000
> For details write
> SIMPSON AND WEIL
> Bankers and Brokers
> Woman's Temple Building
> CHICAGO, ILLINOIS

I'd always known that many people were seeking easy money. But until the replies began to come in I never realized how vast this number was. The volume was tremendous. Anticipating inquiries, we had prepared an elaborate brochure, "The Source of a Tip." In this, we explained how a tip originated (a tip on a fixed horse race), how a tip often was only a rumor, and how we, as owners of many of the nation's finest horses, could furnish genuine information better than anybody else.

We listed two groups of horses: Horses We Formerly Owned and Horses We Now Own. The first was a bunch of dogs. But the second included many of the country's top winners. We had fixed that by making deals with the owners of these horses. For a consideration they had transferred ownership of the horses to Simpson and Weil, and we had transferred ownership back to them. In our vaults we always had papers to prove that we owned the horses we claimed as ours.

The brochure further explained how we, as the owners of the most consistent winners, were in better position than anybody else to know just when these horses would win and what the odds would be. We proposed that the investor send us a hundred dollars to open an account. We would place bets for him on sure winners, using all or any part of his money. Every time we placed a bet, we would make a report of the amount placed and on what horse. We would mail the report immediately so that the investor could check with the postmark to determine that his bet had actually been placed before the time of the race.

We sent one of the brochures to everybody who answered our ad. In those days $100 was a lot of money and we hardly expected to find so many who had that much with which to speculate. But soon our mail was overwhelming. Remittances for $100 poured in. We had to take more space and enlarge our quarters. We put up cages and engaged cashiers and bookkeepers. To all outward appearances we had a real and prosperous bank.

Here is the way we worked. We would put Mr. Smith (who had an account of $100 with us) down on a ten dollar bet on a horse that had won. As soon as we knew the horse had won, we mailed the report to Mr. Smith. Perhaps he checked the postmarks, but he probably didn't. The main thing he did was to check back with the race results and learn that his horse had won.

We kept Mr. Smith's account for a month. At the end of the month, we sent him a remittance for $125, with this explanation:

"We are returning your original investment plus the earnings. We regret that the volume of our business makes it impossible to handle such small accounts.

## *The Get-Rich-Quick Bank*

We did the same thing to every account. Our letters only whetted the investor's appetite. If he had more money, he immediately wrote in to ask how much he would have to invest to have us handle his account. We replied that we could handle nothing under $500. The response to this was so great that we soon raised the minimum to $1,000. We had a few inquiries about taking larger investments — $5,000 or more. I usually went to see these people in person.

Actually what we were doing was paying dividends on old accounts from the monies we received from new accounts — borrowing from Peter to pay Paul. The same scheme was used very successfully by some of the biggest swindlers in history. One man whose name I shall not mention had a few international reply coupons to show as physical assets and another man whose name I better not mention had a few power plants. But in both cases they depended on new money to pay dividends to the old accounts. We too had some assets.

Chief among these was a horse-player who had made a study of horses and their past performances. We engaged him as our expert handicapper for he could predict winners pretty accurately. I sometimes used a customer's money to bet on his advice.

For example, he would figure out a good bet at 3 to 1. I would take $1,000 of a client's money and bet it on the horse. The winnings would be $3,000. But I would write the customer that the horse had paid even money. My profit would be $2,000, the client's would be $1,000. I made enough of these bets so that anyone who chose to investigate could see that we were actually doing what we claimed in our advertising.

But as soon as we had raised the minimum amount to $1,000, we instituted a service charge of ten dollars a month for each account. This eliminated the small fellows and the number of our accounts finally narrowed down to 400 large investors. From these alone we had an annual revenue of $480,000. I don't recall the total amount invested, but we continued to use capital funds to pay big dividends. We seldom reported to an investor that his horse had failed to win. But occasionally we reported a loser to every client. The reason for this was purely psychological.

Perhaps I should explain that in those days there was no way the client could check up on how much his horse had won. The win,

89

## "Yellow Kid" Weil

place, and show horses in each race were published in sport sections of the newspapers, but there was no pari-mutuel system. The only thing the customer could check on was the result. He could learn that his horse had won, but he had to take our word on the pay-off.

Our enterprise became so prosperous that in time we came to refer to it as the "Get-Rich-Quick Bank." Both Romeo and I were getting rich quickly and I can't tell you how much we made. It was the same old story of easy come, easy go. We spent a great deal. It was not at all uncommon for me to squander as much as $1,000 in a night's festivity.

I recall one incident that occurred in 1898 during the Spanish American war.

Nick Langraf had a bookmaking establishment in the basement of Bathhouse John Coughlin's establishment. Diagonally across the street was the saloon of Powers and O'Brien, where a man I recall now only as Andy also made book. Next door was a barber shop. The barber chairs were in the front. In the rear of the shop was a large vacant space that extended to the rear of the building. In the rear was a freight elevator no longer in use.

Nick had a prosperous business, fully equipped with Western Union wire service. One day a fellow named "Fats" Levine came to me and suggested that we go into business "making book." He pointed out the large vacant space in the rear of the barber shop.

"What about the wire service?"

"We don't need that," he said. "If we could only get hold of a telephone."

Then he outlined his plan, and I agreed to go in with him. All telephones were then of the wall type. We scouted around and finally found a telephone, which we "borrowed." Fats Levine affixed it to the wall (though it wasn't connected) and we were ready for business.

I stood at the basement entrance to Nick Langraf's place and told all who were about to enter: "Nick is having his place redecorated and is temporarily closed. You can make your bets in the rear of the barber shop across the street."

I succeeded in steering Nick's customers to our makeshift room

## The Get-Rich-Quick Bank

in the back of the barber shop. They went in and placed their bets with Fats Levine, who stood at the phone and supposedly received the results. Of course nobody ever won. I saw to that. Andy, the bookmaker in Powers and O'Brien, got the results by ticker tape, and it was his custom to pass the tape along to the barber shop.

I acted as Andy's messenger. But between the time I left him and my arrival in the barber shop I cut the tape and switched it in such a way that the winning horse always appeared to be second or third, while the place or show horse appeared to be the winner. Anybody who lost a bet to Fats had only to step up front to the barber shop to check up.

We had one particularly good customer. He was an iceman who had the entire Loop territory. His commissions were high and it was not uncommon for him to bet up to $1,000 a day. He never questioned the results until one day when he happened to go into Powers and O'Brien's for a drink after he had lost $800 to Fats. To his amazement he saw that Andy had posted his horse as the winner.

He came storming back into our place where Fats stood in front of the telephone with the receiver in his hand. He grabbed Fats' collar and demanded an explanation.

Fats started to explain that there had been a slight mix-up with the ticker tape. The iceman was ready to accept this explanation. But in earnestly trying to convince him, Fats stepped away from the phone, the receiver in his hand. The phone was attached only by a nail, and it came tumbling down.

The iceman saw there was no connection and he appraised the situation at a glance.

"Why, you two dirty — "

Fats dropped the receiver and made a dash for the rear. I followed. The only exit was the freight elevator, which was not in operation. It stood empty. We scrambled to the top and began climbing up the elevator cables. We almost reached the next floor when the cables became greasy. We got the grease all over our hands and were stopped. We held on for a few moments, then gradually began to slip.

## "Yellow Kid" Weil

The iceman was a big, husky brute. He waited for us with a murderous gleam in his eyes. As soon as we were within reach, he grabbed us, pulled us down and, handling us as if we were toys, cracked our heads together. Then he gave us both a good beating, recovered his money, and left.

That ended our business. When Nick Langraf heard the story it answered the question in his mind: what had happened to all his customers?

For two weeks after that we didn't go near the Loop. The incident was the occasion for a lot of fun in the saloons and pool rooms in the vicinity of Bathhouse John's. At that time Admiral Dewey was the most talked-of figure of the day. It was the custom for the *Daily Inter-Ocean* to send news bulletins relating to the war to the various Loop establishments. One such bulletin served as a model for the ribbing we took:

"Admiral Dewey has just steamed into Manila Harbor."

Various establishments added their own bulletins to this:

"Admiral Weil and Commodore Levine were seen steaming near 12th Street."

That fiasco still affords me a chuckle.

Fred Coyne owned a restaurant near the barber shop. I ate at his place regularly.

Until the days of the Get-Rich-Quick Bank, I hadn't seen Coyne, though I knew he had become postmaster. One day his superintendent of delivery, Colonel Stewart, called at my office. The postmaster was curious to know what sort of business brought such a tremendous amount of mail.

Of course, I didn't tell the postal representative all that we were doing. But I did give him the story of how we were able to get absolutely reliable inside tips. This was reported to Coyne, who came to see me.

He was enthusiastic about the possibilities and offered to make an investment. I agreed to take him in as a silent partner. He didn't know that the fat dividends we were paying were skimmed from the money that was constantly coming in.

## The Get-Rich-Quick Bank

This money continued to flow in steadily. But both Romeo and I were so intent on having a good time that we became remiss in the matter of paying the investors. We began to get some beefs.

Then one day the mail dwindled to a trickle. For several days there was practically none. I couldn't understand it, until my secretary told me what was happening. Romeo had become involved with several women. He had mistresses in half-a-dozen different places and was supporting them lavishly.

"Mr. Simpson has been coming in early," my secretary said. "He's been getting the mail and taking the money."

I was in a quandary. I called Fred Coyne and told him what had happened. Coyne decided to withdraw and advised that I do likewise.

"Meanwhile," he said, "I'd suggest that you take up quarters somewhere else and have the mail forwarded."

Acting on this advice, I engaged a suite at the Stratford Hotel, taking my secretary with me. I said nothing to Romeo, but soon the shoe was on the other foot. I was getting all the firm's mail. Romeo, who had said nothing before, now wondered what had happened to our business.

"Why the sudden concern?" I inquired. "You've spent very little time around here for weeks. If you had been on the job, you would have known that we haven't been receiving many checks. Frankly, Romeo, I think we're through."

There wasn't much Romeo could say to this. He had devoted very little time to the business. The complaints that began to come in were against me, not him. Those complaints were all from the wealthier investors — the little fellows had been paid off.

And the heavy investors were the ones who remembered me. In every case I had gone to visit them when I learned of their interest and ability to invest large sums.

Within a short time, Simpson and Weil, Bankers and Brokers, had folded up completely.

Both Romeo and I had profited. Besides handsome salaries, we had reaped large dividends for the special benefit of Simpson and Weil. Romeo, who continued to be a playboy even after we entered the business, had squandered all his share.

## "Yellow Kid" Weil

I had spend plenty too. But being the active partner, I had less time to devote to amusement and managed to save a tidy sum.

Finally the complaints got into the hands of the police. I decided that an ocean voyage would be good for me. I told my wife I was going to Paris on business.

I spent several months in Paris having a good time. In those days no passport was required and anybody who had the price of a steamship ticket could go abroad. I had learned German from my father and French from my mother. I now had an opportunity to put both to good use, particularly French.

The nearest approach I made to business was in observing how the French loved the dollars they took from wealthy American tourists. A number of Americans I ran into used Letters of Credit to obtain funds in Paris. I learned all I could about Letters of Credit and later put this knowledge to profitable use.

When my funds became depleted I decided to return to Chicago. I felt enough time had elapsed to allow the investors in the Get-Rich-Quick Bank to cool off and that it was safe for me to go back.

## 9. Red Letter Days

ON THE STEAMER RETURNING TO NEW YORK I MADE THE ACQUAINtance of a distinguished looking man with a beard.

I had noticed that he always dressed in a cutaway coat, usually banker's gray or wood brown, with striped trousers. He had a dignified, almost military, bearing. I decided he was a wealthy capitalist or a banker and that it would be to my advantage to cultivate his friendship.

One day when he was standing at the rail I accosted him.

"Pardon me, but could you give me a match?"

"Of course," he replied. "And I shall be pleased if you will join me in smoking one of my special Havana cigars."

He had taken out his cigar case and opened it. He offered me a cigar and I took it, noting that it was monogrammed with the letter *B*. I noted also that the cigars were of a rare and expensive quality.

"Thank you," I murmured, taking one of the cigars. "My name is Weed — Walter H. Weed."

"Ah, yes!" beamed the bearded man, "I've heard of Dr. Walter H. Weed, the famous mining engineer. It is indeed a pleasure to meet you. I am Captain Ball of Muncie, Indiana."

"Glad to know you, Captain Ball," I said, grasping his hand. I knew quite well that Captain Ball was the head of the Ball Mason Jar company of Muncie, Indiana. I had nothing particular in mind at the time, but I felt it was worth my while to get acquainted with such a prominent — and wealthy — man. "On your way back to Muncie, now, Captain?"

"Not immediately," he replied. "I expect to stop over in New

## "Yellow Kid" Weil

York for a few weeks. There are some new Broadway shows I'd like to take in. And of course one has friends. And you?"

"I'm afraid I must hurry on to Chicago," I said, ruefully. "I had a nice holiday in Paris — so nice, in fact, that I stayed longer than I should have. Now I must get back to my business."

"Of course," said my companion. "One's business is often a cruel taskmaster, isn't it?"

"It is in my case. But I always can manage to take a little time out to show the town to a friend. I do hope you'll look me up when you pass through Chicago on your way back to Muncie."

"I'll be delighted to do that, old chap. If you'll give me your address — "

He cut his sentence short when a man standing behind us let out a loud burst of laughter. We both turned to look at the fellow. I recognized him as Jack Mason, a veteran oceanic card shark, a regular rider on the liners between New York and Cherbourg.

"Well, who's going to lose in this deal?" he inquired.

"Sir," asked the bearded man haughtily, "Just what do you mean?"

"Yes," I said. "What is the meaning of your strange outburst?"

"You've both got a swell line," chuckled Mason, "and I enjoyed every bit of it. Tim," he said to the bearded man, "I want you to meet Joe Weil, better known as the Yellow Kid. Joe, I want you to shake hands with Tim North, con man and card shark de luxe."

Neither of us carried the bluff any further. I dropped all pretense and proceeded to make friends with Tim North. He was indeed a master con man and succeeded in convincing many people that he was Captain Ball — just as he had almost convinced me.

By the end of the voyage I knew Tim pretty well. He came of a good Wisconsin family and his uncle was a banker in Fond-du-Lac. I renewed my invitation that he look me up if he ever came to Chicago. When we parted in New York, I was not to see him again for several months, but he was destined to play a prominent part in my future activities.

Back in Chicago I found that the Get-Rich-Quick Bank was all but forgotten and that I didn't have to worry about complaints. I was at loose ends but not broke, for my wife had saved most of the money

## Red Letter Days

I had given her. Money in my hands was like water, and I always gave a sizable amount to my wife, who invariably saved most of it.

Con men of ability always have certain schemes that are saved for a rainy day — deals that are sure-fire and don't require too elaborate a build-up. These generally don't pay off in big figures but they do help to tide one over dull periods.

One of my favorites was the ring deal. I had a ring with a large diamond setting that any pawnbroker would value at $5,000. When I entered a saloon wearing this ring — as I frequently did — it usually caused envious glances and whispering. One night the idea struck me that here I could capitalize.

I was in the Soft Spot on Jackson Boulevard, accompanied by a very attractive, red-haired young woman. The Soft Spot had a dining room adjacent to the barroom, and we took a table. I saw Jake Hogan, an old partner of mine, at the bar and motioned to him.

He came over, and we conversed for a few minutes. When he returned to the bar, he was besieged with questions: "Who is he?"

"He's young Morton, out for a lark," Hogan whispered. "But it would never do for his father to know he's here."

"You mean his father is the Morton of Bense and Morton?"

"Sure. But don't repeat it. He doesn't want his identity known."

Naturally word spread quickly. It got around to Phil Smart, the man who owned the place. Smart made it his business to cater to me, for it was not often that his place was patronized by the scion of such a wealthy family.

The girl didn't know who I was. For all she knew, I really was young Morton. At least I was not stingy about food or champagne and spent money as if I had plenty. Smart, the owner, personally saw to it that we had the best of service.

When we had completed our dinner, I excused myself and asked the proprietor if I could see him in private. He led the way to his office.

"Mr. Smart," I said, "you have been very kind to me tonight. I wonder if you will do me another favor?"

"I'll be only too happy to do it, Mr. Morton."

"But how did you know my name?" I asked, as if a little shocked.

"Perhaps you are better known than you think."

"Maybe you're right. That's all the more reason for my asking this favor of you. This ring," I said, removing the diamond, "is an heirloom and I wouldn't want to lose it."

"How can I help?"

"I plan to go to a — er — hotel with this young lady. Now I don't know her very well and I don't want to take a chance on losing the ring. I wonder if you would put it in your safe and keep it for me overnight?"

"Certainly," he replied. "I'll be glad to."

So I left the ring with him. Perhaps I took the young woman out — perhaps I didn't. It didn't matter, for I did register at a nearby hotel.

The following day I wrote a note to Smart, sealed it in an envelope, and had it taken to him by a bell boy. The note read:

"Dear Mr. Smart: I find that I am in need of cash and I would appreciate it very much if you would take my ring to a pawnbroker and borrow about $500 on it." He learned the real value of the ring. That was the main purpose in having him borrow $500 on it.

He put the money in an envelope, sealed it, and sent it to me by the bell boy.

The following day I dropped around at the Soft Spot, thanked the man for his kindness, picked up the pawn ticket, and redeemed the ring.

"Glad to help you any time I can," he said.

That was the build-up. I built up three or four similar deals in a week's time at various other saloons. Every owner was impressed by the value of the ring, as well as by the name I used. Hogan usually helped me in each deal. I did not always pose as Morton. I let it be whispered that I was the son of various wealthy Chicagoans.

Then on a Saturday evening I would visit all the places I had built up. I would spend perhaps an hour in each, then depart, supposedly for a hotel, leaving my ring in custody of the saloon owner.

The following day, Sunday, I sent a bell boy with a note to each of the saloon owners with whom I had left a ring. Of course, each ring I had left had a beautiful paste imitation of the diamond I had worn for the build-up.

## Red Letter Days

I knew that the pawnshops were closed. I knew, also, that each of the saloons where I had left a ring had a safe with a good supply of cash on hand. Beforehand I had sized up each owner and had a pretty fair idea of how much he might be expected to have on hand.

In some of the notes, I asked that the ring be sent out to a pawnshop for a loan of $500. In others, I asked $1,000. It all depended on the individual. I must have sized them up correctly, for in every instance the amount I asked for was sent. The saloon owner had already learned the value of the ring. Even though no pawnbroker was open, he advanced the money himself. After all, it isn't often that a saloon keeper has an opportunity to do a favor for the son of a multi-millionaire.

This was a racket that could be worked only so often and no more. For one thing, I had to steer clear of the saloons where the owners had advanced the money: it took them only a few days to find out that they had paid money for a paste diamond.

As I have said, this was a rainy day scheme. After I had got a few thousand from it, I turned to something else.

One day Hogan and I ran into a fellow known as "Red Letter" Sullivan. He was a heavy-set, florid faced fellow, and his clothes were anything but tidy. He was an habitual drunkard. He had gained his nickname because he carried a fountain pen with red ink. Everything he wrote was in red. I don't know why — it was one of his peculiarities.

When Sullivan was sober he was a whiz as a stock operator. He had an uncanny knowledge of Big Board stocks and could make accurate predictions about market trends. The trouble was it was almost impossible to keep him sober.

Nevertheless, Hogan and I decided to try it. We formed a partnership and took "Red Letter" Sullivan in with us. We rented the ground floor of the Western Union building, which fronted on La Salle Street and was not far from the Chicago Stock Exchange.

We installed an impressive array of furniture and all the usual fixtures of the office of a stock broker who is dealing in Big Board issues. This included ten telephones. Then we began hiring clerks and stenographers who were experienced in stock offices.

## "Yellow Kid" Weil

I knew a man named John Blonger in Denver. He owned some mining property he called the Copper Queen. The Copper Queen Mining Company had been incorporated by Blonger for $10,000,000. The company was authorized to issue a million shares of stock with a face value of ten dollars per share.

As far as I know it was purely a stock-selling scheme. I don't believe there was ever any attempt to mine the property, although Blonger did own some property. In those days about all you needed to form a corporation was an excuse, an attorney, and $100.

We made a deal with Old John, as we called him, to buy large blocks of his stocks at one cent per share. We acquired 100,000 shares. There was no law to prevent our selling it for whatever price we could get.

There was a lot of worthless stock on the market then. On fifth Avenue (now Wells Street), in the old Medinah Temple building, was a wildcat exchange where you could buy large blocks of such stock for only a few cents a share. We acquired a supply of various issues at these prices.

We were also equipped to purchase Big Board stock, if the need arose. As a matter of fact, we did occasionally place an order for good stock for a client — for the sake of appearances.

Then we began to publish a weekly magazine called *The Red Letter*. "Red Letter" Sullivan was the editor and wrote most of the stuff analyzing trends in the market. *The Red Letter* was sent to a selected list of clients — mostly professional men like doctors, dentists and lawyers — who had money to invest. The magazine was printed entirely in red ink.

Red Letter Sullivan wrote authentic and up-to-date news about trends in the better stocks. It was my job to write glowing accounts of the prospects for the Copper Queen or for any other stock we decided to feature.

Hogan and I worked mostly by telephone. We would take the telephone book and start on physicians. To give you an example of how we worked, I'll relate the story of Dr. Johnson.

"Dr. Johnson?" I started the conversation.

"Yes."

## Red Letter Days

"This is Hogan, Weil, and Sullivan, stock brokers. I understand that you are interested in making a good investment. Is that correct?"

"Well, yes," Dr. Johnson replied. "I do have a little money I'd like to put in a gilt-edged stock."

"I believe we can work together to our mutual advantage. We have some advance — and strictly confidential — information that Standard Oil of New Jersey is to merge with a large Pennsylvania oil company. Holders of Standard Oil stock will profit a great deal by the merger. I'd suggest that you buy as many shares of Standard Oil as you can afford."

"How much is it selling for now?"

"Twenty-seven fifty a share is the current price. How many shares would you like?"

"Oh, possibly ten shares, which would be $275, wouldn't it?"

"Yes."

"That's about all I can afford now."

"Shall we buy it for you?"

"Don't you want the money first?"

"Oh, we can carry the transaction," I replied. "We'll order the stock at once before the market price changes. You can drop a check in the mail and we'll get it tomorrow."

"Do you trust everybody?"

"Of course not. But one of your standing — well, that's different. We know you are trustworthy."

"Thank you," said the doctor. "I'll mail you my check right away."

Everybody is flattered by the thought that he has good standing in the community. Besides, we didn't have anything to lose on the deal. We didn't buy the Standard Oil stock, whether or not we got the check. If we failed to get the check, we just forgot about it. But in most cases the check came in promptly. In some cases where the victim didn't have a bank account we sent a messenger to pick up the cash.

The first step after completing the call was to send a copy of *The Red Letter* to Dr. Johnson. Having invested his money he was naturally interested in stocks. He couldn't help seeing how the Copper Queen was featured as the best buy of the year.

## "Yellow Kid" Weil

When we had received the doctor's check for $275 we had a bookkeeper enter it to his credit. But we held off buying any stock for him. Instead, a day or two later, one of us called him again.

"A hitch has developed and the merger has been postponed indefinitely," I told him. "I think you could make a better investment. We can dispose of the Standard Oil stock we bought for you and give you a better deal in the Copper Queen."

"I read about that," Dr. Johnson replied. "What do you think about it?"

"I think it is the best stock on the market today. The prospect is for a boom in copper and I think the owners of Copper Queen stock are likely to make a killing."

"What's the price of Copper Queen?"

"The par value is ten dollars per share. But by a fortunate arrangement with the corporation, we have a small block of this stock that we can dispose of at five dollars per share. My advice to you is that you let us sell your Standard Oil and buy Copper Queen. With no additional cost to you, we can buy seventy-five shares of Copper Queen."

"I'll think it over and let you know."

"I feel I should tell you," I said, "that our supply is limited. And we can't guarantee that this low price will continue."

"Oh, all right," said Dr. Johnson. "Sell my Standard Oil and get me the mining stock."

"Very well, Doctor. I shall see that the matter is attended to at once."

That was just one of many such deals. We hired additional telephone men and put them to work on the prospects. Within a few weeks we had an office personnel of seventy-five people. The telephones were kept busy by our solicitors, who went through the telephone book, calling all categories of professional men.

Hogan and I devoted our time to the executive end of the business — and to keeping Red Letter Sullivan in line. We still needed his bonafide stock market analyses with which to surround our own articles of high praise for the stocks we were peddling.

In nearly every instance our solicitors talked the customers into switching to the Copper Queen or some such stock after having placed

## Red Letter Days

an order for Standard Oil or A. T. and T. Hogan and I talked only to the clients who were hard to convince.

There were not very many of these. It doesn't seem reasonable that people would be so gullible. I have often marveled at the number who seem to be waiting for someone to come along and take their money. Beyond the normal, greedy desire to make easy money or to get something for nothing I can't explain it. But I do know that this gullibility exists — and works.

In those early days, I didn't have time to stop and wonder why people could be taken in so easily. Having learned that they could be I used the knowledge to full advantage. Hogan and I, through *The Red Letter* and our telephone solicitations, sold many thousands in worthless stocks before complaints began to come in.

Incidentally, our use of a string of telephones was the beginning of the "boiler rooms" that still exist. In later years the boiler rooms were used to solicit sales of stocks and various other items. Today, their principal use is for solicitation of donations to charitable institutions or to further the cause of some politician.

We ran our stock business and published *The Red Letter* for several months before the "heat" became so intense that we had to close. We had operated within the law, but our clients soon learned that they could expect no return from their stock investments.

It was shortly after this that Hogan, who had been involved in a number of wire-tapping schemes and was sought in several cities, decided that he had made enough money to retire. He went to Paris, bought a villa and, so far as I know, never returned to America.

One day I was walking along Jackson Boulevard when I almost bumped into Phil Smart, upon whom I had worked the ring deal. I didn't see him until I noticed suddenly that a redheaded Irishman with a burly figure blocked my path. For a moment we stood there facing each other. It must have been a sight. We both had red hair. Smart's face, normally red, was livid. Ordinarily he spoke good English, but now, greatly excited, he spoke with a rich Irish brogue.

"So," he said, "'tis the son of Morton ye are. Tis the likes of ye, ye thievin' scoundrel, that makes honest men commit murder. Wait until I get me hands on ye!"

My complexion is normally red, too. But now it was as white as chalk. For a moment I had been rooted to the spot. But as the big Irishman made a lunge for me, I ducked, turned a corner, and didn't stop until I saw that Smart, still red and puffing, had given up the chase. But I doubt if he ever did forget the $1,000 he had paid for one of my paste diamonds.

## 10. Millionaires and Murder

I WENT INTO A SALOON AND STARTED FOR THE BAR. A HAND REACHED OUT and detained me. I turned and recognized George Gross, a former boxer, who had helped me with various deals.

"Too bad we didn't know about you when we had the foot races," he said, laughing. "I bet we could have cleaned up a lot of money on you."

I gave Gross a withering look and strode on up to the bar.

"Whiskey and soda," I ordered. Then as I calmed down I saw a man with Gross. He was a bearded person in a cutaway coat and banker's gray trousers.

"Hello, Joe," he called, sticking out his hand.

"Tim North! Glad to see you," I replied. "What are you doing in Chicago?"

"I'm on my way to Galesburg," he said. "But I stopped off to see you."

"What's up?"

"We've got Galesburg fixed for the fights," he said, "and we need a good steerer. Suppose we go somewhere and talk it over."

Tim North's scheme had started with fixed foot races, which had been promoted on Saturdays in small towns in Missouri. The farmers came to town and, looking for amusement, they were easy victims of the fixed foot races, originated by a couple of old-time track stars.

Gross had worked the fixed foot races in various towns in the Middle West. Then he met North and between the two of them they cooked up the fight racket. By comparison with the fights, the foot races were peanuts.

# "Yellow Kid" Weil

Boxing as an amateur sport was permissible in gymnasiums in Illinois and other states at that time. But in many states, prize fighting was illegal. All prize fighting in Illinois was done under cover, much of it in private gymnasiums.

Nevertheless there was a wide interest in the sport, particularly in betting on the outcome, and that was the basis for the racket. North had contacted certain officials in Galesburg and for a reasonable fee had arranged that there would be no interference from the police. Galesburg soon became known throughout the country as a "fixed town."

North was building up an organization but needed a few more good men. I suggested Big Joe Kelly, whose main asset was his impressive appearance; Jack Carkeek, a wrestler; Old Man Parsons, a con man; and a boxer known as Jack the Kid. North took them all into his outfit.

He offered me 50 per cent of the proceeds of any deal that I steered to him and helped carry through, and I accepted. But I needed a little help, too. I lined up a heavyweight fighter named Sol Frost and made a deal with George Gross. Both worked for me on numerous occasions when we fixed a fight.

Generally I tried to find a wealthy prospect who was interested in prize fighting. But on several occasions my victims knew nothing of boxing. In every case, however, they were rich and were trying to add to their fortunes without risking anything.

Such a man was Sam Geezil. I met him legitimately when I went to look at a two-story apartment building in South Union Avenue which he had offered for sale. My wife and I had looked over the property and decided to buy, if we could get it for a reasonable figure.

Geezil's original price was $7,200. He would accept $3,500 down and the balance in easy payments. I had practically made up my mind to buy the building when one day I ran into George Gross in Hannh and Hogg's saloon on Madison Street. I told him I was dickering for the building.

"Geezil?" said George. "Not Sam Geezil?"

"Yes. Why?"

"Do you know who he is?" Gross asked excitedly.

"No. Who is he?"

## Millionaires and Murder

"Well, he's a millionaire, for one thing. He used to own the Geezil Express and Storage Company. He just sold out last week for $825,000 — cash."

"That's a lot of money." I studied Gross. A light was dancing in his eyes. "What have you got in mind?"

"He's an old man, Joe. A man his age hasn't got any use for all that money. Do you suppose he would go for the fight?"

"It's worth trying," I replied. "I'm on my way out to see him now. I was going to close the deal for that building, but I'll lay a little groundwork first. You wait for me here."

Sam Geezil was a heavy-set German, past middle age. He had devoted practically all his years to the accumulating of money and I doubt if there had been much fun in his life. Even now when he was trying to swing this business deal with me, he should have been in Florida or California for his health. He had recently undergone an abdominal operation and still hobbled about on a stick.

"Well, have you decided to buy the building?" he asked.

"I don't know. How much would you let me have it for if I paid cash?"

"I would knock off the $200," he replied. "But I don't care whether I have it all in cash or not. If you pay half down, then the mortgage will be a good investment at 6 per cent."

"I'd rather pay it all down," I said. "If you can wait a day or two I can get the money."

"Eh?" he rejoined — he was interested in any transaction involving money. "How can you make money so fast?"

"I have to make a trip to Milwaukee," I replied. "A distant relative of mine and I have a business deal of importance to negotiate. I expect to profit handsomely."

"What kind of a transaction is it?" he asked.

"I am sorry, but I cannot discuss it. It is a matter that has to be kept confidential — for the time being."

"I wish you luck, my boy," he said cordially.

"Thank you, Mr. Geezil. I will return in a day or two with the money. Then my wife's dream will be realized. She will have a home of her own."

Instead of going to Milwaukee, I went to Hannh and Hogg's and

107

## "Yellow Kid" Weil

met Gross. I told him of what had happened. He agreed to act as my fighter if the old man went for my story.

George had once been a good middleweight boxer. But now he was past his prime, and wine and beer had taken a toll. He was becoming paunchy, but he could still box.

I waited three days before calling again on Sam Geezil.

"Welcome back," he said, shaking my hand. "Did you have a successful trip?"

"Unfortunately, no," I replied. "The person I went to see wanted to keep the greater part of the profits."

"What sort of a deal is it?" he asked.

"I'm not supposed to discuss this with you without my uncle's permission," I replied. "I hope you will respect my confidence."

"You can depend on Sam Geezil," he assured me.

"My uncle, who is a very brilliant man," I told him, "is private secretary to a coterie of millionaires who have vast holdings in electric roads, coal mines, municipal bonds, and diversified investments. They travel about the country in a private railroad car — a palace on wheels.

"Not only are they big-scale financial operators, but they are also sportsmen who are interested in hunting, fishing, and the fight game, on which they love to wager large sums. Traveling with them is a physical culture man, a boxer. They have matched him in mining camps over the country and have made vast sums of money betting on the outcome of the fights. All the monies, of course, were in private wagers."

"Coal mining camps?" he asked.

"Sometimes. But they also have holding in copper, gold, and silver mines. Sometimes their wagers run into astronomical figures. It is not unusual for them to have a million dollars on a fight. Their fighter has won consistently and they've made millions betting on him, but all he gets is a small salary."

"Don't they ever give him any of the winnings?"

"Not one cent. As a matter of fact, this boxer's sister is tubercular and he has become morose over his inability to send her to the proper climate. He sought a small loan from the millionaires and they flatly

## Millionaires and Murder

refused. On top of that, one of them insulted him one day by asking him to shine his shoes. He has sworn that he will get even with them in some way."

"What was the deal?"

"Several years ago," I replied, "this group of financiers bought a three-thousand-acre tract of marshland on the Illinois River. They used it for a shooting preserve. They built a lodge and clubhouse and had many good times there.

"During the season the ducks were so thick you could reach out and get them with a stick. The club members had a set rule that when they were shooting ducks everybody had to congregate at the clubhouse at midday.

"One day while they were there," I continued, "everybody showed up at midday except one of the financiers and the doctor who had gone out with him in a boat. Alarmed by the absence of these two men, the others organized a searching party.

"It was not until the following morning that they learned what had happened. The boat had capsized and the financier had been drowned. The doctor had clung to a stump and that's where his fellow members found him.

"The loss of their friend and companion so saddened them that they never returned to the lodge. They ordered my uncle, their secretary, to dispose of the tract for whatever he could get.

"The property lay untouched for a few years. Then one day my uncle received a letter from a banker in a near-by town inquiring if the land was for sale. Stimulated by his interest, my uncle went to inspect the property.

"He was amazed to find that a large company which owned the adjoining property had ditched and tilled their land. The result was this swampy land had drained, leaving three thousand acres of very rich farm land, the current price of which was from $300 to $500 per acre."

Mr. Geezil listened with rapt attention. As a matter of fact the rich farm land in the vicinity I had described actually was selling at $300 to $500 per acre, and he knew it.

"My uncle had been ordered to sell for whatever he could get," I went on. "Any loss would be inconsequential to the owners. He kept his discovery to himself and got to thinking. Since his employers had treated the physical culture man so shabbily, it was very likely that my uncle could expect no better treatment from them. He concluded he might as well take care of himself and feather his own nest.

"My purpose in going to Milwaukee was to meet a certain person and have him contact my uncle at a certain place. He was to negotiate with my uncle for the purchase of the property at $50 an acre, which would be $150,000. However, the land is worth $900,000.

"The mission of the Milwaukee man was to meet my uncle, who would give him sufficient money to purchase an option on the land at $50 an acre. He was then to sell the property to the banker for $300 an acre. The profits were to be divided 50 per cent to my uncle and 50 per cent to the Milwaukee man and myself.

"But the Milwaukee man was too greedy. He insisted that he get 50 per cent and that my uncle pay my share out of the remaining 50 per cent. I would not agree to this and broke off negotiations. Now my uncle and I must find a new principal."

"Why not let me do this negotiating for you?" asked Mr. Geezil.

"That's very kind of you," I replied. "For my part, I'd like to have you in the deal but we need a very wealthy man who appears to have some good reason for buying the land."

"Do you know what I'm worth?" he demanded.

"Why, no. I know you own that $7,000 building. But —"

"Young man, Sam Geezil is worth more than a million dollars!"

"Is that so?" I acted polite, but incredulous. This made him all the more anxious to convince me of his wealth.

"I can see you don't believe me," he said. "Did you ever hear of the Geezil Express and Storage Company?"

"Of course," I replied. "Who hasn't?"

"Well, I'm the Geezil who owned that business. I just sold it last week — for $825,000. What do you think of that?"

"Why — why —" For a moment I pretended to be dazed while this stupendous news soaked in. Then: "Mr. Geezil, I am sorry if I have misjudged you. But, of course, I had no idea —"

## Millionaires and Murder

"Oh, that's all right," he assured me. "No harm done. Now, do you think I would put up a suitable front to negotiate the deal with those millionaires?"

"Certainly you would. But I don't know what my uncle would say about it. After all, he has the final word in the matter."

"Well," he urged, "why don't you ask him?"

"Frankly," I replied, "I'm afraid of what my uncle would say if he knew that I had divulged the facts to anybody without his consent."

"All right," he declared, "I know a way around that. Don't tell him I know the whole thing. Just take me to meet him and let him invite me into the deal."

"I don't know," I said hesitantly.

"Where are you to meet your uncle?"

"Out of town," I replied evasively.

Geezil continued to ply me with questions. As I become more vague and reluctant, he became more enthusiastic. He gave me all sorts of reasons why he would be a good intermediary. I let him plead with me for an hour.

Inwardly I was chuckling at this money-mad millionaire who was begging me to lead him to the slaughter. He would enter any kind of scheme to make money. Gradually I weakened before his arguments and finally relented.

"Mr. Geezil," I said, "you have convinced me that you are the right man for this deal. I will take you to my uncle, but I cannot guarantee that he will accept you."

"I'll take that chance," he said. "Just arrange the meeting. And let's not lose any time."

The following day I told Geezil that the meeting had been arranged, and we took the train for Galesburg. George Gross went with us.

"George is a very promising fighter," I explained. "I'm his trainer and I'm taking him along to see that he keeps in shape and doesn't break his training rules."

It was apparent that he knew nothing about sports. He took no notice of Gross's obvious age and his gray hairs. Nor did the old man seem to think it strange that a boxer should be making the trip with us.

We registered at the best hotel in Galesburg and engaged two large

111

connecting rooms. Geezil occupied one and George and I the other.

As soon as we were settled I said, "You'd better get some rest. I'll go over to my uncle's office and see if he will do business with you."

George disrobed and got into his boxing trunks.

"What's he going to do?" Geezil asked.

Gross was standing in front of the mirror punching at an imaginary opponent.

"Oh, he shadow boxes," I explained. "That's part of his training schedule. Just don't pay any attention to it."

The millionaire shook his head and went into his room to rest.

The town of Galesburg was still fixed with all the law enforcement officers. Tim North who had his office in a building not far from the hotel had paid them to ignore our activities.

Tim posed as Mr. Worthington, my uncle, private secretary to the group of capitalists. He was an impressive-looking fellow, with his beard, striped trousers and cutaway coat.

Old Man Parsons also wore a beard. He was tall and slender, dressed in a frock coat, and looked like a man of distinction. He posed as Mr. Mortimer, a financier.

Tom Muggins, who was a heavyweight wrestler, was broad of shoulder and had a fine figure. He wore a van Dyke beard and posed as a wealthy physician, Dr. Jackson.

In appearance Joe Kelly was probably the most impressive of the lot. He was over six feet tall, big and stout without being fat, and had a nice face. He too wore a beard and a frock coat. The worst difficulty with Joe was that his grammar was atrocious. If he ever opened his mouth, you knew at once that he was a native of Chicago's West Side who had little, if any schooling. We called him a "dese, dem, and dose" guy. For that reason he was instructed to say nothing. His silence impressed the suckers all the more. He appeared to be a big man who tolerated small talk in a whimsical way but took no part in it himself.

Phil Barton was an old faro-bank dealer from Chicago. He was tall, bearded, slender, and was formally attired. He posed as Judge Barry, an eminent jurist. Actually he was a man with a small mind and small ideas and was out of place in our group.

## Millionaires and Murder

Jim Andrews was another of our "financiers." Mr. Howard was a fictional member of the group but always missing because he was ailing. This mythical invalid was necessary to our plan.

When I entered their offices, they were seated around a table playing whist.

"Welcome!" called North. "Who have you got?"

"Tim," I said, "I have a man in the hotel who is a millionaire. He has $825,000 in actual cash from the sale of his business. I think we can take half a million dollars or maybe more from him. But I want you to do exactly as I say."

"Of course I will, Joe," he replied.

I should explain here that there were several other setups like Tim North's in the Middle West. While I usually steered my victims to him in Galesburg, I could have taken them to any of the other fight setups on the same terms — 50 per cent of the take as my share.

I should also explain our terminology. We would either "establish" or "send" every victim. This necessitated a fixed bank, which we had in Galesburg. Very few of the victims ever went to Galesburg with a great deal of money.

To "establish" a man, we asked him to go to the local bank and have a specified sum withdrawn from his own bank and transferred to his account in the local bank. Once we had done this we definitely established the amount we could take from him.

But to "send" a man meant that we asked him to go to the local banker and identify himself. We left the amount open. The banker would find out for us how much the victim was good for.

"I want you to send this man," I stated. "Don't establish him under any circumstances."

"That's agreeable to us, Joe," he said. "What's his name?"

"Sam Geezil." I then related all that had happened. "You come over to the hotel in a little while and meet him. But if you try to establish him, I'll take him somewhere else."

When I got back to the hotel Geezil was sitting up in bed watching Gross at his calisthenics. He motioned to me. I went over and sat down on the edge of the bed.

"That fellow there — he worries me. Every few minutes he jumps

113

up from where he is sitting, and starts punching at the air."

"He's got to keep in shape for a match on the Pacific Coast," I explained. "Just ignore him." I could have told George to cut it out and he would have been only too happy to do so, but his apparent eccentricity was a necessary part of the plan I had carefully worked out.

"Did you see your uncle?" Geezil asked.

"Yes. And I have some good news for you. He has agreed to accept you to transact the deal."

"When are we going to get started?"

"Today. He will be over as soon as he can get away from his office."

While we waited we discussed prize fighting. I told him about Gross, the big bouts he had won, what bright prospects he had for the future. Periodically George jumped up and went into his shadow-boxing routine. He made each routine very short however, for he was such a heavy beer drinker that he soon became winded.

After a short interval my "uncle" appeared. I introduced him as "Mr. Worthington."

"Mr. Geezil," he said, "I don't know how far my nephew has gone with you in this transaction. I cautioned him not to go too far because of my position and standing with the men I represent."

He then proceeded to relate all that I had told him about the hunting preserve, the reason for selling it, and its great increase in value.

My uncle continued, "I don't know whether you have a bank account or not —"

"Of course I have a bank account," Geezil interrupted anxiously. "It's at the Englewood National in Chicago. If you want to check up you can communicate with the president of the bank."

"Here is what I suggest," said Tim. "Go to the local bank and draw on your bank in Chicago for say $35,000. Have it placed to your credit here.

"Mr. Geezil," he continued, "I could give you that money and have you deposit it to your credit. But that would not protect me. The only purpose in having your own money actually transferred from your own bank to this one in Galesburg is this: if it should happen in the future that my people learn of the value of the property and want to know why it had been sold so low, I can say I know nothing of the

## Millionaires and Murder

property whatsoever; that you had approached me and were willing to pay the price they had paid for it; and that you had transferred your own money to the bank in Galesburg. This would prevent them from learning of my collusion in the matter.

"The day that you purchase this option," North continued, "I want you to draw your money out of the Galesburg bank and have it transferred back to your own bank."

The idea that the money would eventually find its way back to his own bank served to allay any suspicions Geezil might have.

When Tim had gone I asked him what he was going to do.

"There's only one thing to do," he replied, "and that is what your uncle suggested."

We walked down to the bank and Geezil talked to the president. He produced his credentials.

"I'll be glad to attend to it, Mr. Geezil," said the banker. "I'll call you at the hotel as soon as I have some word on it."

We thanked him and left. The old gentleman, tired because of his recent operation, went back to the hotel. I went over to the offices of the pseudo-millionaires. They were waiting for me.

"Tim," I declared, "what in the name of creation ever possessed you to establish that man? I've got a notion to take him away."

"Joe," he replied, "I didn't know you smoked the pipe."

"What do you mean?"

"Well, you must, because you're having pipe dreams. That man doesn't have a nickel!"

"Who told you that?" I demanded.

"Barton. He knows a lot more about suckers than you do. He's acquainted with this Geezil and he's poorer than either of you."

"Is that so! Well, I happen to know he just got $825,000 from the sale of his business."

"Yeah," said Barton. "But did you know his wife is divorcing him?"

"No."

"Well, she is, and she's tied up every penny of his money."

I didn't know what to say to that. There was a chance that he was right. I returned to the hotel somewhat confused, wondering if Geezil had lied to me.

Gross was going through his routine again and the other man was lying on the bed, watching him nervously.

"Did you see your uncle?" he asked.

"Yes. Mr. Geezil, this transaction at the banks — are you sure your banker will respond?"

"Certainly. Does your uncle have some doubts about me?"

"No, of course not. I guess I'm just a little overanxious. This is my chance to make a killing. And I've always wanted to own my own home. I'd hate to go back and tell my wife there wasn't going to be any new home."

"Don't let that worry you," he replied. "The amount I asked for is insignificant. I've got nearly a million dollars on deposit there."

Just then the telephone rang. I answered it.

"Mr. Geezil?"

"Yes," I replied.

"This is the bank. Your money is here any time you want it."

"Thank you," I said and hung up. "It was the bank," I told the old man. "They've got your money."

"I knew they'd get it," he replied.

"My uncle thought maybe I was a little overenthused about you. I'd like to have you draw that money out and show it to him."

He didn't much like the idea of walking to the bank again but he wanted the deal to go through and agreed. After we got the money, I told him:

"Tomorrow will be a very strenuous day for you. I think you'd better go to the hotel and rest. I'll take the money over and show it to my uncle."

"All right," he agreed. "I am worn out."

He handed me the money, done up in a neat bundle of large bills, and I slipped it into my pocket. He went back to the hotel and I called again at North's office.

"Tim," I said, "I owe you an apology. That man hasn't got it and can't get it."

Barton jumped up and shouted, "What did I tell you?"

I reached into my pocket, withdrew the sheaf of bills and handed them to North. "Would you mind counting this money for me, Tim?"

## Millionaires and Murder

He counted it, then stood regarding me in amazement.

"Jeez!" he said. "Where did you get this?"

"Geezil got it from the bank," I replied. "I've never seen a man get money so quickly from out of town."

All eyes turned on Barton. They knew that if he hadn't insisted that Geezil's money was tied up, Geezil wouldn't have been established and we might have been able to take a great deal more from him.

Muggins jumped up and gave Barton the worst beating I've ever seen a man take. He whined for mercy, but Tim said, "You get out and don't ever come back." Muggins caught the blubbering Barton by the collar and pulled him to the door, then kicked him down the stairs.

"Just wait," he whined, "I'll get even with you for this!"

We laughed at him and promptly forgot about him.

When I returned to the hotel I showed Geezil that I still had the money.

"My uncle is convinced, all right. He has no more doubts. Now I think we'd all better turn in early, because we have a strenuous day ahead."

The following morning my uncle was at the hotel early.

"You are to be prepared to meet the wealthiest men in the United States," he said. "I don't want you to act out of the ordinary. Just be yourselves. After all, they are only human, no better than you or I. When you get the option," he said to Geezil, "I want you to be sure that you dispose of it at not less than $300 an acre."

That was agreed, and presently the pseudo-millionaires came in. My uncle introduced them, and Mr. Geezil beamed at the thought of mixing with so much wealth.

"Mr. Geezil would like to buy an option on your hunting preserve," my uncle explained.

"Haven't we sold that yet, Tim?" Mr. Mortimer asked, as if he really didn't keep up with such trivial matters.

"No," Tim replied. "I've been trying to make the best deal possible. After all, your investment — "

"Hang the investment!" Dr. Jackson exclaimed. "We don't care about that since poor Horace lost his life at the accursed place. Isn't that the way you feel, Joe?"

"Yes," the other replied and said no more.

"It's the way we all feel about it," muttered Mr. Andrews. "But naturally we would expect to get our original investment out of it."

"Mr. Geezil is willing to pay $50 an acre," my uncle offered. "That was the original price."

"Yes," said Geezil. "I'm going to use it for a hunting club and sell memberships."

"An excellent idea," approved Mr. Mortimer. "I think there can be no objection to selling him an option. Do you gentlemen agree?"

The others readily agreed, and my uncle was directed to act as their agent.

"You can deal with Mr. Worthington," said Dr. Jackson. "And I for one wish you luck in your new venture."

"There's just one detail that has to be settled," my uncle hesitated. "That's the abstract. It will take me two or three days to have that drawn up."

Geezil hadn't quite expected this, but he knew enough about real estate to realize the deal couldn't be completed without an abstract, so he made no objection.

There was a lull in the conversation. Just then Gross jumped up and started going through his shadow boxing routine.

"Say," Dr. Jackson commented, "that man looks like a fighter."

"Yes," I replied. I motioned to George and he came romping over to where we sat. "I want you gentlemen to meet George Gross. He is preparing for a bout on the Pacific Coast. I am his trainer."

"How interesting," said Mr. Mortimer. "While we're waiting for that abstract, maybe we can arrange a match. We own a fighter, you know."

"Is that so?" I said. "Who is your fighter?"

"Jack the Kid."

"I've heard of him and I think my man can beat him."

"There's just one way to find out," challenged Dr. Jackson.

"The match can be arranged," I said, "provided you gentlemen are prepared to make a substantial wager."

"Nothing I can think of that we would like better," said Mr. Mortimer. "Tim, you draw up the articles of agreement."

## Millionaires and Murder

With that the millionaires departed, leaving North behind. As soon as they had left he whirled and faced me angrily.

"Who do you think you are?" he demanded. "Where will you get the money to bet? You know they wager hundreds of thousands on the fights."

"I know what I'm doing, Uncle," I replied. "Mr. Geezil hasn't paid over his $35,000 yet. We can put $15,000 with that and have $50,000 to wager."

"And how," my uncle asked sarcastically, "do you propose to cover hundreds of thousands with $50,000?"

"By pyramiding the bets," I replied. "Did you ever hear of that?"

"No, I don't understand what you mean."

"It's simply a matter of arrangement. You can have yourself designated as the stakeholder, can't you?"

"Yes, that will be easy enough."

"All right, here is the way it will work." I explained my plan in detail. Geezil listened attentively and did not bat an eye at the crookedness of the scheme.

"Is that satisfactory to you?" my uncle asked him.

"Perfectly," replied this law-abiding, respected member of his community. "There's just one thing. How can we be sure that Gross will win?"

"Jack the Kid has been looking for an opportunity to get even with these men," Tim replied. He then told the story about the fighter's tubercular sister. "I'll get him over here and we'll have an understanding with him."

All this was what we called the switch. We had switched Geezil's interest from the original deal to the boxing match. The switch is an important part of nearly all good confidence games.

Tim sat down and wrote out the articles of agreement. These provided for a fight to the finish between the two boxers; for a purse of $500,000; that Mr. Worthington, my supposed uncle, was to be the referee and stakeholder; that if either side failed to put up its share of the purse, any monies wagered would be forfeited; that either side would be given twenty-four hours in which to raise its share of the purse. The match was to be staged in a private gymnasium.

## "Yellow Kid" Weil

Next we contacted the other boxer — who was waiting to be called — and arranged for him to throw the fight. He and Gross rehearsed the bout up there in the hotel room. They made it look realistic for five rounds. The Kid was to take a dive in the sixth. To Geezil the setup was foolproof.

When the millionaires returned to the hotel the stage was all set. Mr. Worthington sat at a table inside the communicating room which Geezil had occupied. The old man sat at a desk in front of Worthington. In front of him was Gross at another table.

On the other side of the room was a larger table around which chairs had been drawn. The capitalists were seated at this. My uncle, the solicitous private secretary, had provided glasses and a couple of bottles of wine.

Mr. Mortimer signed the articles of agreement for the millionaires and Geezil signed for our side. The old man didn't have an opportunity to read this paper very carefully, otherwise he might have asked some questions.

At the side of his desk, Geezil had a satchel containing the $50,000. He was so placed that he was only partially visible to the group at the big table, whose backs were half turned. They were drinking wine and discussing the latest trends in the stock market, thus deliberately creating an atmosphere of confusion in which it seemed plausible enough that they wouldn't notice just what we were doing.

The capitalists opened the betting with a wager of $50,000. Mr. Geezil took our $50,000 from the satchel to cover. I acted as messenger. First I took the money to Gross' table where he tabulated the bets. Then I carried it to the table where Mr. Worthington sat. That is, I was supposed to. But instead of giving him $100,000, I slipped $50,000 into Geezil's satchel as I passed. Only $50,000 was in sight, but nobody appeared to notice.

When the wagering first began we started out counting each bundle of money. This was a tedious process. Soon my uncle said:

"There's no need of counting this money. It was put up at the bank. The amount is printed on the wrapper and each wrapper has the teller's initials on it. We're just wasting a lot of time."

"I agree with you," said Mr. Mortimer. "What do you men say?"

## Millionaires and Murder

Everybody agreed that counting the money was unnecessary. This was to allow for the use of "boodle." Practically all the money used was "boodle," done up in neat bundles, with good bills only on the top and bottom.

The money Geezil had was all good and the other men had used a few thousand dollars in good money while we were counting each bundle. Thus, the first wager consisted of about $75,000 in good money and the balance in "boodle." About $50,000 of this was loose money, from bundles that had been broken open. The balance was in bundles done up in bank wrappers.

Having this much loose money enabled me to cover up in the pyramiding of bets that followed. The betting was continued as soon as it had been decided not to count all the money in the bundles.

When the next wager for $50,000 was made, Geezil reached in the satchel, produced the money I had dropped in there. I took it over to have George tabulate it and the Kid brought a like amount from the millionaires' table. Then we took it over to my uncle. But instead of giving it to him, we dropped it in Geezil's satchel. The other men were drinking and talking about the stock market. Only $50,000 was in sight on the table, but part of it was loose money. They didn't seem to notice the discrepancy.

In this way we covered all bets until the amount had got to $400,000. Then Mr. Mortimer said, "Just a minute. I think I gave you $50,000 instead of $25,000 as my part of that last wager."

"We can't stand a count," I whispered to Geezil.

"A count will soon tell us." Dr. Jackson said. "Count the money, Tim, and see if you have an extra $25,000."

"There's no need of going through such a tedious task as that," he replied. "Why don't we put it in a safety deposit box and count it after the fight?"

"An excellent idea," said Mr. Mortimer. "Go put it in the box. If your friends win, they can count the money to see if there's an extra $25,000. If we win we can count it at our leisure. We will keep one of the keys and Mr. Geezil can keep the other. Whoever loses will turn his key over to the winner."

That was agreed and my uncle was delegated to take the money to

121

the bank. While he had been talking he had wrapped part of it in a newspaper. The balance he had put in Geezil's bag. The bundle wrapped in newspaper he had placed under Geezil's chair.

He picked up the bag and started to the door.

"Just a minute," I said, pointing to the bundle under the chair. "You've forgotten something."

Tim, obviously embarrassed, returned and picked up the bundle, stuffing it into the bag.

"What's the matter, Tim?" asked Mr. Mortimer. "Don't you feel well? Perhaps I should go with you so that nothing happens to you."

They left and his other companions, accompanied by Jack the Kid, left for the gymnasium.

"We'll come as soon as Mr. Worthington gets back," I said.

When Tim returned, he was alone, Mr. Mortimer having gone to the gymnasium.

"What's the matter with you?" he demanded, facing me angrily. "I knew I left that money under the chair."

"Oh," I said meekly. "I just thought you had forgotten it."

"We're in a fine mess now. If I had gone to the bank alone, I could have kept both keys to the safety deposit box. But as it is I had to give one of them to Mr. Mortimer. Besides, I had $250,000 in that bundle. What are we going to use now to cover the purse?"

"I never thought of that," I said meekly. "Maybe they'll forget about the purse."

"I hope so," my uncle said frigidly, "but I doubt it.

So, Tim, Gross, Geezil and I went to the gymnasium. Jack the Kid was in the ring and the stage was all set. I acted as second to George and Dr. Jackson acted as second to the Kid.

The bout was ready to begin when Mr. Mortimer interrupted.

"What about the purse?" he asked. "That hasn't been covered."

"Well, what difference does it make?" Mr. Andrews wondered.

"I promised Mr. Howard, who is ill, that he could put up the money for the purse, since he wouldn't be here and would be unable to bet. I feel a responsibility to him."

"That's different," agreed Dr. Jackson. "If we win, then you'll have to give him what we win on the purse."

## Millionaires and Murder

"That's right," said Mr. Mortimer. "And I don't feel that I want to take the responsibility if there isn't any purse."

"The purse is in the articles of agreement," volunteered Dr. Jackson. "The fight can't go on until it is covered."

The fighters climbed out of the ring and we all went back to the hotel, where a general discussion ensued.

"According to the articles of agreement," said Mr. Mortimer, "you forfeit all the money you've bet if you can't cover the purse."

"I can cover the purse," Geezil spoke up. "Our share is $250,000. I'll give you my check for it."

"No!" insisted Mr. Mortimer. "The agreement stipulates cash."

"Well," I broke in, "the articles of agreement also gives us twenty-four hours to raise the purse. We can have the cash in that time."

"We certainly can," said Geezil.

While the millionaires were discussing this, the old man whispered to me: "I'll go back to Chicago and get it if necessary."

It still seemed possible that we would make a big haul from him. But Tim now made his second mistake. He persuaded his friends to forget about the purse and let the fight go on. I could have kicked him, for I am certain that Geezil would have raised the money if we had waited.

But they didn't want to wait, so the purse was waived and we went to the gymnasium again. The fighters got in the ring and the bout began.

They traded terrific punches that looked very convincing, though each fighter caught the blows on his arms and shoulders. The fight was even for two rounds. Then in the third, Jack the Kid was knocked down several times. In the fourth he was down again, this time for a count of eight.

Geezil was jubilant. He was so sure now that he was going to clean up that his only regret was that he hadn't bet more. He taunted Mr. Mortimer about it.

"I still think our fighter will win," returned Mortimer. "I'm willing to bet more money on it."

"How much?"

"Oh, a quarter of a million."

123

## "Yellow Kid" Weil

"I'll take that," said the old man, "if you'll accept my check."
But Mr. Mortimer wouldn't accept a check.
"Fighting in Illinois is illegal," he reminded Geezil. "I wouldn't care to be involved through a check."

In the fifth round the Kid was down several times but he managed to hang on. At the beginning of the sixth Dr. Jackson, his second, slipped a ball into his mouth. It was about the size of a golf ball and it was made of fish skin. It contained chicken blood that had been mixed with hot water. Gross landed a terrific punch to the Kid's mouth and he was down for a count of eight. As he went down he bit into the ball and blood poured out of his mouth and down his neck and chest.

At the count of eight, he got up blindly to his feet and wove out toward Gross, who wound up and swung with terrific force. He missed the Kid altogether, spun around, and fell on his back. As he spun, he bit the ball I had placed in his mouth.

Blood began to gush from his mouth in great quantity. It spurted in the air and covered his face. Dr. Jackson rushed to the ring and wiped the blood from his face. Then he sponged Gross' face with water, managing at the same time to slip another of the balls into his mouth.

Blood began to gush anew. It ran all over his head and was a messy sight.

"This man is having a hemorrhage," Dr. Jackson declared gravely.

"I think he is dying," he remarked, as he worked frantically to check the hemorrhage. The blood continued to flow freely.

The group in the gymnasium was now silent. Even Geezil had turned pale and begun to tremble. Suddenly Gross coughed and lay still.

Dr. Jackson bent over him with his stethoscope. Then he stood up and shook his head.

"This man is dead!" he quavered.

Pandemonium broke loose. Everybody began to scatter. No one wanted to be mixed up in this prize fight — especially since a man had been killed.

"We've got to get out of here," I whispered to Geezil. He was shaking like a man with palsy.

## Millionaires and Murder

We returned to the hotel room as quickly as possible and, shortly afterwards, my uncle came in. He showed Geezil one of the keys to the safety deposit box.

"I'll get the other key from them," he said. "I'll take the money and meet you two in Chicago."

"But we didn't win," Geezil pointed out.

"No. But they will find out about the shortage if I stay with them. I would lose my job anyway. I might as well quit now. I'll stay with them until I get the money, then we'll meet and split it."

"What about the dead man?" Geezil asked fearfully.

"Let them worry about it. They've got plenty of influence. Now you two had better catch the next train back to Chicago."

A train was due out in half an hour. We had scheduled the fight so that it would end just before train time. Geezil and I got our bags and went to the station.

On the train going into Chicago he fretted a great deal about the "murder" and the possible consequences. I was worried too, but it was mainly about the problem of how I was going to get away from the old man.

He solved that problem for me.

"Suppose they've decided to look for us," he shuddered. "You'll be very conspicuous in that topcoat. They'll spot us the minute we get off the train."

I was wearing a topcoat of London smoked melton.

"What do you want me to do?" I asked.

"Leave that coat on the train when we get off."

"I can't do that!" I protested. "It cost me a lot of money and I can't afford to lose it."

"Well, I can't afford to be seen getting off the train with you in it," he retorted. "I'll tell you what. We're not far from Kewanee. Why don't you get off there and come to Chicago on another train?"

This suited me fine, but I made a pretense of objecting.

"Suppose my uncle comes to Chicago looking for us before I get there?"

"Your uncle won't be there. When those men calm down, they'll demand a count. Your uncle might as well kill himself."

## "Yellow Kid" Weil

"How am I ever going to face my wife? She had her heart set on owning that home."

"I'll give it to you, if that's all that's worrying you," said the old man. "My God, I've got something more serious than that on my mind. Now you get off. I'll call you up in a few days."

With apparent reluctance, I got off at Kewanee, which is about 135 miles from Chicago. That was the last I ever saw of Sam Geezil.

I didn't steer any more victims to Galesburg. George Gross had taken several to the Mayberry setup and I made the mistake of going there. A federal grand jury in Council Bluffs, Iowa, indicted George and thirteen others. Jack Carkeek and I were indicted at the same time.

Gross was caught and went to trial with the Mayberry crowd. Carkeek escaped to California and I fled to Chicago. I hid behind a beard and plain-glass spectacles. These disguised my naturally youthful appearance.

When we kicked Phil Barton out of the office in Galesburg, we forgot about him. But we were soon to have cause to remember him.

Barney Bertsch, who had a saloon on the corner of Randolph and Wells Streets, next door to the Detective Bureau, was Chicago's big fixer. His place was a rendezvous for the underworld, but the law never touched him. In my opinion — and a lot of other people shared it — Chicago has never seen a lower criminal than Barney Bertsch.

Phil Barton remembered that Old Man Parsons held the purse for Tim North's ring. Parsons had a money belt, and usually carried about $25,000 around his waist. Barton, determined to get his revenge relayed this information to Barney, who was always looking for a way to make a dishonest dollar.

Barney called in three crooks — his brother, Joe, who did anything from a street stick-up to a mail robbery, a safecracker named Jake Lukes, and a burglar named Andy Philson who was known as the "Gimlet Man" because he used a gimlet to bore around the latch of a window to break in.

At Barney's instigation these three thugs went to Old Man Parson's room in Galesburg. They posed as federal officers. Parsons knew that others had been indicted and wasn't surprised. He went along

## Millionaires and Murder

quietly. The three men took him to the tracks of the Burlington railroad.

At a dark spot on the right-of-way, they took his money belt and the $25,000, and tied him to the track, as Barney had instructed them. They left him there to be run over by a train — just as they used to do to the beautiful heroine in the old-time melodrama. Fortunately for Old Man Parsons, the thugs didn't know much about their surroundings. They tied him to a sidetrack instead of the main line and two hours later he was released by a couple of railroad men.

The three men kept $5,000 each and gave $10,000 to Barney Bertsch, who probably cut it up with Phil Barton. But Barney wasn't satisfied. He decided to try for more of the swag.

At Riverview Amusement Park he had a concession called "Bosco the Snake Eater." One night, he invited Andy Philson, the burglar, to see the show. The place was crowded at every performance. Andy had no way of knowing that the crowd consisted of "shills" whom Barney had hired for the occasion.

"I got so many irons in the fire," he told Andy, "I don't have time to look after it. I'll let you have it dirt cheap — $2,500. You can see for yourself how much money it takes in."

Andy was impressed and bought the show. He soon discovered he had bought a flop. He went to Barney's saloon to demand an accounting.

Barney had sharp eyes. He saw Philson entering the Randolph Street entrance. He went out the Wells Street door and hurried to the Detective Bureau. There he enlisted the help of Detectives Russell and Stapleton.

Philson was standing at the bar waiting for Barney. The detectives approached him one from each side.

"Have a drink," invited Stapleton.

"I don't drink with strangers," Philson replied suspiciously.

"Nice ring you have there," said Russell, grasping Andy's left hand on which was a large diamond.

Philson backed away from the detectives into a booth opposite the bar. The detectives drew their guns. Andy drew his and fired. Russell went down, dead. Stapleton was shot and dropped to his knees.

127

Still shooting, Philson started to back out the door. But Stapleton fired and got him in the abdomen. Both men were taken to the hospital and eventually recovered.

Philson was indicted for the murder of Russell, was tried in Criminal Court, and sentenced to life in Joliet. It was while he was in the county jail, waiting to be transported to prison, that Philson's mother appealed to Clarence Darrow, then a law partner of Edgar Lee Masters, the poet.

Darrow examined the record and agreed to take the case. He appeared before Judge Scanlon and asked a new trial. The motion was denied. Darrow then filed notice of his appeal to the Supreme Court.

"This is a clear case of prejudiced conviction," Darrow told Judge Scanlon. "I intend to make of it a monument of law. If the Supreme Court doesn't reverse the conviction, I'll quit."

"If it does reverse," said Judge Scanlon, "I'll resign from the bench."

Several weeks later the Supreme Court reviewed the evidence, reversed the conviction, and ordered a new trial. Judge Scanlon reconsidered his rash promise and continued on the bench.

At the second trial, with Darrow defending, it was a different story. Philson testified that he did not know the two men were officers, since they were in plain clothes and displayed no badges. He contended that he thought they were a couple of thugs intent upon taking his diamond ring. He was acquitted.

## 11. I Tried To Go Straight

HANNH AND HOGG'S SALOON, BARNEY BERTSCH'S CRYSTAL PALACE, and other Loop barrooms were the hangouts for the "sporting crowd." This included con men, prize fighters, wrestlers, jockeys, bookmakers, and some actors, not to mention a few safecrackers and stick-up men.

It was but natural that I should get acquainted with most of them. Here I met John Strosnider, a well-known swindler, who later worked for me, and also Old John Snarley, the original gold-brick man. Snarley seemed to like me particularly.

I never could understand why he didn't give up. The greater part of his life had been spent in prison. He was known to everybody as a man who was "stir-crazy." Indeed, he was in so many prisons that he developed a great interest in them.

Many years later Fred Buckminster and I had just completed a deal in Missoula, Montana, and were driving out of there as fast as we could. Old John Snarley was with us. We had heard that Montana had just built a new state prison.

"Boys," Old John proposed, "let's drive by and see what that new pen looks like."

"I should think," growled Buck, "that you've seen enough penitentiaries to last you the rest of your life."

"Besides," I said, "if we go that way, it will be a hundred miles out of our way."

"Just the same," Snarley insisted, "I'd like to see what it looks like. Who knows? Maybe I'll be sent there some day."

"What do you say, Joe?"

## "Yellow Kid" Weil

"All right," I agreed. "We'll humor him. Besides, if they're looking for us, they would hardly look for us near the penitentiary."

We drove one hundred miles out of our way so that John Snarley could see what the penitentiary looked like. We parked opposite it for fifteen minutes while he gazed admiringly at the structure.

Tim North's fight scheme had been copied by numerous other con men. Soon there were similar setups in fixed towns throughout the Middle West. One of the most active was operated by Fred Ventnor with thirteen associates, at Council Bluffs, Iowa. Hundreds of con men, prize fighters, and wrestlers were steering victims to these setups. Ventnor and his thirteen associates were the first to be indicted.

The law hadn't reached me yet and I decided it would be a good idea to stay out of the fights until the heat cooled off. My wife was urging me — as she always was — to get into something legitimate.

One day I saw my chance. I met a couple of fellows who had the makings of a machine for vending chewing-gum. They offered to sell me the dies for $200. I accepted the offer. I knew an inventor named Davis and I took the dies to him. He succeeded in building a very practical vending machine with two plungers of cold rolled steel and nickel. He said he could turn out as many machines as I wanted for $5.00 each.

My wife was very enthusiastic. "Joe," she declared, "this is your chance to be a real business man."

I agreed, and started my new business with every intention of going straight. I rented a suite of offices in the National Life building and organized a company I called, "The National Gum Company."

I had Davis build me several vending machines, which I placed in my display room. I got an idea if I offered something free with each package of chewing-gum I could sell a lot more. At the Far East Trading Company I bought a wide variety of inexpensive but nice-looking articles, to be offered as premiums. These were also put on display in my office. I had them all photographed and made up a nice premium catalog. As far as I know this was the first time that premium coupons had ever been offered as an inducement to buy merchandise. As I had planned, every package of chewing-gum sold through the vending machines would contain a coupon. A certain

## I Tried to Go Straight

number of coupons would bring the customer a free article listed in the catalog. This system of premium coupons was later widely used for every sort of merchandise from soap to silverware.

I contacted four Chicago chewing-gum companies and arranged to buy gum from them. I was now all set to start, except for financing the machines. I decided the best way to do this was to vend the gum through district managers. I inserted ads in all the newspapers for men to manage the vending machines.

The response to the ads was overwhelming. I decided not to sign anybody up until I was ready to operate. Every time an applicant called, I told him:

"You're a little late, but if you'll leave your name and address, we'll get in touch with you as soon as there is a vacancy."

Then I explained the proposition:

"You will be required to put up $120 cash bond. That will be a deposit on twenty machines at $6.00 each. We'll assign a territory to you where the machines may be put up. Each machine will have $50 in it when the gum has all been emptied out. You make a profit of $20 every time a machine empties. Do you think that would interest you?"

I signed about 2,500 men to contracts. Then I got an idea. I formed the National Association of Gum Manufacturers. All the gum companies in Chicago, except Wrigley, joined it. The Association was given exclusive use of Mintleaf gum for the vending machines and all the participating companies agreed to give the Association first call on its gum products.

By the time I was ready to call in the men I had signed up, I was in a position to exercise a good measure of control over all the smaller chewing-gum manufacturers. I had plans to put the vending machines out all over the country.

My own name had become so well known — and so unfavorably — that when I entered this venture I used the name James R. Warrington. But the police had been keeping an eye on me, particularly since Snarley had found out about my new business.

Any day that Snarley had nothing else to do, which was often, he and Strosnider dropped in to see me. They hung around for hours.

## "Yellow Kid" Weil

Snarley and Strosnider were a good deal hotter than I was.

I'm sure the police checked up on every detail of my enterprise. The only thing they could find that might be called a con-game was my deal with the district managers.

I had held off on these men because I needed the machines before the deal could be completed. And it was a very good thing I did.

One day Snarley came over early. He said, "Joe, you don't suppose the cops have got a dictaphone planted in here, do you?"

"No," I replied. "Why should they?"

He pointed to a spot on the wall just above my chair. A bit of plaster had peeled off. "What's making your plaster come off?"

I got up and examined the plaster more closely. It was a dictaphone all right. The wiring had been cleverly concealed, but I was able to follow it. It led straight into the office of the superintendent of the building.

"Well," I breathed to Snarley, "I haven't done anything wrong this time. They haven't got a thing on me. I'm on the level this time and I'm going ahead. But you and Strosnider better quit hanging around. It gives the place a bad name."

But I had made that decision too late. Snarley and Strosnider quit coming, but the police were convinced that I was getting ready to make a big haul. I had signed up 2,500 men and each would post a cash bond of $120. That would be a total of $300,000. The police could not believe I was going to use that much money legitimately. I couldn't blame them, in view of my past activities.

One day Tom Guerin, brother of Eddie Guerin — the notorious escapee from Devil's Island — dropped into the office.

"Joe," he said, "I was just talking to Inspector Petey O'Brien. He told me to give you a message. He said, 'Tell Joe not to take any money.'"

Petey O'Brien was then Chief of Detectives. He had investigated my proposition and could see that it might be on the level. On the other hand he could also see where it might cause me a lot of trouble. O'Brien was a square shooter. He was warning me while there was still time. The chances are that if I had continued I would have been arrested and charged with operating a confidence game!

## I Tried to Go Straight

I knew that Petey knew what he was talking about. There just wasn't any sense in bucking the odds when the cards were already stacked against me.

One of the larger companies which had signed up with me took over the Mintleaf patent and began to manufacture Mintleaf gum. The National Association of Chewing-Gum Manufacturers was allowed to die, although the Association was later resurrected and now flourishes as a group devoted to the advancement of the industry.

Mintleaf was the flavor that later became so popular as Wrigley's Spearmint. I heard that the Wrigley company paid $2,000,000 for the formula.

Shortly afterwards, premiums were offered with various sorts of merchandise and the premium coupon idea has been widely used ever since.

At any rate, even though I was prevented from going into a legitimate enterprise, the ideas I evolved apparently were sound, for they were widely used.

This episode was sound proof of the old adage: "A man is known by the company he keeps." I am convinced that the presence of Snarley and Strosnider around the office caused the police to intervene in the most *legitimate* undertaking of my career!

On more than one occasion I have had cause to regret that I was acquainted with criminals who had records.

The Butterine Kid was one of them. I don't know what his right name was. He was a small-time racketeer whom I had met casually in a Loop saloon. Forty years ago oleomargarine was known as "butterine." The manufacturers were not allowed to color it, though it was used widely as a butter substitute.

The Butterine Kid made his living by buying butterine, adding color to it, and peddling it in pound squares to the smaller shops and from house to house. He sold it as pure creamery butter at less than the current market price of butter.

The Butterine Kid's racket afforded him a living, but not much more. At its worst, the crookedness of his scheme was petty. Occasionally I met him on the street, sweating as he pushed his cart of butterine from house to house and from shop to shop.

Far worse than his butterine racket was the Kid's habit of shooting with loaded dice. No matter who you were or where he met you, he would try to inveigle you into a crap game in which you didn't stand a chance. On a number of occasions when I met him he was broke, and I befriended him. I was to live to regret it.

With an indictment for participating in the fight racket hanging over my head, I did not engage in any business at the time. However, I had been around to numerous furniture dealers to pick up articles for our home. In those days, a piano was essential to every well-appointed home and I began to look around for one. I finally bought an oak upright for $350.

Some years earlier when I had been a partner in the Get-Rich-Quick Bank, it had been my custom to eat at Metzger's restaurant on Monroe Street. It was a combination bar and café, a glass partition separating the two sections.

On the walls of the restaurant hung numerous enlarged photographs of two coffee plantations which Metzger owned at Jalapa and Vera Cruz in Mexico. He served coffee from these plantations and had a quantity for sale in his restaurant at three pounds for a dollar.

The coffee, which had a fine flavor, was one of the drawing cards. His place was also noted for its rare wines; many of the big financiers dined there regularly.

One day shortly after I had bought the piano I dropped in, for I used to enjoy the coffee. I glanced around at the pictures I had seen so many times before, but it was only then that an idea bloomed. As soon as I had finished my meal I sought out the restaurateur.

"My name is Richard E. Dorian."

Metzger was a heavy-set, distinguished looking fellow. He wore a pince-nez and a well-tailored business suit. I knew he was wealthy.

"Glad to know you," he smiled, shaking hands. "I've seen you here but never learned your name. What can I do for you?"

"I'm interested in your coffee plantations," I replied.

"In what way?"

"The output, primarily. Also I was wondering where you dispose of your coffee."

## I Tried to Go Straight

"As a matter of fact," he replied, "I've done very little with it. Except for the small amount I use here in the restaurant and sell to my customers, I haven't done anything. I haven't exploited the plantations because I haven't found anybody who wants to buy raw coffee beans. And I know little about the business myself."

"Then perhaps we can get together. Would you be interested in leasing your plantations?"

"Perhaps. What's your proposition?"

"How would you like to have somebody take over the plantations and operate them so you would have nothing to worry about and still get a good revenue?"

"Sounds interesting," said Metzger. "You have a plan?"

"Yes. As you know, there is plenty of good coffee already on the market. Just to bring out another brand would not be anything new. Furthermore, to build up such a new brand would require a great deal of capital — for advertising and promotion."

"That's correct."

"I have very little capital," I continued, "but I do know how to promote and I have ideas. Suppose that we produce coffee that compared favorably with all the better brands, but gave something free in addition — we ought to clean up."

"It all depends," said Metzger, "on what you give away. Do you have something in mind?"

My eyes roved about the room. They lighted on a piano in the corner.

"Suppose," I replied "we give away pianos. That ought to get us plenty of customers."

"Pianos?" he exclaimed. For a few moments he stared at me, as though wondering if he had been wasting his time on a lunatic. "Man, are you crazy?"

"Of course not. Don't you think pianos would be good premiums?"

"Certainly. But you apparently don't know the value of a piano."

"Yes, I believe I do. The fact that they are so costly is all the more reason why they would be good premiums and would attract a lot of customers."

"All you say is true," Metzger admitted, about ready to tear his hair. "But would you mind telling me how you plan to make money on such a scheme?"

"Isn't it reasonable to suppose," I returned, "that people would pay a few cents more for a pound of coffee if they knew they were going to get something for nothing?"

He reflected. "Yes, I guess it is," he said. "I think most people will go to great lengths to get something for nothing."

Now he was thinking. I already know a great deal about how far the average person would go to get something for nothing. But my task was to sell Metzger the same idea. "I believe you're right," I went on. "Here is my idea: we will pack a really good blend of coffee and sell it three pounds for a dollar. With each purchase of three pounds, there will be a premium coupon. When the purchaser has 150 of these coupons, he will be entitled to a piano absolutely free."

"But that means buying 450 pounds of coffee," Metzger objected. "That's more than the average person uses in ten years."

"True," I agreed. "But, as you know, the cost of the average piano is more than $150. A family could get all the coffee it needs for a long time and still have a piano. Some people will buy the coffee — even if they don't use it — just to get the piano."

"There's one thing you haven't explained to me," he frowned. "How are you going to give these pianos away when one of them costs more than the entire amount you'll get for the coffee?"

"I can get the pianos wholesale. But I need to get the coffee at a low price. That's where you come in."

We discussed this at some length. Finally Metgzer agreed to let me take over both his plantations and put them into production at once. As I had it figured, the coffee would actually cost me less than one cent a pound. Metzger, for purposes of negotiation and advertising, agreed to permit me to say I owned the plantations.

Having settled this detail, I went to see a music dealer. At his place, a few days earlier, I had seen a cheap piano for sale. Now I examined it again. It was no different from the standard instrument, except that the wood was inexpensive scrub oak. However, only discriminating people would have noticed it. The retail price was $150.

"Suppose I wanted to buy these in wholesale lots," I told the dealer.

## I Tried to Go Straight

"Do you suppose I could get them at a reasonable figure?"

"You could get them for less than a hundred dollars," he said. "They are manufactured by Biddle Brothers in Rochester, New York."

I gathered up a few hundred dollars in good money and wrapped it around $5,000 in boodle. Then I went to Rochester and called on Biddle Brothers. I talked to them for several days and they finally agreed to furnish me with their pianos for $45 each. I convinced them that my demand would be so great that they agreed to sell me their entire output.

I showed them the packages of boodle I carried to convince them I had capital. But I explained that this would be needed to get my campaign started, and they didn't press me for an advance deposit. They shipped two of the pianos to me in Chicago to be used for display.

Back in Chicago my plans began to shape up. I knew of a coffee roaster on River Street named Martin. I had used his coffee and I knew he was an expert blender and roaster. I gave him the details of my plan and he became enthusiastic, especially after he had seen pictures of the plantations in Mexico.

"It's only fair to tell you," I said, "that I am doing all this without much capital. But I am so sure that it will go that I am counting on the backing of a few trustworthy men like yourself."

"You can count on me," returned Martin. "If you need credit to get your plant in operation, refer to me."

I made a deal with Martin to blend, roast, and package all of my coffee. It was to be put up in three-pound canisters. The beans would be shipped from the Mexican plantations to Chicago. Martin would grade them, select the proper blends, and supervise the roasting and packaging.

But I had to have a plant. After looking around, I found a millwright building at 14 North May Street that was for sale. The owner's name was Morgan.

I proposed to buy the building from Morgan but frankly admitted I hadn't the cash to pay for it. In my negotiations, I used the names of Metzger and Martin freely. After he had checked with these two, Morgan was ready to sign a contract.

137

I was to take possession of the building at once; no cash would be required for the first six months. Thereafter monthly payments would take care of the balance. Some remodeling was necessary and Morgan lent me the cash to have this done.

I arranged for the remodeling of the first floor, which became my office and display room. Martin determined how the remainder of the building was to be, since he was the coffee expert. He also advised me what sort of machinery to buy. This was bought and installed on credit, with the help of Martin and Morgan.

The office and display room were outfitted by Zimmerman, a prominent Loop firm. The display room was very attractive and eye-catching. There we had the two pianos from Biddle Brothers on display.

While the rebuilding was going on, I devoted my time to planning a campaign. I had a trademark and letterhead designed. It was in colors and showed a picture of Uncle Sam carrying two large cans of coffee.

We discussed the merchandising at some length. It was decided to adopt the slogan: "From plantation to consumer. Eliminate the middleman's profit." Then, for the premium offer: "No breakfast is complete without coffee. No home is complete without a piano."

The advertising campaign I planned was to get us off to a good start. I would take space in leading newspapers throughout the country. A full page was planned for *The Chicago Tribune*. I figured that once the sale of our coffee had gained momentum, it wouldn't be necessary to advertise. I was confident Martin would pack a good blend that would advertise itself. And the free piano would be a big inducement.

Most families with modest incomes, however, were buying pianos on the instalment plan — generally, ten dollars a month. Few of them would be able to put out $150, even if a free piano was involved. I decided to meet this situation to compete with the instalment plan. As soon as a purchaser had acquired ten premium coupons, that is had bought ten dollars worth of coffee, the piano would be shipped to his home, with the understanding that he would be required to turn in at least ten coupons each month thereafter until a total of 150

## I Tried to Go Straight

coupons had been remitted. Then the piano was his to keep.

Actually what this amounted to was that any family could buy a piano, ten dollars down and ten dollars a month for fifteen months, with all the coffee they could use, free. It was an appealing proposition, entirely legal, and I didn't see how it could miss fire. Neither did my backers, Metzger, Martin, and Morgan.

Everything had been arranged except the actual exploiting of the plantations. Martin lent me $2,000 to go to Mexico to inspect them and get them to production at top capacity.

My wife, who had constantly pleaded with me to stay in some legitimate business, was very happy. I was, too. Once again I thought the future held great promise and that I was through with confidence games.

One day in a Loop saloon, when I stopped for a glass of beer, I ran into the Butterine Kid. He asked what I was doing and I told him. He hit me for a ten dollar loan. I was feeling pretty good and let him have it.

One morning a few days before my scheduled departure for Mexico, Morgan was in the office. He was well pleased with the way things were shaping up. He suggested we all get together for a conference later in the day.

"Splendid!" I agreed. "I have to go down in the Loop to see the printer. Suppose you call Metzger and Martin and arrange for them to come over."

This was agreed, and I left for my meeting with the printer. I was gone for perhaps three hours. When I walked into the office an irate group faced me. My three backers, Morgan, Metzger and Martin, were pacing the floor. In the corner sat an unhappy, abject figure, the Butterine Kid.

The three men faced me and all began to talk at once.

"Come in, Mr. Richard E. Dorian!" Martin said sarcastically. "Alias Joe Weil, alias the Yellow Kid."

"So it's all a skin game," said Metzger. "Using my plantations for a skin game!"

Morgan's remarks are unprintable. He had spent about $120,000 for remodeling and for equipment. He was in a rage, and if I had waited for him to get his hands on me, he probably would have torn me apart.

But I didn't wait. I didn't try to explain. Even though this was another time I had a legitimate scheme, I knew that they wouldn't believe me. My reputation was even bigger than my plans. So I turned and left, and that ended my career in the coffee business.

I later learned what had happened:

Martin, Metzger, and Morgan had gathered in the office for the meeting. They were waiting for me when the Butterine Kid breezed in. He was there, he told me later, to borrow $20.

"Where's the boss?" he asked.

"He'll be back soon," Martin replied. "Have a seat."

The Butterine Kid sat down, but he was a restless type. He put his hand in his pocket and it closed over some dice.

"Say," he said, "would any of you fellows like to roll 'em while we're waiting?"

Metzger and Morgan weren't interested but Martin agreed to shoot with the Kid to pass the time. The Kid pulled out his dice and they began to roll. Martin lost consistently. The Butterine Kid was getting quite a roll, when Martin, who was no fool, thought that the dice he was shooting with seemed to be a little different from those the Kid was using. The next time the Kid rolled 'em Martin reached out and grabbed the dice. He discovered at once that they were mis-spotted.

"I was playing to be sociable," he growled. "I don't like to be cheated."

He took his money back and clipped the Kid on the jaw.

"You can't do that to me," the latter whined as he got up off the floor. "Just wait till Joe gets back."

"Joe? Who is Joe?"

"Joe Weil. He's the boss here, ain't he?"

That was the tip-off. The three men began to question him, and soon learned my real identity, which they had not suspected before. They backed him into a corner and made him tell everything he knew about me. So when I showed up I didn't stand a chance.

## 12. *Easy Money on Rainy Days*

As I walked back toward the Loop I felt pretty despondent. It was like waking from a long, beautiful dream. The turn of events was so unexpected I hadn't the slightest idea what I would do next.

Suddenly a bulky figure blocked my path and a big voice boomed: "Hello, Joe! Why you so sad, Joe?"

I looked up into the good-natured face of a con man known as The Swede. He was a big, heavy-set fellow, with white, close-cropped hair and a ruddy complexion. He wore a cheap, baggy suit and carried a suitcase. He might have been a farmer in town for the day or he might have just got off the boat.

Briefly I told him what had happened. He seemed sympathetic and asked me to help him on a few deals. I had no plans at all so I agreed.

The case of Schwartz, the bondsman, will illustrate how we worked. Schwartz always had considerable cash on hand. His place was not far from Riverview Amusement Park. One day the Swede walked into Schwartz's saloon, laid his suitcase on the counter, and opened it. He had an array of cheap merchandise such as pencils, shoestrings, and combs. Schwartz bought a few articles and the Swede ordered a drink. After he had a couple of drinks he noticed the ever present dice at the end of the counter.

"I shake you for the drinks."

"Okay," said Schwartz. "Shoot."

The Swede shook them and lost.

"I shake you for a dollar," he proposed.

## "Yellow Kid" Weil

The dice were rolled again, and once more the Swede lost. He made several additional rolls until he had lost five dollars.

"Ay tank ay go home," he said. When he paid he peeled the money off a big roll of bills. It might have been his life savings. Of course Schwartz saw the big roll.

The Swede closed up his suitcase, put his roll back in his pocket, and departed, muttering to himself in Swedish.

A couple of days later in Schwartz's place, I sat at the counter, eating a hot dog and drinking a glass of beer.

"Nice place you have here," I remarked. "I work at Riverview."

"Yes, I have a lot of customers from Riverview," he replied.

We engaged in small talk and became friendly. I was complimenting him on his excellent hot dogs when the big Swede walked in.

Or perhaps I should say the Swede staggered in, for he pretended to be intoxicated. He put his suitcase down on the bar and leaned over it in a drunken manner.

"Well," said Schwartz, who hadn't forgotten the big roll, "here's the Swedish tradesman."

"Yah," grumbled the Swede. "Gimme drink."

Schwartz put a bottle on the bar. With unsteady fingers, the Swede poured out a drink and gulped it down. He followed it with another. The Swede appeared to be becoming more inebriated by the minute. When he had finished the third drink, he opened his suitcase and spread it so that the wares were revealed.

"Wanna buy something?"

I took a pencil and Schwartz selected a pair of shoestrings. The Swede closed the suitcase slowly and strapped it.

"Lost my money in here," he smiled at Schwartz. "But I'm gonna win some day."

"Would you like to shake now?" asked Schwartz, no doubt thinking of the Swede's big roll.

"Not on bar," said the Swede. He carried the suitcase to the counter near where I was seated. "Shake on grip," he proposed.

"What's the difference?" Schwartz shrugged.

"Shake like in old country," said the Swede.

"How's that?"

## Easy Money on Rainy Days

"I show you." The Swede picked up a tumbler from the counter and put the dice in. "Got handkerchief?"

"Sure." Schwartz winked at me as he handed over the handkerchief.

I winked back. After all I was supposed to be just an amused spectator.

The Swede, reeling drunkenly, had a very serious expression on his face as he carefully wrapped the handkerchief around the glass. Then he shook the glass and put it top down on the grip. The dice were in the glass.

"Bet odd or even."

"I'll bet odd, said Schwartz.

"I take you," growled the Swede. "I bet a dollar."

The bet was made and Schwartz lifted the handkerchief. The dice were odd up and the Swede lost. In this manner he lost four dollars more. Then, apparently disgusted, he gathered his suitcase and left.

Schwartz and I chuckled over this seemingly illiterate and naïve foreigner. I ordered another hot dog. I hadn't finished eating when the Swede staggered back into the place, drunkenly placed his suitcase on the counter, and flopped over the bar.

"Gimme 'nother drink," he said thickly. Then, after he had gulped it down: "Wanna shake again?"

"Sure," Schwartz agreed. "How'll it be — Swedish style?"

"Yust like in old country," said the Swede.

Schwartz handed him the glass, the dice, and the handkerchief. Very clumsily, the Swede spilled the dice on the floor. But he was not so clumsy as he picked them up and switched to the loaded set he carried! I could see it, but Schwartz on the other side of the counter could not.

After fumbling around a while, apparently retrieving the dice, the Swede stood up and reeled back to the counter. He dropped the cubes into the glass, carefully wrapped the handkerchief around it, and handed the whole thing to Schwartz.

"You shake."

Schwartz shook, then put the glass, open end down, on the suitcase. The handkerchief was wrapped around the glass so you couldn't see the dice.

"How do you want to bet and how much?" asked Schwartz.

"I see," said the Swede. He turned his back and dug into the inner recesses of his clothing.

While his back was turned, I lifted a corner of the handkerchief and peeked at the dice. Schwartz shot me a questioning look and I formed the "even" on my lips.

The Swede took out his roll and laid it on the counter.

"How much you bet?"

"How much you got?" Schwartz countered.

The Swede untied his roll and began to count his money. The bills were all old and dogeared, as if he had been hoarding them for many a day.

"I got $1,275," he said. "I bet you all."

"It's a cinch," Schwartz whispered. He went to his safe and counted out $1,275.

"What you bet," asked the Swede, "odd or even?"

"Even," said Schwartz grinning at me.

The Swede placed his money on the suitcase. As he did so, he grasped the handle. Schwartz had no way of knowing, as the Swede and I did, that this handle was really a switch that controlled a battery concealed inside the suitcase. No matter how the dice fell, when the battery was turned on they came up odd.

Schwartz unfolded the handkerchief and lifted the glass, fully confident he was the winner. He could hardly believe his eyes when he saw three aces up. Grudgingly, he handed over his cash to the Swede, who carefully rolled it up, tied a string around it, and put it away in an inner pocket of his coarse suit.

"Ay tank ay go home now," he said. He gathered up his suitcase and weaved out of the saloon, still pretending to be drunk.

As soon as he was out of the door, the saloonkeeper whirled on me. "I thought you said to bet even."

"No, indeed," I replied. "I whispered to you that they were odd." Actually, I hadn't whispered at all. I had merely formed the word "even" with my lips.

## Easy Money on Rainy Days

Schwartz shook his head in confusion. "I could have sworn you said even."

"I really shouldn't have said anything," I told him as I paid for my hot dogs and left. "After all, it was a game of chance."

Later I met the Swede and we split the profit. I had no compunction at all in a deal of this nature. For Schwartz had fully expected to fleece the Swede and the tables had been turned.

There were not many suckers like him. The Swede concentrated on saloons and few saloonkeepers had that much money on hand. The Swede's average haul was about $20 and he usually played a lone hand.

It was not very long until somebody caught on to his battery trick, and pretty soon the cigar counter of every saloon in Chicago had a battery attachment.

The Swede's dice-in-a-glass game was the forerunner of today's "26-games," without which no barroom is complete. The circular dice-box used in the "26-game" undoubtedly evolved from the Swede's dice-in-a-glass.

There was not enough in the Swede's line to keep me occupied. I was at loose ends and went back to my first love, the horses. I had a quantity of green cards printed. These purported to be courtesy cards issued by the American Turf Association and extended to the bearer extraordinary privileges at any racecourse.

I hired a stooge, and the scheme I evolved was so ridiculous that I can't, even now, see how the most gullible would be taken in by it. I posed as a representative of the American Turf Association and my stooge was my assistant.

My victims were importers of olive oil. The case of Nicholas Zambole and Company will serve as an example.

My stooge, John, and I entered Mr. Zambole's office. After I had produced my credentials the office girl showed us in to see the proprietor of the firm.

I said, "My name is Warrington — James R. Warrington — and I represent the American Turf Association."

"The American Turf Association?"

"Yes. We control all the better race tracks in the country."

## "Yellow Kid" Weil

"I know that," said Mr. Zambole. "But I was wondering what I could do for you?"

"You import fine olive oil, don't you?"

"Yes, that's our business."

"We're in the market for some olive oil," I explained, "and I came to get prices from you."

"I'll be glad to quote prices," returned Zambole. "But would you mind telling me what use the American Turf Association has for olive oil?"

"Of course. Our trainers use a great deal of it every day to rub down the horses. Surely, you've noticed that every horse's coat is shining when he prances out to take his place at the post?"

"Yes."

"Well, that sheen is produced by olive-oil rubdowns."

"So that's how it's done!" Mr. Zambole reflected for a moment. "I've often wondered how they get those horses to shine so. And now I know."

"Naturally," I continued, "with so many horses running every day, we use a great quantity of olive oil. I'd like to have your prices in carload lots."

"I'll make you a very good price," Mr. Zambole spoke happily. "Suppose we go down to the stockroom. I'd like to show you what fine oil we sell."

"My assistant, Mr. Sims, will go with you," I said, indicating my stooge. "I'll join you in a few minutes. I have to make a telephone call."

"Why don't you use my phone, Mr. Warrington? You are quite welcome to do so."

"This call is rather personal," I hesitated. "If you don't mind, I'll step out to a public phone."

"As you like. When you get back, come on downstairs to the stockroom."

"Thank you. I'll be back in a few minutes." Then to my stooge: "You know the grade of olive oil we will require, John."

"Yes, sir."

With that I departed to make my supposedly personal telephone

## Easy Money on Rainy Days

call. Actually I went around the corner and waited ten minutes while my stooge worked the switch on our victim.

As they walked to the stockroom, Zambole said: "I wonder what kind of call he's making that is so personal."

"I'll tell you something," John offered in a confidential tone, "if you won't tell the boss."

"I won't tell him," the merchant promised.

"He's gone to phone his betting commissioner. He has to go and make a call every day about this time. But he ain't got me fooled. He's cleanin' up on the ponies."

"What makes you so sure of that?" asked Zambole.

John glanced about him to make sure he wasn't observed. Then he reached into his pocket and pulled out a clipping.

"Look," he said. "I cut this out of *The Racing Form,* but he doesn't know I got it."

The clipping was a half page from *The Racing Form* — or appeared to be. Actually, it had been made up especially for such occasions. The headline read:

WARRINGTON STUMPS THE EXPERTS

HANDICAPPER MAKES ANOTHER KILLING

In the left column was my picture. The story related how I had made one killing after another at the tracks, always betting on long shots that the experts said didn't have a chance. There was glowing praise for my infallible judgment.

Zambole was quite impressed. "I wonder how he does it."

"I can't prove it," muttered John, "but I got my ideas about how he does it."

"How?" Zambole prodded.

'You're sure you will keep this confidential and won't repeat it?"

"You have my promise not to tell."

"All right. He works for the Turf Association, don't he? Okay. He knows all the big shots. So they give him inside tips and he cleans up. But he lets everybody think he's an expert handicapper. At least that's the way I got it figured out. And if that ain't so, why does he have to go make a telephone call every day?"

147

## "Yellow Kid" Weil

"Sounds like you've got it figured out all right," agreed Zambole. "Doesn't he ever give you an inside tip on races?"

"No. Oh, sometimes he says, kind of casual, 'Johnny, that horse looks like a good bet.' I ask him if it's an inside tip and he always says, 'No, Johnny, it's just a hunch.'"

"Do you ever bet on his hunches?"

"I sure do. And I always win, too. That's why I say —" He broke off in the middle of the sentence. "Look, I'm supposed to be down here looking at olive oil. Maybe you better show me some before Mr. Warrington gets back."

By the time I reappeared, John had picked out the three top brands of olive oil that Zambole had in stock. I looked over what he had picked out, sampled each, and rubbed some on my hands. Finally, I selected the most expensive brand and ordered five carloads of it to be shipped to various tracks, throughout the country.

Then, as a gesture of friendliness, I made out a courtesy card and gave it to Zambole. We went back up into his office, where I gave specific directions as to where the olive oil was to be shipped and the dates on which I wished it shipped.

"John," I ordered, "go over to the printer and see if those tickets I ordered are ready. I'll see you at the hotel."

"Thank you very much," said Zambole, as I started to shake hands and leave. "Are you in a big hurry?"

"No, not especially," I replied. "I have an appointment in an hour, but I'm free until then."

"Come and have a drink with me."

This was what we had been building up to.

"I hear you're pretty good at picking winners," he began.

"Why, who told you that?" I appeared startled.

"Nobody. But I read *The Racing Form* occasionally."

"Oh, that," I said in an offhand manner. "They rather overdid the piece, don't you think?"

"No, I think a lot of credit is due a man who can judge horses so accurately."

"It was luck, Mr. Zambole. Pure luck."

"Maybe so," he said, obviously not convinced that a man could be

## Easy Money on Rainy Days

so consistently lucky. "There weren't any inside tips in those deals, were there, if I may ask?"

Acting good-natured about it, I laughed. "I like your frankness and can see that you are a man one can't fool. Yes, I did have a few inside tips."

"I'd like a chance to clean up on one of those races," prodded Zambole. "How about giving me a winner?"

"Oh, I couldn't do that. That would be violating a confidence."

"Here's the way you can do it," Zambole proposed. "You can make the bet for me."

I considered this for a few moments. "Yes," I said slowly, "I guess I could do that. But you understand that I couldn't divulge the name of the horse."

"That's all right, as long as we make a killing. How much do you generally bet?"

"Five thousand, as a rule."

"That's a little more than I can afford to gamble. Suppose you split a five thousand dollar bet with me?"

I finally agreed.

We went back to Zambole's office. He took the money out of a safe — $2,500 — and handed it to me.

"If you want to see your horse win," I told him, "be at Hawthorne tomorrow for the fifth race."

"Thank you very much, Mr. Warrington. And where will I see you?"

"I'll join you in the clubhouse, between the fifth and sixth races."

I don't know whether Zambole went to the track or not. He didn't have to wait until the fifth race to learn that he had been the victim of a con game. If he presented the courtesy card at the gate, he found out then.

I heard that he was furious about the horse deal. He complained to the police and swore out a warrant for my arrest. But I was already on my way.

## 13. A Deal with Father Flanagan

FOUR MEN WHO HAD BEEN INDICTED FOR PARTICIPATING IN FAKED prize fights were at large. All the others had been tried and convicted. Those still to be caught included myself, Jack Carkeek, the Honey Grove Kid (I never knew his real name), and Hot Springs Ryan. Carkeek had been caught in California and had languished for twenty-eight months in the Los Angeles county jail while he fought extradition. I had hidden behind my beard and eluded detection. But the Honey Grove Kid and Ryan finally gave themselves up and were taken to Council Bluffs, Iowa, for trial in the Federal Court.

The government men redoubled their efforts to find me and to extradite Carkeek. Chicago was becoming uncomfortably warm, so I told my wife that I was going to Paris on a business trip and booked passage on the *Berengaria*. I appeared on the passenger list as James R. Warrington.

While I was away the case went to trial in Council Bluffs. The prosecuting attorney asked the judge to convict us on the grounds that he had previously found our associates guilty.

Judge MacPherson rejected this plea, and the reply he made is a classic:

"I do not choose to cultivate wings and a halo on the one hand nor horns and hooves and swinging tails on the other. It is a case of the pot calling the kettle black. Bailiff, make wide the windows. Let this foul air out of the courtroom. Case dismissed!"

This meant that I had been acquitted for my part in the fight racket. It also meant freedom for Carkeek, who was released from the Los Angeles jail.

## A Deal with Father Flanagan

Since this was the main thing I had to worry about, I decided it was safe to return to Chicago. On the boat coming back, I made the acquaintance of half a dozen "boat-riders," that is transoceanic cardsharps.

When I got back to Chicago, I had no definite plans. I still was well fixed financially, but my wife wanted me to get a job. I didn't think much of that idea, but at the same time I wanted to please my wife.

I went to work peddling books. The books I sold were sets of the *Catholic Encyclopedia*. But I didn't just go out cold. First I changed my name to Daniel O'Connell. Then I got some credentials and went to work.

One warm day in July I called on a priest, whom I shall call Father Flanagan, in Flint, Michigan. I was neatly dressed and carried a brief-case under my arm.

When the priest came to the door, I doffed my hat and said politely, "Father Flanagan? My name is Daniel O'Connell."

"Daniel O'Connell?" That was a highly respected name in Catholic circles at the time. "Won't you come in?"

I followed him into his study and laid my brief-case on his desk.

"Now what can I do for you?" he asked when we were seated.

"I have been sent here on a mission of the utmost importance. Perhaps you have heard of the *Catholic Encyclopedia*?"

"Yes, though I'm not very familiar with it."

"As you probably know," I continued, "it is the only commercially produced work that has ever received the unqualified endorsement of the Holy Father."

"No," he replied, "I wasn't aware of that."

I reached into my brief-case and withdrew some papers. I handed them to Father Flanagan.

"This," I said, "is the Pope's letter. And the others are letters of commendation from Cardinal Farley and Cardinal O'Connell."

Father Flanagan read the papers carefully. They were photostatic copies of genuine letters the publishers had received.

"These are extremely interesting," he said. "What can I do to help you?"

## "Yellow Kid" Weil

I reached into my pocket and produced a Pope's token, which I had picked up in a pawnshop. On one side was a likeness of the Madonna and on the other a profile of Pius X.

"I recently received this from the Holy Father," I said. "At the same time he expressed a wish that I place the *Catholic Encyclopedia* in at least 2,000 homes in Flint."

Father Flanagan examined the token with considerable interest.

"To help me accomplish this," I continued, "I would like you to be the first subscriber. If you subscribe there will be many others who will follow your lead."

"What does the *Catholic Encyclopedia* look like?" he asked with much interest.

I reached into the brief-case and withdrew a bound volume.

"These are specimen pages," I told him. "They have been reproduced in the actual size. Of course it would be impossible for me to carry the entire set around with me."

He studied the pages. "I'll be glad to subscribe," he finally declared. "What is the price?"

"Ninety dollars for the entire set. This is payable twenty dollars with the order and the balance when the books are received. In the case of those who can't pay that much at one time, convenient terms can be arranged."

"Very well," said Father Flanagan. "You may write out an order for me."

I produced an order pad and I wrote out the order in duplicate. Father Flanagan signed it, and I gave him the carbon copy.

We conversed for a few minutes and I departed, to begin my house-to-house canvas. People were impressed by the Pope's token and by the three letters. But these were not sufficient to induce them to place an order. The clincher was the signed order of Father Flanagan who, I soon learned, was highly respected in Flint.

My commission from the sale of the *Encyclopedia* was the twenty dollars I received when the order was placed. By the end of the third day, I had placed eighty sets, far from the goal of 2,000 supposedly set by the Pope.

I was about to quit for the day when I met Father Flanagan on

## A Deal with Father Flanagan

the street. It was no chance encounter, I soon learned.

"My son," he said, "I would like to talk to you. Will you be good enough to call on me this evening?"

"I'll be delighted, Father," I replied.

After dinner I called on Father Flanagan. He semed in a jovial mood.

"Come down into the cellar with me. I'd like you to sample some of my wine."

I accompanied him to the cellar. He produced glasses and went to a cask and drew two glasses of fine sherry.

We sipped wine there in the cellar while Father Flanagan talked about topics of the day. Then he filled our glasses again and we went back upstairs to his study.

I was wholly unprepared for what followed when we had seated ourselves.

"Daniel O'Connell!" Father Flanagan declared suddenly. "It's a fine name."

"Thank you, Father."

"Oh, don't thank me. I know now that it isn't your name. I've been doing some checking up. You are a cunning fellow and you have a clever scheme."

"What do you mean?"

"I mean that I know all about you. I know that you really are selling the *Catholic Encyclopedia* — an excellent work. But your name isn't Daniel O'Connell and that story that the Holy Father wants you to sell 2,000 copies in Flint is pure fiction. You did a good job of misleading me. Now I want you to return that order I signed and get out of town."

"But — I don't understand. If that's the way you feel, why are you giving me wine?"

"That," said Father Flanagan gently, "is just my way of turning the other cheek."

I gave him back his order and that night, I left Flint. I decided I had enough of bookselling. My profit for three days' work was about $1,600. This was pretty good pay, but I knew that without Father Flanagan's endorsement the picture would be much sadder.

## 14. Some Credit—and Lots of Cash

I RETURNED TO MY FAMILY IN CHICAGO. I HAD ACCUMULATED SOME money, but I got rid of it even faster than I got hold of it. When I spent an evening at one of the gay spots, it was not unusual for me to spend $500. This was in the days when the average worker considered $500 fairly good pay for six months' work.

I knew my failings. That is why, when I made a good score, I turned a major part of it over to my wife, Jessie. She was wise enough to know it was best to put our money into something tangible.

Thus, at her behest, we gradually acquired considerable property in Chicago. Some of it was in vacant lots expected to increase in value. But most of it consisted of income-producing property such as apartment buildings. If I had followed the course my wife had charted, I might have escaped poverty in my old age — who knows?

At that time we owned a three-story apartment building on Pratt Boulevard in the Rogers Park section of Chicago. We occupied a nine-room apartment and rented the rest of the building.

Not so far away on North Broadway was Johnny Butterley's buffet, a gathering place for many people of unusual talents — confidence men, actors, writers. I went there because it was close to home and I liked rare wines — and Johnny served the best. The actors and writers came from the old Essanay Studios near by where they were doing the pioneer work in the motion picture industry. The con men liked Butterley's because of its atmosphere and its location, far from the territory of the Central Police, where the Detective Bureau was located.

I was seated here one day, when "Big John" Worthington came in. I had christened Big John "the Wolf of La Salle Street" and the appella-

## Some Credit—and Lots of Cash

tion stuck. He was a big fellow, about six feet tall, with broad shoulders and an imposing manner. His features were broad and stern. He dressed well, but conservatively. He bore a strong resemblance to the late J. P. Morgan and could easily have passed for the financier, except among Mr. Morgan's intimates.

Big John looked around and, seeing me, sidled up. He asked in a whisper, "Joe, how would you like to be vice-president of a LaSalle Street bank?"

"Me, the vice-president of a bank?" I retorted. "Do you know any more jokes, John?"

My attitude seemed to annoy him. "Are you questioning my sincerity?" he demanded. A flush of anger crossed his stern features.

"If you were sincere, John, I'm sorry," I replied. "But surely you must realize what would happen if I became an official of a bank. There would certainly be a run, followed by the complete collapse of the institution!"

"On the contrary, Joe," he said, "the depositors would feel that your acumen would safeguard their interests."

"Tell me more."

Briefly, he told me: The American State Bank, at 10 South LaSalle Street, could be purchased. (This bank had no connection with the present American National Bank in Chicago.) All the stock could be purchased for $75,000. He proposed that we invest $37,500 each and share the control. He would be president and I vice-president.

Big John was acquainted with Melville Reeves, known as the Skyscraper Burglar. Reeves had come into the possession of millions of dollars worth of bonds that had been stolen. It was Worthington's idea that we could buy these bonds from Reeves at a small fraction of their actual value.

"Assuming that we bought the bonds," I mused, "what would we do with them?"

"Accept them as collateral for loans," he replied. "Of course, we could use fictitious names for the borrowers. And we would always have good collateral to show what had happened to the depositors' money."

"I'm sorry, John," I said, "but such a proposal doesn't interest me.

These transactions in stolen bonds would have just one result: they would take us out of circulation for a long time."

"Then you won't go in with me?"

"Perhaps. But it must be understood that there will be no dealing in hot bonds."

"You mean you think we can make money running an honest bank?"

"Perhaps not. But I think I have a plan that will reap us considerably more profit — and with far less risk — then your scheme."

"What is it?"

"Did you ever hear of letters of credit?"

"Yes, but I don't know much about them."

"I do. My trips abroad have familiarized me with their uses. Through letters of credit, I think we can clean up."

It was agreed that we would buy the stock, though Big John did not fully realize the scope of my plan. I didn't understand his ready acquiescence until he said:

"Joe, I'm broke. If we go into this, you'll have to advance me $37,500."

I agreed and gave him a check for $75,000. He purchased the stock and we took over the bank. It was an old-fashioned, gray stone structure and was comparatively small. An iron stairway led from the sidewalk to the entrance.

We decided it was best to retain all the personnel with whom the patrons were familiar — tellers, bookkeepers, and other employees. We made only three changes: Big John became president and I was named vice-president. A disbarred attorney, whom I shall call Newman, we made cashier. In our plans, the cashier was the key man.

Big John was a natural for the job of president. Not only did he look the part, but he was well versed in financial operations and was a graduate of Harvard.

Nobody misses a vice-president, so that fitted into my plans. As long as John's imposing figure could be seen at the president's desk, my own absence would not be noticed.

We agreed that all our American business would be conducted legitimately in accordance with general banking practices of that time.

## Some Credit—and Lots of Cash

Worthington took care of all the routine matters requiring official attention.

I went to work on a scheme that, as far as I know, had never been tried up to that time. Using the bank's best engraved stationery, I wrote out six letters of credit, each for $100,000. They were signed by Newman, the cashier, and the bank's seal was affixed.

A letter of credit is just what the name implies, and there are two kinds. One is a letter from a bank or mercantile house, addressed to a specific correspondent or affiliate, authorizing a certain designated party to draw drafts for certain sums.

The other—the kind I prepared—is a circular letter of credit. It is addressed to bankers and merchants at large and authorizes the designated party to draw any sum up to the limit fixed in the letter. Each bank or mercantile establishment honoring a draft writes the amount on the back of the letter. For example, when ten entries of $10,000 each have been made, a $100,000 credit is exhausted. The last banker to honor the letter takes it up and forwards it to the issuing bank.

Circular letters of credit have been in wide use, both at home and abroad, for many years. They have been developed into very fancy documents, with engraving, embellishments, and paper as hard to imitate as federal currency. But at that time they were not so well protected, and mine looked as authentic as any.

Armed with the six letters, I left for New York, where I contacted six men—all well-known boat-riders or transoceanic cardsharps and swindlers: The Harmony Kid, Bill Ponds, George Barnell, Max Cott, Bud Hauser, and Henry Smart.

They all agreed to try my plan, and we sailed for Europe. We dropped Ponds at Liverpool, from whence he proceeded to London. The rest of us went on to Paris, with which I was quite familiar and there set up headquarters for our venture.

Each of the six men was given one of the letters of credit. Each engaged the services of a young woman; that was necessary to our scheme. Henry Smart remained with me in Paris, while the other four went to Rome, Vienna, Budapest, and Antwerp, each accompanied by the girl he had engaged.

## "Yellow Kid" Weil

In Paris, Smart and his girl visited such places as Cartier's, Poiret's, and Schiaparelli's, buying expensive jewels and fine furs. Smart and the woman posed as wealthy American tourists. Parisians dearly loved the American tourist, especially for his money.

The woman made the selections and Smart paid with a draft against the letter of credit. It was not unusual for American business men to take their wives for spending sprees in the Paris shops. And they presented letters of credit more often than they paid in cash.

If the purchases the woman had selected amounted to $2,500, Smart wrote a draft for $5,000. He received the change in currency and no questions were asked. In this manner, he drew until the entire $100,000 had been exhausted.

We were prepared in advance for any inquiry. If any banker had cabled to Chicago to see if the letters of credit were good, our cashier, Newman, was ready to cable back that they were. But nobody made inquiry.

We had to work fast. One of our drafts might clear within six weeks. As each draft came in, it was turned over to Big John, who protested it. But by the time the draft got back to Paris or whatever other European capital it had been drawn in, we were back in the United States.

Within a few weeks, Barnell and Hauser joined us in Paris and we returned to New York, where the Harmony Kid, Ponds, and Cott were waiting for us. It had been agreed that each man would keep 40 per cent of the net proceeds. Some of them sold the furs and jewels on the return trip, in a few instances getting more than they had paid. They all had channels to dispose of the merchandise in New York at a discount.

When an accounting was made, we found it had been a very profitable venture. The total amount turned over to me was $292,000. This amount I took back to Chicago, dividing with Big John, who was now able to repay the $37,500 I had loaned him to go in the banking business.

I had been back only a few days when the first complaint came in. It was from Barclay's of London. I had anticipated this, however, and had already sent Newman to Mexico City, where he took up residence

## Some Credit—and Lots of Cash

under an assumed name. He was supplied with sufficient money for expenses and his salary was paid regularly.

The complaint was referred to Worthington.

"This letter of credit was issued without my knowledge," Big John replied. "Obviously it was a fraud perpetrated by the cashier, who signed it. The cashier has absconded and we have been unable to locate him."

The next complaint was from the Banque de France. Others came subsequently from Vienna, Antwerp, Budapest, and Rome. Big John made the same reply to all. No one was able to prove that he was not telling the truth. Newman, who had signed all the letters, was nowhere to be found. There was no evidence to connect Worthington with the transactions. Strangely enough, nobody thought of blaming me. We continued to support Newman in Mexico City until the affair had been forgotten.

Our bank prospered, but the profits were not spectacular. Big John was not satisfied. He was impatient for big money. One day he asked me into his office.

"Joe," he said, "I saw Melville Reeves last night."

"What about him?"

"He offered to sell me a million dollars worth of bonds at ten cents on the dollar."

"And every one of them registered?"

"Yes, but — "

"Don't be foolish, John," I returned earnestly. "Those bonds can all be traced. You'd be paying $100,000 for a ticket to the pen."

"If we made loans on them and locked them in the vault, how could they be traced? Everybody doesn't have the combination to our vault."

"Have you forgotten about the state bank examiners?"

"They probably wouldn't even look at the numbers," he argued.

"But they might. No," I insisted, "I'm not having anything to do with stolen bonds."

"Well, I will," he grumbled defiantly. "I got enough money to buy 'em myself."

"Go ahead, John. But count me out. I'm willing to take chances, but I'm not willing to do anything so foolhardy."

"I'm ready to take the chance. Do you want to sell me your stock?"

"Yes. I'm tired of this business, anyhow."

The transaction was completed then and there. Big John Worthington paid me my original investment of $37,500 and my connection with the bank ceased.

He went ahead and made the deal with Reeves. He milked the bank of all its funds and eventually it was forced to close. But the bond gang had no intention of letting him get away with the money. They kidnapped him and did not let him go until he had parted with the money he had taken from the bank.

Big John was broke when the kidnappers released him, and he never recovered. A few years later he died penniless. He was saved from a grave in potter's field by a collection among con men to give him a decent burial.

## 15. The Man with a Beard

For several weeks after I had left the bank I was at loose ends. One summer day I was sitting in the lobby of the Metropole Hotel in downtown Chicago when a man named Sam Banks came in. He had a very prosperous business in the London Guarantee Building on North Michigan Avenue. It was so prosperous, indeed, that Sam had opened a branch office in Boston.

"Hello, Joe," he cried, shaking hands. "What are you doing now?"

"At the moment," I replied, "I am free. Did you have something in mind?"

"Yes. How would you like to make a trip to Baltimore?"

"You know me, Sam," I told him. "I always like to travel. What's the deal?"

"You can make your own deal," declared Sam. "I'll give you the layout and you can work it any way that you like. Come over to the office with me and I'll tell you all about it."

Sam was in the fortunetelling business, which has always been popular. He had been so successful in his predictions that his clientele had gradually changed. Now, he had only the wealthy people from the Gold Coast. Numerous stockbrokers came to him for advice about the market.

Seeing the way his business was going, Banks made a special study of stocks. He read the financial pages regularly. He knew as much as any intelligent analyst about stock trends — what was likely to be a good buy, what was likely to drop. With this information he was able to forecast trends with fair accuracy.

But Sam's modus operandi made his predictions seem supernatural.

## "Yellow Kid" Weil

A man seeking information about stocks was put through the same hocus-pocus as any other man or woman who came to have a fortune told.

He acted as the "medium" for these high-priced clients. The fee was from $1,000 to $5,000. First the client was asked to write his questions on a square of blank paper about three by three inches in size. Then he handed the paper to the medium, who said: "I will lie on this couch and put the paper on my forehead. Then I will go into a trance and your questions will be answered."

The medium reclined on the couch. He put the square of paper on his forehead — or so the victim thought. Actually, it was a different square, of the same size and appearance, which had been substituted by the medium. He slipped the paper on which the questions had been written through a slit in the curtain and an accomplice picked it up.

The turban that covered the head and ears was a part of the medium's equipment. This had a two-fold purpose. One was to give him an Oriental appearance. But the main reason was to conceal the telephone headset that was clamped over his ears.

The wire from the headset went down the back of his neck to metal connections in the heels of his shoes. At the foot of the couch were other metal connections. These were hooked to wires that led into the adjoining room where the accomplice had a telephone.

As soon as the accomplice had the slip of paper, he read the questions over the phone. The medium received them through the headset as he lay on the couch, supposedly in a trance.

With his eyes closed, the medium removed the paper from his forehead. Holding the paper in his right hand, he reached out and held it over the flame of a candle that burned on a table beside the couch. As soon as the paper had been burned, the medium spoke:

"You have asked what stock you should buy today. Buy American Telephone and Telegraph. The market will rise today and you will make a cleanup."

That was all there was to it. When the question had been answered, the medium lost no time in coming out of his trance. He collected his fee and was ready for the next victim.

## *The Man with a Beard*

There were many wealthy women. Each usually asked about affairs of the heart, what sort of man was coming into her life, how to hold the affections of a husband or sweetheart, and other feminine questions. Banks gave common-sense answers, and that probably accounted for his success.

After he had shown me how he operated, he led me into his private office and told me about the Baltimore deal.

A week before in Boston, a wealthy spinster named Dora Albright had come into his office. Sam had conversed with her before going into his trance.

"I need some advice," she said.

He was quick to take advantage of anything that made him appear to have supernatural powers. He shrewdly noted her Southern accent.

"Miss Albright," he murmured, "you are not a Bostonian, are you?"

"No, I'm not."

"Are you just in town for a visit?"

"Why, yes. I came here to see about some investments and I heard about you. I'm from Baltimore."

"Yes, I thought so," Sam replied. The impression on her was profound. "You are, perhaps, the head of the family?" This was a guess, but based on sound reasoning.

"Yes," she said, even more impressed. "There are only two sisters, Clara and Emma. I'm the head of the family because I'm the oldest."

"I'll be happy to help you in any way that I can," Sam offered modestly. He handed her a square of paper. "Please write your questions here."

While she wrote, he stepped into his inner sanctum where he donned the turban and a flowing tunic. When he emerged his appearance had changed drastically. He lighted the candle on the table near the couch, and turned out the lights. The heavily draped room was in eerie semi-darkness.

Reclining on the couch and closing his eyes, he took the paper from the awe-stricken spinster. He made a few supposedly magic motions with his hands, sweeping them up and down in a wide arc. (This enabled him to slip the paper behind the curtain.) Then repeating a few words of gibberish he placed what she thought was the original

## "Yellow Kid" Weil

square of paper, on which she had written, on his forehead.

With his hands folded across his breast, he lay quite still and went into his trance, pushing his feet hard against the foot of the couch. That was to complete the telephone connection.

He lay thus for five minutes, while Dora anxiously watched his motionless face. Then slowly his right hand went to his forehead, removed the slip of paper, and held it to the flame of the candle.

"You say," he spoke, "that you and your sisters have about $200,000 in cash. You wonder if you should put this in a savings bank or if you should seek an investment. My advice to you is this. Don't do anything now. I see a man coming into your life. This man wears a beard. I can't tell you when or under what circumstances you will meet him. Nor can I tell you what he will advise. But heed him! For the bearded one holds the key to your fortune. That is all."

The spinster was old-fashioned and somewhat emotional. Sam could see that she had been shaken but was very pleased with his performance.

"She's ripe for plucking," he told me as he finished the story. "I checked up and found out that the family is quite wealthy, with a large estate outside Baltimore. This $200,000 she mentioned must be some loose money she wants to put to work. Do you have any ideas?"

"Plenty," I replied. "Want to hear them?"

"No!" he retorted. "I'd rather not know any of the details of your scheme. All I want is a twenty-five per cent cut. Whatever you get and how you handle it is up to you."

"I can manage it," I said. "Think I'll take a trip to Texas."

"Texas? But these sisters live in Maryland—"

"Yes, I know. But Texas fascinates me right now. There's something there that I want."

"Well, do it your own way, Joe."

Twenty-four hours later I was on my way to Texas. Before leaving Chicago I had looked up the locations of various properties owned by the Standard Oil Company and by the Texas Company, producers of the Texaco oil products. Finally I found what I sought. The two companies owned tracts that were very close to each other in the same part of the state.

## The Man with a Beard

I bought maps of the property owned by the two companies, with the adjoining territory. By putting the two maps together, I got one big map that showed Texaco's holdings on the east and Standard's on the west. Between the two of them were many acres of land not connected with either company. There were no markings on the Standard and Texaco tracts, which indicated that both, while owned by the oil companies, were not being exploited.

This suited my purpose admirably. I made plenty of markings of my own on the territory that lay between the two oil company tracts. One indicated the location of a "mother pool," while various others located spots where wells were expected to come in.

When I had completed drawing my symbols, I had the whole thing reproduced on one big map. I had several copies of this new map made and took them with me to Texas.

I had no trouble locating the property. I found that it was all pretty scrubby, including the tracts owned by the two companies. It was not uncommon for the big oil companies to buy up or lease large tracts of land which they held for years without drilling. Such was the case with the Texas lands I have mentioned.

Since no oil had been discovered, the value of the land had not soared. I was able to purchase 1,500 acres at a dollar an acre without any trouble. As soon as I had obtained an abstract and a deed and had recorded the purchase under the name, Dr. Henri Reuel, I set out for Baltimore.

My car was a Fiat, imported and custom built. It was expensive, powerful, and luxurious. I drove to Baltimore leisurely and sought the road on which the Albright sisters had their home.

It was a huge estate, a few miles outside of Baltimore. The big colonial mansion was built on a hill in a clump of trees, some distance back from the road. A gravel drive led from the road to a wide-columned porch. After looking over the setup, I drove back to Baltimore, checked in at a hotel, bathed, and had dinner.

It was after nightfall when I again drove to the Albright home. The big house was on a little-traveled country road and there was practically no traffic.

I drove over to the side of the road and pulled the choke to flood the carburetor. The motor sputtered and died. I got out and raised the hood — for effect — and doused the lights. Then I approached the mansion.

It was an eerie sight. The whole countryside was bathed in darkness. The only light was in the big house. A gleam came from the center of the house on the first floor and lights could be seen from two upstairs windows.

As I walked toward the house, the only sounds that pierced the calm of the black night were the crunch of my feet on the gravel drive and the singing of the crickets in the thickets that lined the driveway. I must confess that I had some misgivings as I walked that lonely quarter of a mile.

After what seemed an eternity, I finally reached the wide veranda. I saw immediately that this house was not run down. Indeed, it was in excellent state. The whole exterior had been freshly painted and the grounds were well kept.

I went to the front door, lifted the brass knocker and knocked. A colored servant, dressed in a frock coat, came to the door. He was skinny and old and his shoulders were stooped. There were wrinkles around his eyes and a fringe of white hair around his bald pate, which shone in the dim light like polished ebony.

"Could I see the master?"

"Ain't no mastuh," he replied in a high-pitched voice, "Jest Miss Albright."

"Then may I see Miss Albright? I'm Dr. Reuel."

"Come in an' I'll see."

I followed him into the drawing-room and took the chair he indicated. The chair was an antique with a scrolled back, but it was comfortable. I glanced about the room and saw that it was filled with priceless furnishings. The only illumination came from an elaborate partially lighted crystal chandelier.

The negro butler shuffled out of the room.

In a few moments I heard the swish of skirts. The woman who came toward me was not tall, but she was slender and her long dress gave her a stately appearance. I judged that she was in her late forties. Her frock was obviously expensive, but it was simply cut.

## The Man with a Beard

"I am Miss Albright," she announced. "Did you wish to see me?"

"Yes. I'm in a quandary. I was motoring past when my car broke down. I'm not much of a mechanic, I'm afraid, and I can't get it started again. May I use your telephone? I'm Dr. Reuel — Dr. Henri Reuel."

"Of course, Dr. Reuel," she replied. "This way, please."

I followed her into another room, which appeared to be a sort of library. In the center was a long counting-house table of shining mahogany. In one corner was a writing desk and on it a phone.

"Do you have a directory?" I asked.

"Yes, right here."

"Thank you. Do you happen to know the name of a good automobile repair shop in Baltimore?"

She named one and I looked up the number. I called this number but there was no response.

"Probably," said Miss Albright, "they are closed. You ought to be able to get somebody tomorrow, though."

"Tomorrow is Sunday," I reminded her. This was part of my plan. I knew that no mechanic would be available on Sunday, and that's why I had picked Saturday night for the breakdown.

"That's right," she agreed. "I'm afraid it looks as if you may not be able to get any mechanical help before Monday." She did not seem at all unhappy at the prospect. I knew that she had been observing my bearded countenance.

"Is there no way I can get into Baltimore tonight?"

"I don't know of any," she replied, "unless you walk. Is it necessary that you be in Baltimore tonight?"

"Well, no, but — "

"Why not be our guest over the week-end since there is no immediate solution to your problem? I'll have Ned prepare a room for you. My sisters and I will be happy to have you here until you can get your car repaired or secure transportation to Baltimore."

"That is very kind of you. Under the circumstances, I must avail myself of your hospitality."

I followed her back into the drawing room, and she summoned the negro butler.

167

## "Yellow Kid" Weil

"Ned," she told him, "prepare a room for Dr. Reuel. Where is Sam?"

"Back in de kitchen, Miss Albright, I reckon."

"Tell him to go with Dr. Reuel to get his luggage out of the car."

"Yessum."

I knew now that she was convinced I was the mysterious man with a beard the fortuneteller had predicted.

Sam, I later learned, was the gardener and man of all work. His wife, Lulu, was maid and cook. They were younger and more active than old Ned, but I learned that all three of them had grown up as part of the household.

Sam went back to the car with me. I locked the ignition, put the hood down, and took out two bags. Both bags were covered with labels from various European countries. As we re-entered the house, Miss Albright was waiting. She looked with considerable interest at the bags.

"Dr. Reuel," she said, "unless you plan to retire early, my sisters and I will be happy to have you join us in the drawing-room this evening."

"I'll be delighted," I said.

Sam led the way up a carpeted stairway whose polished mahogany bannisters gleamed in the dim light. I could see, as we passed through the house and up to the second floor, that costly and exquisite bric-a-brac was everywhere.

I unpacked my bags and put everything into the spacious drawers of the dresser. The room was large and well furnished, with a comfortable four-poster bed. I changed into evening clothes, and combed a few kinks out of my beard. When I went downstairs to join the Albright sisters I was immaculate.

Dora introduced me to her younger sisters. Emma was about thirty-five and Clara about thirty. They were attractive girls but their high priced costumes were severely tailored. It was obvious that the sisters lived sheltered lives.

Clara and Emma acknowledged the introduction, but had very little to say. Dora, being the oldest, was spokesman for the family. Occasionally she would turn to her sisters for confirmation of something

## The Man with a Beard

she had said, more out of politeness than anything else.

Our conversation began with trivialities. Ned, the butler, brought in some fine sauterne wine. Eventually Dora Albright got around to the question that had been on her mind since I had first appeared at the door:

"Are you going to Baltimore on business, Dr. Reuel?"

"Yes," I had my answer ready. "I represent European capital. As you know, the clouds of war are now forming over Europe. My principals have extensive holdings of valuable oil lands in this country, but it now appears that events in Europe will prevent them from exploiting these lands. I expect to dispose of a considerable amount of their holdings in Baltimore."

"How very interesting," said Dora, turning to her sisters, who each nodded.

"Have you traveled extensively in Europe, Dr. Reuel?"

"Yes," I admitted, knowing she had seen the European labels on my luggage. She was trying to draw me out.

"Won't you tell us something about the countries you've visited?"

"Gladly."

For an hour I told them stories about my ocean trips, about conditions in England, France, Germany, Italy, and the Balkans.

"War in Europe is almost inevitable," I said. "The interests I represent will surely be involved. They had made extensive plans for exploiting the fabulously rich oil lands they hold in Texas. But they cannot be bothered with this work, now that they are so busy with affairs of state. They have instructed me to dispose of the lands even though it will mean a great loss to them."

"Do you expect to sell it all in Baltimore?" asked Dora.

"I don't know," I replied. "I have offers from various firms for all but about 1,500 acres."

"I don't suppose you'd want to sell any of this land to private investors?"

"Perhaps. Do you have somebody in mind?"

"Yes. We have some money that we would like to invest in something gilt-edged. Do you suppose your principals would allow us to buy some of this oil land?"

"They have left the matter entirely up to me."

"Dr. Reuel, would you be willing to sell us some of the land?"

"Not knowing that you might be interested, I hadn't thought about it," I replied. "But I see no reason why you shouldn't be allowed to get in on a good thing. As a matter of fact I'd like you to have the opportunity, in view of your kindness to me."

"Suppose you tell us more about it, Doctor."

"I'll be glad to," I said, rising. "I have maps of the property in my bag. Will you excuse me while I get them?"

I went upstairs and got two of the maps. When I returned, Dora suggested that we go into the room she used as an office.

We went in and Dora sat down at the head of the counting-house table. Emma sat at the foot and Clara on one side. I spread out one of the maps in front of Dora and the other was shared by Clara and Emma.

I pointed out the locations of the lands of the Standard Oil Company and Texaco. Then I pointed to the "mother pool" on our property, as well as the various spots where producing wells were expected to come into production.

"This field is so fabulously rich," I said, "that the owners will gain wealth beyond their dreams. If I were seeking an investment for myself, I would look no farther."

"It sounds very good," murmured Dora, looking at her sisters, "doesn't it?"

"Yes, Dora," they replied.

"How much are your principals asking for this land?"

"I have the handling of all negotiations," I went on. "I intend to dispose of it for $120 an acre. That makes it a real buy for the purchaser, but time is an element with me."

"Do you suppose we could buy the 1,500 acres that you said you still have left for sale?"

"I see no reason why it could not be arranged."

"I'm in favor of buying it," said she. "What about you, Emma?"

"Yes, Dora."

"Clara?"

"Yes, Dora."

## *The Man with a Beard*

"Would you be willing to arrange it for us, Doctor?"

"With pleasure, I'll do so as soon as possible," I replied.

I folded up the maps and gave one to Dora. We had more wine and the sisters became a bit gayer. I had drunk just enough to give me a fine glow when I retired.

I spent a very quiet Sunday with the ladies. In the morning, after breakfast, Ned hitched up two bay mares to the family brougham and we drove to church two miles away. The sisters had on their plainest dresses. I wore striped trousers and a morning coat. I sat with them in their reserved pew and could feel curious eyes upon me. It was easy to see that the Misses Albright were the dominant figures — and probably the main support — of this little church.

We had an excellent Sunday dinner, and I spent a leisurely afternoon and evening with the Misses Albright.

The following morning, I called Baltimore and a mechanic came out. It didn't take him long to discover the two ignition wires I had disconnected. I left the women with a promise to return that evening.

In Baltimore I fixed up a deed to the 1,500 acres I had purchased in Texas, making it out to Dora Albright. That evening, I was back at the estate.

We met again in the room with the counting-house table.

Dora sat at the head as before. Beside her was a strong box. I gave her the deed and she counted out $180,000, each movement of her arm casting a weird, moving shadow on the wall. She put the deed in her strong box and I put the cash in my brief case.

"I suggest that you have this recorded as soon as possible," I urged. "It will protect you against encroachment."

"Thank you, Doctor," said Dora. "I can't tell you how glad I am to have had this good fortune."

All the sisters importuned me to stay another night, but I pleaded that I must be on my way to keep other business engagements.

There was nothing the Albright sisters could have done to me even if they had wanted to. For all I know, there really was oil on the land I had sold them. At any rate the sale was bona fide and the land actually existed. Whether they later tried to develop it for oil, I don't know. I never heard any more about them.

## "Yellow Kid" Weil

I returned to Chicago and gave Sam Banks his 25 per cent cut. He was having his troubles. Barney Bertsch, who had protected him from police interference, faced charges of bribery and corruption. Barney, in an effort to save his own hide, had announced that he was going to "sing" about all those he had shielded.

Banks decided the wisest thing to do was to close shop. I had no more dealings with him. But then it was unlikely that he would ever run across another perfect setup like the Albright sisters.

## 16. The Faro Bank Pay-off

THE CONFIDENCE GAME KNOWN AS THE PAY-OFF HAS BEEN WORKED by many con men throughout the world. Undoubtedly the reason the pay-off has been operated so successfully in so many instances is that it is a game of chance where the victim stands to win a lot of money. There is perhaps no other lure known to man that has so much appeal — the chance to risk a little and win a lot.

Aside from the natural animal instincts that are inherent in every normal person, I believe nothing else is so powerful as the urge to gamble. That is the reason there have been so many attempts to legislate gambling out of existence. My own opinion is that you can do this about as easily as you can change human nature.

I venture to guess that there have been more laws against gambling than any other crime, with the possible exception of homicide.

These laws may have changed our habits, but they haven't done much to stop gambling. The net result is that we do our wagering furtively, just as we drank under cover during Prohibition. If gambling houses and bookmakers were licensed and allowed to operate openly and legally, some measure of protection for the public would be possible.

As it is now, the only "protection" is for the gamblers — against being raided. If a man is the victim of a dishonest gaming house, he can't protest to the law, because he was engaging in an illegal activity in the first place.

There are a number of reasons why gambling hasn't been legalized. One is that certain groups — generally, the same that forced Prohibition upon us — are against it. Another is that the racing interests, composed of influential people, do not want the handbooks legalized for fear that they could cut into their own fat revenues. These people oppose the legal book from purely selfish motives and not for any moral considerations.

Another group opposing legalized betting consists of politicians. They are the people who receive the protection money, which would stop coming in if the bookies became legal.

Now suppose we faced this realistically and recognized that you cannot stop gambling. Suppose we allowed each community to decide for itself whether or not it would have gambling. Those deciding in favor of it could license each establishment, as taverns are licensed.

There would be some abuses, of course. But one important element would be removed — the muscle man. Gambling is about all there is left to the powerful syndicates which flourished during Prohibition. Repeal reduced these gangs, and the number of murders they committed, and even caused the complete collapse of the smaller gangs. The licensing of gamblers would remove their last fertile field.

Moreover, the fees that would be collected by each city could be used for many good purposes. It has been estimated that Chicago alone could collect about $3,000,000 a year from gambling licenses.

The situation boils down to this. People want to gamble and they will, even though it is unlawful. Police have confessed that they are powerless to stop it. Then why not do the most sensible thing — make the gamblers pay for the privilege?

One of the oldest gambling games is faro bank. I don't know just when it first became popular. But I do know that it dates back to the Pharaohs of ancient Egypt, from whom the name was derived. It has long been popular in France.

In the early days faro was dealt from an open deck, without the box. Louis XIV was one of the first to try to legislate it out of existence. The French nobles gambled so recklessly and lost so consistently at faro bank that many became penniless. Louis issued a decree banning the game, but still it flourished. For centuries, it has been a favorite of Parisian and other French gaming resorts. It became a major attraction at Monte Carlo. In the early days of the United States, faro bank was popular in the frontier towns.

My own experience with the game began soon after my return from

## The Faro Bank Pay-off

Baltimore. I was in Tommy Defoe's tailor shop in the Railway Exchange building. Tommy's place was a regular hangout for con men. If we wanted to pass the word along to a fellow worker, Tommy always obliged.

John Strosnider, who could be as smooth as silk, was sitting at a table shuffling cards. He was a wizard at cards. He could deal from the bottom and the average person would never know it. He also had a gadget for pulling a card up his sleeve which consisted of a wire extending from the foot, up through the trousers, under the shirt, through the sleeve at the shoulder, and out the coat sleeve. On the end of the wire at the sleeve was a clip-like finger. With this, John could palm the card he wanted and make any other card disappear faster than you could see it.

Now he was shuffling the cards, doing tricks and playing with his faro box. He had two new gadgets he was demonstrating. Both were bits of wire he manipulated with his left hand. He called one "the thief" and the other "the knife." With "the thief" he could remove any card he wanted from the deck, with "the knife" he could cut the deck and put the bottom card on top. He was practicing various other manipulations.

After a while I tired of watching him and picked up a newspaper. I turned to the classified column. I soon came across a want ad that interested me.

A Mrs. Kingston was going to California for six months and wanted to lease her nine-room apartment on the Gold Coast. I lost no time in calling on Mrs. Kingston. She showed me the apartment.

It was furnished luxuriously, and in excellent taste. The floors were covered with fine Oriental rugs. The large drawing-room was hung with priceless oil paintings. The other rooms were elegantly appointed, and there were two bathrooms.

The kitchen was completely equipped. Next to the pantry, there was a wine room.

It was an ideal setup. I succeeded in convincing Mrs. Kingston that I would take good care of her furnishings — and this was a prime consideration. I agreed to the $200 a month she asked, and paid her six months rent in advance.

175

## "Yellow Kid" Weil

Returning to Tommy Defoe's tailor shop I found Strosnider still practicing with his cards. I told him of the apartment and of my plans for it.

"We need a couple more good men to complete our organization," I added.

"How about the Deacon and Jimmy Head?" he proposed.

I had known Fred "The Deacon" Buckminster, one of Chicago's top confidence men, casually for a number of years but had never worked with him. Buck had been doing errands for Barney Bertsch, Chicago's big fixer. But things were hot for Barney, and Fred was ready to pull out.

He was a big, portly fellow, with the most innocent face you ever saw. Looking at him you would have sworn that he could not be anything but honest. His eyes were as innocent as a baby's and his features were positively cherubic. His demeanor was so decorous he actually radiated an air of piety. This had earned him the sobriquet "The Deacon" by which he is still known, although he is now an old man.

"He is a good detail man," Strosnider told me.

Fred seldom slipped up on the small things which are very important in any good con game.

Jimmy Head was from Texas. I have heard that he was from a good family and that his real name was not Head. He was a medium-sized man, nearing middle age, with a mild and pleasing manner and a slight Southern accent. In any crowd he would be inconspicuous, for he was a good example of the average citizen.

Head was also smooth. He was polite and his soft-spoken pleasantries made a favorable impression on the victims. He was the sort of fellow you would have expected to find in a teller's cage at your bank. We engaged a private room and I told Strosnider, Head and Buck of my plan. We would set up an establishment more lavish than any gambling club in Chicago. The story to our victims would be that it was a club maintained by the Jettison estate — one of a chain of such clubs scattered throughout the country.

They were enthusiastic about my scheme and agreed to play the roles I assigned to them.

## *The Faro Bank Pay-off*

As soon as Mrs. Kingston had vacated the apartment, we moved in. Of course there had to be some rearrangement. Buckminster arranged for a roulette wheel and I had a number of tables brought in. In addition to the roulette table, we set up tables for poker and dice and, of course, a table for faro bank.

In a corner near the entrance we set up a cashier's cage and installed Jimmy Head as cashier. He also kept the register and the membership book. This roster contained most of the biggest names in Chicago. Jimmy was supplied with large stacks of boodle, which were always in plain view. A victim always believes he has a chance of winning if there is a lot of cash in sight.

Strosnider was to be the manager of the club and also was to deal the faro bank game. Buckminster was the "overseer," an official whose headquarters were supposedly in New York. The story was that he went from club to club, checking to see that each was being operated properly.

The apartment was ideal. Only a very wealthy person, such as the millionaire Jettison, could have assembled such rich furnishings. It was not difficult for an outsider to believe that the club was frequented only by the socially elite. Indeed it would have been hard to convince the average person that anybody other than a millionaire was behind the club.

Strosnider became "John Steele," manager of the club. Buckminster became "Mr. McFetridge," the director from New York. My own place in the scheme was to pose as an outsider with inside connections.

As first victim I selected a man named Orville Hotchkiss. I had met him a year before when for a short time I operated a paint factory. Hotchkiss owned a retail paint store and had bought products of the factory. I knew he had no money to speak of, but I also knew that he was a fast friend of a man named McHenry, a sports promoter in Aurora. Though I brought in Hotchkiss, my ultimate victim was to be McHenry.

"Orville," I told him when I called, "I want you to help me out."

"Sure, Jim. What can I do?" Hotchkiss knew me as James R. Warrington.

177

"I have an uncle," I said, "who is the manager of one of the gambling clubs operated by the Jettison estate. You've heard of these clubs, haven't you?"

"Of course."

I knew he hadn't, but I also knew he had heard of the Jettison estate and the fabulous man who had founded it.

"My uncle has been with Jettison for twenty years," I continued. "He's served faithfully. He expected to get a raise last week, but what happened? They gave him a cut. He's plenty mad about it and wants to quit. But before he does he wants to make a killing.

"He knows that the New York overseer, a man named McFetridge, is back of it. McFetridge doesn't like my uncle and that's the reason for the cut. At the first opportunity he'll fire my uncle. But my uncle isn't going to give him a chance. He's going to clean up and retire."

"I don't blame him," said Hotchkiss. "What do you want me to do?"

"I want you to go in and make a big wager at the faro bank table. My uncle will be dealing. He'll let you make a killing — providing you split with him."

"Why don't you do it, Jim?"

"I would," I replied, "but they know me at the club. They know that Mr. Steele is my uncle. I couldn't get away with it."

"It's all right with me," returned Hotchkiss, amiably, "but what am I going to use for money?"

"Don't worry about that. My uncle will tell you how to do it."

I arranged a meeting with "Mr. Steele." He brought the faro box along.

"It's a case of rank ingratitude, Mr. Hotchkiss!" Strosnider said heatedly. "I've given Jettison the best years of my life. I certainly was entitled to a raise, if anything. But no, I get a cut." Strosnider was a good actor and there was bitterness in his voice.

"That's too bad," Hotchkiss commiserated with him.

"It's a rotten shame," Strosnider said with feeling. "But I don't intend to let them rub my nose in the dirt. I'm going to get even. Do you blame me?"

"Of course not," Hotchkiss replied.

"Ordinarily I wouldn't consider doing anything dishonest," John

## The Faro Bank Pay-off

went on, "but this is different. I feel it's what I've got coming to me." He shuffled the cards. "Do you know anything about faro bank, Mr. Hotchkiss?"

"No, I don't."

"Well, you will when I get through."

For two hours Strosnider rehearsed Hotchkiss in how to play. He showed him how, by shielding the cards with his big hands, he could always see what was coming out before it was dealt. He arranged a series of signals so Hotchkiss would know how to bet. They went over it time after time, until Hotchkiss was letter perfect in receiving the signals.

"Now, I'll let you win all through the deck," Strosnider said, "but wait until the last turn to bet all your chips. I'll give you the signal just before the deal. Now is that clear?"

"Yes," Hotchkiss replied, "but there's one thing that isn't. What am I going to use for money?"

"You can write a check, can't you?"

"Sure, but it wouldn't be any good."

"Don't let that worry you," said John. "You can cover it the next day. It'll be plenty good with all the money you'll win."

"Suppose they won't take a check?"

"Oh, they'll take it. All the big men who come to the club write checks. You just hand me a check for $50,000 and I'll give you the chips."

Strosnider produced two elaborately engraved guest cards. He wrote "James R. Warrington" on one and "Orville Hotchkiss" on the other and handed them to us.

"Come in about ten," he said, shook hands and left.

Promptly at ten that evening we were at the Gold Coast building that housed the Kingston apartment. Hotchkiss knew he was in an aristocratic section. He knew also that only wealthy people inhabited this building.

We were admitted by a man in an impressive butler's outfit. He took our hats and escorted us to where the manager sat. Strosnider got up, shook hands, and greeted us profusely.

"We're happy to have you gentlemen as our guests," he declared.

179

## "Yellow Kid" Weil

He led us across the room towards the kitchen. The activities of the club were in full swing. My friend's eyes popped when he saw the lavish appointments. About two dozen men in evening dress were at the various gaming tables and with them a number of women in formal gowns.

Hotchkiss thought he had indeed landed in the very midst of Gold Coast society. He had no way of knowing that the men were all stooges, minor con men hired for the occasion. Each was paid $25. Each man furnished his own clothes and his own woman companion. I've no doubt that many of the girls thought the place a swank gambling club, just as Hotchkiss did.

Each man was plentifully supplied with chips. They strolled about the room, trying their luck at all the games. It didn't matter whether they won or lost. The chips weren't worth anything. But Hotchkiss didn't know that. He gaped at the piles of crisp greenbacks in Jimmy Head's cage.

We made our way across the room in leisurely fashion so that our guest could absorb all the atmosphere. Then, we went through the kitchen and into the wine room where we found a bottle of champagne in a bucket of ice. The chef — a genuine chef, incidentally — was preparing sandwiches to serve the "club members."

Strosnider poured the champagne. "Here's to the Jettison Club!" he cried. We drank the toast.

"You gentlemen make yourselves at home," said Strosnider. "I have to see if there is anything I can do for the guests. When you feel like it come over to the faro bank table and we'll have a little game."

For perhaps a half hour we wandered about the big room, watching the various games. The butler came in with a big tray of sandwiches and passed them among the "club members." Later he returned with the beverages. Hotchkiss was thoroughly sold on the idea that it was a high-class club.

"I see my uncle is not occupied now," I told him. "Suppose we go over and play."

Hotchkiss agreed, and we walked over to the faro bank table.

"I'd like to buy some chips," he said. "I don't have much cash with me. Will a check do?"

## The Faro Bank Pay-off

"Of course," said Mr. Steele (Strosnider). "How much did you wish to play?"

"Fifty thousand dollars."

"Just make the check payable to cash." He began to count out chips with an expression that implied this club thought nothing of a mere fifty-thousand-dollar bet.

Hotchkiss wrote the check and Strosnider handed him the chips.

"Step up, gentlemen, and place your bets," he said briskly.

Two or three stooges at the table put chips down on the board. Hotchkiss won small bets consistently, aided by Strosnider's signals, and had $75,000 in chips when the last turn came.

"The last turn, gentlemen," Strosnider called. "There are three cards left. You must call the first two to win. The winner gets four to one."

But the other players apparently had had enough. They left the last turn entirely to Hotchkiss. Strosnider signaled, and he put his chips down on low-high. The last turn was dealt and the first two cards to appear were Four-Queen.

"I congratulate you, sir," said Strosnider, pushing $300,000 in chips to Hotchkiss. "You have been — "

He didn't finish the sentence. He looked up and there, standing behind Hotchkiss, was a big, imposing figure. He was immaculately groomed and he watched with great interest as Hotchkiss picked up the chips and walked to the cashier's cage.

"Hello, Mr. McFetridge," Strosnider greeted him with a sickly grin. "This is an — ah — unexpected pleasure."

"Mr. McFetridge" nodded curtly and followed Hotchkiss to the cashier's window.

Hotchkiss unloaded his chips and Jimmy Head counted them. "Three hundred thousand," he said. "Is that correct, sir?"

"Yes," Hotchkiss replied, obviously with a lump in his throat. You could tell that the mere thought of $300,000 all in one bundle frightened him.

Jimmy Head reached for the pile of boodle and started counting out crisp hundred-dollar bills.

"Just a moment!" It was the commanding voice of Mr. McFetridge.

"Mr. McFetridge!" Head exclaimed. "When did you get in?"

181

## "Yellow Kid" Weil

"I just came in as this gentleman called the last turn," the big fellow replied. "Are you a new member, sir?" he asked Hotchkiss. "I don't seem to recall you."

"Why, no," Hotchkiss replied. "I'm a guest."

"I see," said McFetridge. "I was over at the faro bank table and I noticed that you bought your chips with a check."

"Yes. Isn't that all right?"

"Of course," Mr. McFetridge replied. "Our members do it regularly. But we know them and we know their checks are good. But the rules of the house require that a guest pay cash for his chips."

"I can do that," Hotchkiss retorted crimsoning. "If you'll just wait until I collect my winnings, I'll be glad to redeem the check in cash."

"I'm sorry," said Mr. McFetridge, gently but firmly. "That's against the rules of the house too. I am sure that you can see our position. Suppose you had lost. Would the check have been good?"

"Certainly it would!" I cut in.

"I have no doubt that it is good. But we must be sure before we can pay your winnings."

"What do you want me to do?" asked Hotchkiss.

"Just let us put your check through the bank," the overseer said amicably. "It will take only a couple of days. Then we'll be very glad to pay you your $300,000."

"In other words," I said, "if Mr. Hotchkiss can prove he had $50,000 in cash, you will pay him?"

"Certainly," said the overseer. "The money is his. He won it. All we ask is that he demonstrate his ability to pay if he had lost."

"Then why not give him back his check? He can cash it and return tomorrow with the money."

"That is agreeable to me," said Mr. McFetridge. "If he brings in $50,000 in cash tomorrow, we'll gladly pay him what he won." He turned toward the faro bank table. "Oh, Steele!"

Strosnider came over, a hang-dog look in his eyes.

"You know the rules of the house," McFetridge said sternly. "You know that only members are allowed to use checks to buy chips."

"Yes, sir," the other murmured abjectly. "But Mr. Hotchkiss has a guest card — "

## The Faro Bank Pay-off

"I have no doubt that Mr. Hotchkiss is as good as gold," McFetridge cut him off. "But the rules of the house must be obeyed. I'm afraid I'll have to report this infraction of the rules to the New York office."

"I'm sorry," the faro bank dealer apologized.

"Now give Mr. Hotchkiss his check back," the overseer ordered.

Strosnider handed the check to Hotchkiss.

"We'll be in tomorrow with the cash," I said. "Please have the money ready."

"It will be ready," returned the big fellow, with a sweep of his hand toward the pile of boodle in the cashier's cage

Once we were outside I muttered, "It would be just our luck to run into that overseer."

"What are we going to do now?" Hotchkiss asked.

"What can we do?" I shrugged. "I haven't got $50,000 and I don't know anybody who has."

"Well, I do," he said. "And I don't intend to pass up my share of that $300,000."

"You do know somebody with that much money?"

"Yes. You remember McHenry?"

"McHenry?" I hesitated. "McHenry. Oh, you mean the man who helped you in the paint deal?"

"Yes. He's got $50,000. If I give him half of my share, he'll come in with me. Or I think he will."

"So what are you going to do?"

"I'm going to Aurora first thing in the morning."

"Good! We'll put one over on that McFetridge yet."

I parted from Hotchkiss after arranging to meet the one o'clock train from Aurora on which he expected to return. As I have said, we had slated McHenry as the real victim and Hotchkiss was doing exactly what I expected him to do.

When the train came in I was there. Hotchkiss got off and so did McHenry. We shook hands and went into the station restaurant for lunch.

We discussed the deal and McHenry took the bait. "Suppose we go up there now," he proposed. "Will anybody be in?"

"Yes," I replied. "My uncle is always there in the afternoon."

"All right," said McHenry. "Let's go."

We took a cab to the Gold Coast apartment. Strosnider admitted us. I introduced him to McHenry and said: 'We've come to collect. Mr. McHenry has the $50,000."

"McFetridge isn't here, the dirty rat!" Strosnider said bitterly. "He's got all the funds locked in the vault. You'll just have to wait until he comes. He's threatened to fire me."

"Well," I declared softly, "after this deal you won't have to work for him, Uncle John."

"I have a better idea," offered Strosnider. "You gentlemen come with me."

He led the way to a sun room which was comfortably furnished with tables and chairs. "Have a seat and I'll be right back."

When he returned he had his faro box.

"Do you know anything about faro bank?" he asked, addressing McHenry.

"Not much," McHenry admitted.

"Well, we've got plenty of time. I'm going to teach you."

"What for?"

"I'm going to give that McFetridge a real double-crossing," Strosnider replied. "You've got $50,000 in cash. You can buy chips with that and I'll let you win. You can win $300,000 and give Mr. Hotchkiss $50,000 and let him collect his bet, too."

All afternoon Strosnider rehearsed McHenry in how to play faro bank, how to bet, and the signals. Finally McHenry said he had practiced enough.

"Are you sure you understand it?" John asked.

"Positive," McHenry insisted.

"All right but I don't want any slips. Are you sure you don't want to go over it again?"

"No. There won't be any slips. I understand it perfectly."

He didn't, of course, but we didn't want him to. Strosnider wrote out a guest card for McHenry and we departed. I took them to dinner and at nine that night we went back. Our purpose in going early was to allow McHenry to make his play before McFetridge showed up.

## *The Faro Bank Pay-off*

The same group was on hand, going through the same motions. McHenry, like Hotchkiss, was very much impressed. But there was a difference between the two men. Hotchkiss frankly admitted he didn't know his way around gaming circles. But McHenry was the type that would today be called a "wise guy." He looked upon everything with a knowing eye.

When he approached the faro bank table he was set for the kill. He put down $50,000 in cash and received the equivalent in chips.

The game started, with a few stooges playing alongside McHenry. They all dropped out before the last turn. He won regularly with the help of Strosnider's signals. He had more than $75,000 in chips when the last turn came.

"Step up, gentlemen," Strosnider called. "It's the last turn. You can bet any of six ways. There are three cards remaining in the deck — a King, Ten, and Ace. You can call it high or you can call it low. If you call the cards, you get four to one."

This was the signal for McHenry to bet. The cards were in the box exactly as Strosnider had called them. But McHenry got his signals mixed when John said, "You can call it high or you can call it low." That was in reality the signal that high card would be first.

McHenry put all the chips he had on Ace-King to show in that order. Strosnider started to deal, then looked up. Behind McHenry was the formidable bulk of Buckminster (Mr. McFetridge). Strosnider signalled frantically to McHenry to withdraw. This was to make it seem realistic to McHenry.

Buckminster spoke up. "The bet stands," he said icily.

Strosnider hesitated, looking from McHenry to McFetridge, with a harried expression.

"Deal the last turn!" McFetridge commanded.

"Sure, go ahead and deal," McHenry said confidently.

Strosnider dealt the cards. The first was a King, the second a Ten, the last an Ace.

Sorrowfully, Strosnider raked in the chips. McHenry turned pale, as if he could not believe his eyes.

"I've been cheated!" McHenry muttered.

"Come on," I said, grabbing his arm. "Let's get out of here."

"You can go with them," said McFetridge. "Steele, you're fired!"

The three of us went out and stopped in the nearest buffet.

"Whatever possessed you to bet on Ace-King?" Strosnider demanded as soon as we had been seated.

"You signalled to bet on the high card," McHenry defended himself.

"Certainly I did," Strosnider replied. "Why didn't you?"

"But I did. I bet on the Ace —"

"The Ace? Why, you stupid idiot, everybody knows that the Ace is low card in faro bank."

"I didn't."

"Well, why didn't you ask?" Strosnider demanded bitterly. "I thought you said you knew everything about this game."

"I'm sorry that I muffed it."

"A lot of good that does now. Not only did you muff our chance to make a killing but you caused me to lose my job. I hope that I never run into anybody like you again!"

On this note we parted company. I later saw Hotchkiss many times. He laughed about the whole thing when he learned my real identity.

There was almost a serious sequel to the McHenry episode. It was only a few days after we had taken the Aurora sport's money. I had just finished shaving when Buckminster dropped in. He'd had another quarrel with his girl friend and had been chased from their apartment.

"Had breakfast yet?"

"No," I said. "Won't you join us?"

"Thanks. I'll read the paper while you're getting dressed."

*The Chicago Tribune,* still rolled as the boy had delivered it, was on the table. Buckminster picked it up and opened it.

"Holy smoke!" he exclaimed. "Joe, look at this!"

He held out the front page. Across it was a two-inch headline that read:

WEIL-STROSNIDER GANG SOUGHT FOR MURDER

And under it was another headline:

THREE CON MEN SUSPECTED IN SLAYING OF
RED-HAIRED TANGO DANCER

*Jimmy Head, con-man confederate of the "Yellow Kid" for many years.*

*"Yellow Kid" Weil as he looked in the early 1920's.*

## The Faro Bank Pay-off

Buckminster rolled up the paper and jammed it in his pocket.

"Come on," he snapped, "we've got to get out of here."

"But I'm not fully dressed — "

"You're dressed good enough." He grabbed my arm and propelled me unceremoniously to the door. I had on socks, but still wore bedroom slippers.

Buckminster pulled me out the door and started cutting across the lawn to a back street. My wife had a glass-covered hothouse and in the excitement I stepped in that. Buck kept me from going through, but I lost my slippers.

We made the back street and I walked a dozen blocks in my stockings without any shoes. Finally we came to the rear of Johnny Butterley's saloon.

In there we had a slight breathing spell. But Buckminister was sure the cops were hot on our trail. He phoned for a cab and we took that to a hotel on the northwest side. Every time Buck saw a car he was sure it was the police.

As soon as we were settled I phoned my wife, told her where we were, and asked her to bring me some shoes. Buck had breakfast sent up. Then we read about the murder of which we had been suspected. This is what we learned:

It was near 8 P. M. on an evening two days before. Dusk was merging into darkness. Mrs. Frank Pratt, whose husband managed the Dunham farm near Wayne, Illinois, was hurrying homeward when she saw a couple.

Even in the semidarkness, she observed that they were a handsome pair. The man was of medium build and slender. The woman, dressed in a blue serge suit, wore a large hat with a bow, a pink rose, and ostrich plumes over her long red hair. They were leaving a bypath and walking toward the road to Wayne.

"This way, sweetheart," said the man.

"All right." The woman laughed happily and added, "It's dark, but I'm not afraid as long as I'm with you."

Mrs. Pratt continued on to the farm. The last she saw of the couple, they were walking down the road, not far from the tracks of the Elgin, Joliet and Eastern Railroad. She thought little of the incident, since

## "Yellow Kid" Weil

many Chicago people had summer homes in the vicinity and strangers were common enough.

As she neared her home Mrs. Pratt heard an explosion. But she dismissed this with the thought that it was a torpedo — a signal in wide use by railroads at that time. She thought no more of it until the next day.

Early that morning a woman had been hit by a train in the vicinity of the Dunham farm. At first Wayne authorities regarded it as a regrettable accident. But when the body was examined by a coroner's physician he found a bullet hole in the head. He said that the woman had been murdered before the train hit her.

When Mrs. Pratt heard this she told of the chance encounter the night before. Police renewed the search of the ground. They found a calling card bearing the name Mildred Allison. On the back was a penciled notation. "Frank L. Oleson, Felicita Club." Searching further the police found some bits of paper — evidently a letter that had been torn up and scattered on the tracks.

They carefully pieced together the bits of paper and this is what they had when they had completed the jigsaw puzzle: "In the hands of three confidence men named Weil, Strosnider, and Buckminster."

The investigation was immediately shifted to Chicago. The Felicita Club was a dance hall known as a "tango palace." Frank L. Oleson was the manager. He said that he had employed Mildred Allison as a tango-dancing instructor.

Persistent work by Captain John Halpin, then Chief of Detectives, brought out some facts about the murdered woman. Her name was Mildred Allison Rexroat and she had been married to a man named Allison, by whom she had three children, the eldest a boy of seventeen. But she had become enamored of the tango palaces and spent a good deal of her time there.

At the Felicita Club, she had met Rexroat. After a clandestine affair she had divorced her husband and married Rexroat, a farmer from downstate. But she had lived with him only a few weeks on his farm, tired of him, and returned to Chicago, where she had been engaged as an instructor by the Felicita Club.

Inquiry at the club brought the information that the red-haired

## The Faro Bank Pay-off

woman had been seen frequently with a slender fellow of medium build known as Mr. Spencer. There were various opinions as to Mr. Spencer's character.

One woman said that he was a confidence man; another that he was a blackmailer; a third that he was a leader of the Black Hand. Others said he was a bond salesman and a gambler.

While none of these descriptions fitted me exactly, nevertheless the physical description was close. The police were none too sure about my occupation, but they had ideas. Further, it was known that I was fond of red-haired women.

None of this would have made the police look for me on the face of it. But the letter that had been found near the body made the trail lead straight to me. Or it would have if I had been at home.

Fortunately for me, Captain Halpin was a conscientious worker. He kept looking for the mysterious Mr. Spencer. Finally the rooming-house where the man lived was located. The police laid a trap for him and captured him within a matter of hours. Spencer confessed, was convicted, and died on the gallows.

After Hotchkiss learned who I really was he told me how our names became linked with the affair. He had received a bitter letter from his friend McHenry in which the Aurora sportsman had complained that he had been in the hands of three confidence men named Weil, Strosnider, and Buckminster. Hotchkiss had the letter with him on a week-end trip to Wayne. While walking down the track he had torn the letter into bits. Most of it had been scattered by the wind, but the bits containing the two sentences that implicated us still remained near the murder scene.

Buckminster and I had to hide out only about two days before the murder rap was lifted. We weren't questioned at all, though the newspapers made a lot of the story.

I still had Mrs. Kingston's apartment and I saw no reason to discontinue the "club." But I made a rule then, and I have stuck to it ever since. I decided all my victims must be from outside Chicago.

There would be much less danger of my encountering them later if they were outsiders. This worked out remarkably well and is probably the reason that I had comparatively little trouble over the years.

## "Yellow Kid" Weil

Through an agency, I had want-ads inserted in newspapers in other cities. The ad read:

MONEY TO LOAN — Retired multi-millionaire will make business loans to responsible concerns for expansion. Must be bona fide. Give full details in first letter. Address Box J-215.

These ads brought an avalanche of mail and provided us with many wealthy victims. We brought each victim to the Jettison Club and worked the faro game on him while he was waiting for a decision on his loan. To make it realistic, we always sent auditors to go over his books and look into his bank credit. Most of our victims didn't learn they had been tricked until much later.

But in this, like everything else I have undertaken, I soon had many imitators. Faro bank gambling clubs sprang up all over Chicago. We talked it over and when the small fry began to move in decided it was time for us to quit.

## 17. Meet Me in St. Louis

FRED "THE DEACON" BUCKMINSTER AND I DECIDED TO STICK TOGETHER. We both lived in Chicago and were fond of excitement. Either of us could have retired and lived a legitimate life many times, but we craved excitement.

One of our stooges in the faro bank venture owned some Alaskan mining stock. We bought it from him for $500. We found out that it was worthless, though perfectly legitimate, because the mining property actually did exist.

The beautifully engraved certificates gave me an idea which I discussed with Fred. The plan required considerable forethought and it was several months before we were ready. But when we finally did complete the scheme we had something that was to be a gold mine for more than twenty years.

The first concrete step was to have stock certificates printed. We had an ample supply of the most magnificent stock certificates you ever saw. The stock was so beautifully engraved that it looked like money in the bank. The borders were gold leaf.

The certificates were all shares in the nonexistent "Verde-Apex Copper Mining Company" and the equally nonexistent "Verde-Grande Copper Mining Company."

Gene Boyd, who lived in East Chicago, Indiana, was lined up to "hold the rag," which means holding a block of worthless stock. John Snarley, the gold-brick specialist and John Strosnider, who was ready to participate in any kind of skin game, also became rag-holders. They were all given detailed instructions.

Jimmy Head, the most dependable man of the lot, completed our organization.

## "Yellow Kid" Weil

At this time I had become involved with a young woman in Chicago who had taken my attention a little too seriously. I decided that a drive to St. Louis would be good for me.

Buckminster wasn't doing anything, and accepted my invitation to go along. We drove in my Fiat roadster.

We were approaching Alton, which is not far from St. Louis, when we saw a big, run-down plant. It was not in operation and was in a state of dilapidation. Weeds grew unchecked on the grounds around the building. The fence was falling apart and most of the windows were broken. Across the side of the building was a dirty sign: THE ALTON IRON WORKS.

"That," I said to Buck, "ought to be a good investment for our European associates."

"It might," he agreed. "But I'll bet it's in hock."

"Shall we find out?"

"Sure. It might be a good bet."

We drove on into Alton and stopped at a hotel dining-room for lunch. I inquired of the waiter, and we received the complete story of the Alton Iron Works.

"It started out big," he told us. "A lot of people worked there and the whole town was proud of it. But something went wrong. The owner was a man named Gibbons. He was a partner in the Third State Bank. Gibbons went broke and had to borrow money on it. He lost all of that and then he hocked his house. When all the money from that was gone he had to close up. I guess the disappointment killed him."

"Who owns the plant now?"

"Mrs. Gibbons, I suppose. But there's a big lien on it and she'll never get anything out if it."

"How about the man who holds the lien?"

"He'll get something out of it," said the waiter. "I don't know how, but I bet he will. He was Gibbons' partner in the Third State Bank but wouldn't go in the Iron Works. When Gibbons needed money he went to the bank. This fellow — his name is Hoffman — lent him the money — first on the plant and then on the house."

"What makes you think he won't lose any money on it?" I asked.

## Meet Me in St. Louis

"Him lose money? Mister, he's the tightest man in the world. He never lost money on anything."

"Thanks." I slipped the waiter a five dollar bill and paid the check, and we left for the Third State Bank.

It was a modest building. There was no pretentious lobby, no wasted space. Five tellers' cages were all on one side. At the end of the room the banker sat on a platform in front of his private office.

This was the man — Marvin Hoffman — whom we had come to see. He was of medium height and build. A frugal man — you could tell that just by looking at him. He wore the cheapest clothes I ever saw on a business man. The suit was plain gray of very coarse material. The coat was ill-fitting and the trousers were baggy. He looked like anything but a banker.

Hoffman had a thick moustache, obviously dyed. My own reaction was that he had used black shoe-polish. On top of his head was a toupee, also black, the most ill-fitting toupee I had ever seen. You could spot it a block away, for it looked like the stuffing out of a cheap mattress.

"Mr. Hoffman?" I approached him.

"Yes." He stood up and surveyed me with a critical eye.

"I am Dr. Weed and this is my associate, Mr. McFetridge. We represent European capital. To be exact, our principals are important figures in Europe."

"I'm honored, Dr. Weed," he said, shaking hands. He beamed at us cordially. "What can I do for you gentlemen?"

"As I said, our principals are important figures in Europe. They are none too sure that Germany and her allies will win the war. If something should go wrong they want to have something to fall back on in this country. They have entrusted us with the task of selecting some worthwhile investments."

"Can I help you with an investment?" Hoffman inquired.

"Perhaps. I understand that you own the Alton Iron Works."

The banker's rotund face lighted up. His dyed moustache almost brushed against his nose as he parted his lips into a smile.

"I don't own it," he began. "But I do have a lien on it. And I am empowered to negotiate a sale."

193

"Excellent," I said. "How much do you think the owner would want for it?"

"I believe," he replied, with a perfectly straight face, "that he would be willing to sell for $500,000."

"H-mm!" If I had been seriously considering buying the place, I would have laughed in his face. But, very solemnly, I turned to Buck. "What do you think, Mr. McFetridge."

"That's about the figure we had in mind," he replied. "I think it will make a good investment."

Hoffman looked us over again. I am not very large, but I was well-dressed. My beard was well-groomed. Buckminster's clothes had been cut by a good tailor. His figure was big and impressive. I looked distinguished and Buck imposing. Hoffman thought he had hit the jackpot. We gave every tangible evidence of being big business in person.

I stroked my beard thoughtfully. "There is another thing we have to consider. It will require some additional capital to get the plant into shape. How much do you think would be required for that?" I asked Hoffman.

"Not so much," he replied. "Maybe $50,000."

"We'll plan on a hundred thousand," I said. "Suppose you talk to the owner and get the necessary papers ready. We'll go on into St. Louis and I'll contact my principals. We'll see you again next Tuesday — a week from today."

"I'll arrange everything," said the overjoyed Hoffman.

We shook hands and left.

"How much do you expect to get out of him?" asked Buck, as we drove into St. Louis.

"Not much," I replied. "But we ought to be able to make our expenses."

"He's a tightwad if I ever saw one," said Buck. "We'll be lucky if we take him for $25,000."

We registered at the Jefferson Hotel in St. Louis and took a suite with a sitting room and two bedrooms.

The following morning, I read the financial pages of a St. Louis morning paper. One item that interested me particularly was that

## Meet Me in St. Louis

Bright and Company, a large brokerage house, was going out of business. I called the item to Buck's attention.

After breakfast we went downtown. The brokerage house of Bright and Company was a beehive of activity. I asked for the manager and was shown into his office.

"Yes," he affirmed the report, "we're liquidating this office."

"I represent the brokerage firm of Farson, Clark, Hamill Company," I told him. "We plan to open an office in St. Louis. What do you plan to do with your furnishings?"

"Sell them, I suppose," the manager replied.

"How would you like to rent the whole thing, completely furnished?"

"I think that could be arranged. But it will be two weeks before we'll be out. Our clerks will be busy until then, getting the books in order."

"That would be all right," I said. "I suppose you'd have no objections to our bringing in some of our own clients if you're not out by the time we're ready to move in?"

"No, of course not."

I arranged to lease the place and paid a month's rent in advance. Then I called Jimmy Head in Chicago and told him to come on to St. Louis.

Buck and I surveyed our new offices with undisguised satisfaction. The place was completely equipped for handling stocks. The board was still in operation. Quotations from the New York Stock Exchanges were coming in as usual. All around us clerks were busy over ledgers. It was agreed that we could have the use of one of the offices until the company closed its affairs.

This settled, Buck and I set about the business of relaxing, which had been our original purpose in coming to St. Louis. We attended a performance of *The Passing Show* and went to a cabaret.

People have often asked me what I did with all the money that came into my possession. A little impromptu party we gave offers a good example of how the cash melted away. We often entertained on a lavish scale.

Friday night we were in the elevator going up to our room when

195

## "Yellow Kid" Weil

I noticed a beautiful red-haired girl. I recognized her as the star of *The Passing Show*.

On an impulse I approached her. "I beg your pardon, Miss, but what are you doing tonight?"

She looked up in surprise. "Why, I'm going to my room."

"Won't you join us?" I said. "This gentleman" — I indicated Buckminster — "and I are having a little party. I have five bottles of imported champagne and a feast of English pheasant."

"Why, I don't know — " the girl hesitated.

"We expect another young woman to join us," I added hastily.

"I suppose it would be all right."

"Excellent. You go along to your room and get ready. We have some preparations to make. We'll call you as soon as everything is ready."

The girl got off the elevator and we went on up to our suite.

"What's the big idea?" Buck demanded, "telling that girl you've got a feast. Why, you haven't even got a bottle of wine."

"No, but I'll get it. How about you getting a girl?"

"That's easy," Buck replied. "I can get that blonde from Fogarty's show. And that reminds me. I'm giving a party for Fogarty's entire show Saturday night. Do you want to come along?"

"Certainly. And maybe I can bring along a few of the cast of *The Passing Show*."

"The more the merrier," said Buck.

I hurried back downstairs and talked to the night clerk. All liquor stores were closed then, as was the hotel dining room. But for a consideration, the clerk got into the dining room and found some roast chicken in the icebox. He also got the keys to the liquor stock room. He returned with three bottles of champagne and a bucket of ice.

Within half an hour I had the feast spread on a table in the sitting room of our suite. Then I called the redhead and she came up. Within a few minutes Buck was there with the blonde from Fogarty's show.

We had a gay time that lasted well into the morning hours. Before I had parted with the girl I had arranged to take part of her company on our party the following night.

196

## Meet Me in St. Louis

We had selected Saturday night because there was no performance on Sunday. It was well after midnight when we got going. Buck and I hired a dozen cabs to take us to a roadhouse just outside St. Louis. The place was about ready to close, but we persuaded the proprietor to let us in.

A ten-piece band was on the point of leaving. But a little cash, with promise of more, induced them to stay on. There was plenty of food and plenty of wine.

It was probably as merry a party as had ever been staged at that roadhouse. The gayety lasted through Sunday and Sunday night and until late Monday afternoon. We consumed great quantities of food and many gallons of wine. We finally had to call a halt because the players had to get back into St. Louis for their shows.

The band had stuck with us all through the week end, as had the employees of the roadhouse. When it came time to settle the bill Buck and I paid out more than we hoped to take from Hoffman. We made money in large amounts and we spent it that way. We cared for money for only one reason — the fun and the things it would buy.

We were exhausted after the party and went to the hotel to sleep. We slept until Tuesday evening and got up with hangovers. Tuesday was the day we were supposed to go back to see Hoffman. There was nothing we could do now but make it the next day.

Hoffman greeted us effusively when we entered his bank the following morning.

"I'm sorry we were not able to get back on Tuesday," I told him. "But I was delayed by another matter in which I am extremely interested."

"Oh, that's all right," said the banker, obviously relieved that we came back at all.

"Do you have the papers all drawn up?"

"Yes, everything is ready," he replied. "I have a bill of sale, free of all encumbrances. Did you contact your principals?"

"Yes. They think the site is excellent and are quite ready to complete the transaction at the figure you mentioned. But it will be necessary to take the papers to New York where they can be inspected by the man who will direct the property in America. His name is Hans

197

Luther and he has just arrived in this country from Europe."

"You mean I have to go to New York?" asked Hoffman.

"Would it be inconvenient?" I countered.

"I'm afraid so," he replied. "I have nobody to run the bank."

"Suppose," I said, "that we let Mr. McFetridge take the papers to New York and close the deal?"

"That's all right with me," Hoffman replied.

"An excellent idea," Buckminster approved. "I ought to be able to get the whole thing settled in a week."

"Meanwhile I'll stay here," I said.

"I'd ask you to stay with me," frowned Hoffman, "but my house is rather small—"

"I wouldn't think of it." I told him. "As a matter of fact I have already engaged a suite at the Alton House."

Buckminster took the papers and went back to St. Louis, supposedly to take a train for New York. He drove the Fiat, leaving me without transportation. I registered at the Alton House and welcomed the opportunity to get some rest at this quiet hotel.

During the ensuing days I spent a great deal of time with Hoffman. He had a Toledo touring car, which I think was the worst automobile I've ever been in. He took me to the iron works, and showed me how to make the necessary repairs.

One day while I was waiting for him to go to lunch he left the bank early, saying he wanted to buy a suit. I went along. He first tried the town's leading haberdashery. But the cheapest suit this store had cost twenty-three dollars and that was more than Hoffman was willing to pay.

We went to several other stores, walking up and down side streets, until Hoffman finally found a suit that he felt he could afford. It was a ghastly color, poorly cut and of the very cheapest material. But the price tag was nine dollars, and that was what appealed to Hoffman. He bought the suit and wore it to church the following Sunday.

On the way to church Hoffman picked me up. While there were curious glances directed my way as we sat in Hoffman's pew, there were no friendly advances. As far as I could see Hoffman had not a friend in the entire town. I had already seen some of the reasons for this, but as we drove back to town he gave me an even more revealing clue.

He pulled up to the curb in front of a house.

"See this place?"

"Yes."

I couldn't have missed it. It was a beautiful home, a two-story house of face brick which stood on a promontory. The lawn surrounding it had been terraced and the grass was very green. A winding driveway led to an arched portico on one side. On the other side was a greenhouse and a summer house. There were several fine trees on the grounds.

"That is the show place of Alton," said Hoffman, "and I expect to move into it in a few weeks."

"Did you buy it?" I inquired, very much surprised.

"Yes, in a way," he replied. "I hold a mortgage on it. It was built by a man named Gibbons. He used to be my partner. Then he built the iron works and our partnership was dissolved. After I lent him the money on the iron works he wasted it all and came to me for more. I lent him $35,000 and took a mortgage on this house."

"And does he still live there?" I asked, knowing the answer perfectly well.

"No, but his widow does. And she hasn't been able to raise enough money to pay the mortgage."

"You mean you're going to foreclose on the widow?"

"I certainly am." There was no hint of leniency in Hoffman's manner — only greed. "It's not my fault she can't raise the money."

"Well, you'll have a beautiful home, Mr. Hoffman."

"I sure will. And when I move in, I want you to come and visit me some time, Dr. Weed."

"That's a promise," I agreed. "After you have taken up your residence in that house I promise to come and stay a week!"

And I meant that. For an idea had begun to crystallize. Maybe it was idealistic. I didn't know Mrs. Gibbons, but I felt that she could not possibly deserve to lose her home at the hands of this miser.

The following day, while we were having lunch, I said to Hoffman: "You remember the mining deal I mentioned to you?"

"Oh, you mean the one that delayed your coming back?"

"Yes. Well, I'm rather concerned about that. I need some advice."

"Maybe I can help you," the banker offered. "What is this mining problem."

"You've probably heard of the Verde-Grande Copper Mining Company of Jerome, Arizona?"

"Of course," he replied. I knew he hadn't, because no such company existed except on our stock certificates.

"This mine gave promise of being very rich. But suddenly, when the miners got to the boundary of an adjoining mine — owned by the Morgan interests — they found that the vein went over into the next mine and that their own ore had been exhausted. They shut the mine down until they learned of the Law of the Apex."

"What is the Law of the Apex?" Hoffman asked.

"Just this: the property where the outcropping is of the higher point shall be entitled to all bodies of mineral ores lying therein and boundary lines may be disregarded."

"What does that mean to the Verde-Grande mine?"

"It means that it is fabulously rich. For the vein that extends across the boundary was higher than the outcroppings in the other mine and it was one of the richest veins ever discovered."

"What is your idea of a solution to the problem?" Hoffman asked thoughtfully.

"The Morgan interests, knowing that they will lose a great deal if the Verde-Grande stands on its rights, are trying to gain control of the mine before the stockholders find out what happened. Their brokers have asked me to help buy up the stock. They have offered to buy all I can get for two dollars a share."

"What brokers made you the proposition?"

"Bright and Company."

"Why, they have an office in St. Louis," the banker exclaimed.

"Yes. As a matter of fact that's where I expect to sell the stock if I can get somebody to help me buy it up."

"Do you know who has the stock?"

"I have one or two leads. And from what I have heard I think I can get the stock for ten cents a share."

## Meet Me in St. Louis

"And sell it for two dollars?" There was a greedy gleam in the banker's eye.

"Yes."

"Why don't you let me help you?"

"I will. But first there is the deal for the iron works. As soon as I have closed that, then I'll let you help me."

"Why wait on that? It may be a week before your friend will get back from New York. And in the meantime the stockholders might get wind of what's happened and then maybe you can't get their stock so cheap."

"But you don't know me very well, Mr. Hoffman. I —"

"Ha!" he broke in. "I know you maybe better than you think. I say let's go get that stock while we can."

Reluctantly I acquiesced. The next morning we set out for East Chicago, Indiana, where Gene Boyd was waiting with 12,500 shares of Verde-Grande stock. The Toledo sputtered every mile of the way. We were beset with engine trouble and numerous flat tires.

We found Gene Boyd's home — he was an East Chicago policeman — and inquired about his stock.

"It's no good," he said disgustedly. "You can have it for anything you want to pay."

"We'll give you ten cents a share," I offered.

"It's a deal."

I counted out $1,250 and handed it over to him. Gene slipped $1,000 of it back to me before we left, keeping $250 for his services.

We proceeded at once to St. Louis. Jimmy Head had installed himself in the one office that we were to use until Bright and Company had finished their business.

I led the way into this office and introduced Head as manager of Bright and Company. Hoffman never doubted it. He looked about him and saw the clerks busy at their ledgers. Quotations from the New York Stock Exchange were coming in and Hoffman didn't miss that either. It was one of the largest and busiest financial offices he had ever seen.

"I'm glad to see you, Dr. Weed," said Jimmy, shaking hands. "Did you have any luck?"

**201**

"Some," I replied. "I picked up 12,500 shares."

"That's only a drop in the bucket," Head remarked. "But I'll buy it from you at two dollars a share, as agreed." I handed the stock over and he counted out $25,000. Hoffman's greedy eyes glistened as he watched me making money so fast.

"I have another prospect," I said, pocketing the money. "I understand he has 250,000 shares."

"Just bring it in, Dr. Weed," Jimmy said, smiling expansively. "We'll have the money ready for you." He turned to Hoffman. "I'm very glad to have had the opportunity to meet you, Mr. Hoffman. You say you're in Alton? Maybe we can get together later on a stock transaction."

We left and Hoffman walked as if his head were in the clouds. I could tell that he was overwhelmed.

"When do we see that fellow with the big block?" he asked.

"Well, you have to get back to Alton, don't you?"

"I'll run in there tonight and we can start tomorrow morning."

"All right, Mr. Hoffman. I think I'll stay overnight in St. Louis. I'll meet you tomorrow morning at the Jefferson Hotel."

Buckminster was waiting for me at the hotel. With him was a big, bluff, red-faced fellow to act as Hans Luther. This fellow participated in dozens of swindles but was never touched by the law.

The next day Hoffman and I drove to Logansport, Indiana. I directed him to the livery barns of the O'Donnell Transfer Company, owned and operated by John O'Donnell.

O'Donnell wasn't in his office, as I knew quite well. But John Strosnider was there. One look and I could tell that he had a hangover.

"I beg your pardon," I said. "Are you Mr. O'Donnell?"

"Yeah. What do you want?"

"Do you own some stock in the Verde-Grande Copper Company?"

"No, I don't."

"I am Dr. Walter H. Weed," I said. "I happen to know that you hold 250,000 shares."

"Well, what if I do?"

"I am prepared to buy the entire lot," I removed my gloves, laid

**J. P. Morgan & Co.**
*Bankers*
*Broad & Wall Street*
*New York*

MEMBERS
NEW YORK STOCK EXCHANGE
BOSTON STOCK EXCHANGE
CHICAGO BOARD OF TRADE
NEW YORK COPPER EXCHANGE
NEW YORK COTTON EXCHANGE
NEW ORLEANS COTTON EXCHANGE
WINNIPEG GRAIN EXCHANGE

PRIVATE EXCHANGE HANOVER 5160

September 19, 1934.

Mr. James A. MacDonald,
United Verde Copper Co.,
Jerome, Arizona.

Dear Mr. MacDonald:

As much as we regret to acknowledge our decision of closing down for an indefinite period the Verde properties yet we feel we can at least compel our adversary to visualize the folly of his senseless and dilatory tactics toward a friendly settlement. What can it avail anyone insofar as gain is concerned to permit such an enterprise to remain idle? And idle it shall remain unless all persons interested shall be in accord with the future developments. We are willing to go before any recognized committee and adjudicate the claims of our opposing factions but we do not intend to relinquish our equities nor do we intend to pay an exorbitant demand.

We cannot understand why or how there has been confession of defeat coming from those to whom we have previously entrusted the commission of buying up the stock of the Verde-Apex. I do not say they were not aggressive or inefficient yet they have failed, and for this reason I shall have the well known brokerage firm of THOMSON & McKINNON, Lincoln Bank Tower, Ft. Wayne, Indiana, through their manager Mr. Connor, handle the situation.

Today Mr. Elihu Root paid me the compliment of his august presence and urged that we merge our interests, coupling our corporations together; if we cannot obtain control of the Verde claim then we have no alternative. I had rather paid the real value to the holders of the Verde stock than agree to his demand.

When you have received any news of definite importance communicate it to me at once.

Very sincerely yours,

J. P. MORGAN & CO.

By *J. P. Morgan*

JPM/PG

*Forged letter and signature used in the Verde-Apex stock swindle.*

*Impressive-looking but worthless Verde-Apex stock certificate.*

them on the desk, and took out the $25,000 I had received from Jimmy Head. "I'll give you $25,000 for your holdings."

"$25,000?" Strosnider spat viciously. "Get out of here. I won't even talk to you for that. The stock cost me a dollar a share."

"But you know it's worthless now—"

"If it's worthless, why are you so anxious to buy it?" he demanded. "There must be something up. I don't want to sell."

"All right," I said, "I'll give you $25,000 for a forty-eight-hour option to buy it for twenty cents a share."

"I won't sell for twenty cents. And why should I give you an option? Nobody gave me an option when I paid a dollar a share for it."

"Would you sell it for a dollar a share?"

"I tell you I don't want to sell. But if I did, I wouldn't consider less than a dollar."

"I'll give you a dollar," I said. "But I'll need time to raise the money."

"Nobody gave me time to raise the money when I bought the stock," he said irritably. "I had to put cash on the line."

"But I'm willing to put this $25,000 down—"

"Get out!" he barked. "I don't want to talk about it."

Hoffman and I returned to the car. His spirits were very low. He got in and I was about to follow when I noticed that I had left my gloves behind. Hoffman said he would wait while I went back for them.

I stayed fifteen minutes and when I returned my manner was jubilant.

"I talked him into selling," I told Hoffman. "He has agreed to give me an option for $50,000. I gave him the $25,000 I had and he agreed to wait until this afternoon for the other $25,000."

"I wouldn't take that old drunk's word for anything," Hoffman said. "Where are you going to get the $25,000?"

"I'm going to wire my principals. Please drive me to the Western Union office."

He drove me to the telegraph office and parked in front while I went in. I sent a fake message to Buckminster, then came back out and told Hoffman there would be a wait of about an hour until I got a reply. I went back in the Western Union office and engaged the manager in conversation, telling him I was going to build a factory in Logansport. After conversing for a while I induced him to accompany me to a near-by bank. Hoffman saw this, though he didn't know what it was about. The Western Union manager introduced me to the president of the bank, to whom I told the same story. The whole thing was just to fool Hoffman into believing we had gone to the bank to get money.

I returned to the car and showed Hoffman $25,000. It was the same $25,000 I had supposedly given O'Donnell on the option. But he didn't know that; he thought I'd got it by wire.

We went back to the O'Donnell place and gave the $25,000 to Strosnider. He wrote out an option to buy his stock for $200,000 balance if purchased within forty-eight hours. Then he managed to slip the money back to me.

We started driving back to St. Louis.

"I can raise $140,000," I told Hoffman. "But I need your permission."

"Why my permission?" he asked.

"It's part of the money that will go into the iron works. It was entrusted to me by my employers. I know that there is no risk, but I can't use the money without your sanction.

"You remember Mr. McFetridge went to New York to see a man named Hans Luther? Well, Mr. Luther is going to be the managing director of the iron works. He will need a home near the plant. He comes from an aristocratic German family. They always lived in a castle and he will require a pretentious home in America."

"How soon do you think you could make the deal?"

"I don't know, but we haven't much time. You drive me by the hotel and I'll stop and see if there is any word from McFetridge."

In St. Louis Hoffman drove me to the Jefferson. I went up to our suite, where I found Buck and the stooge who was taking the part of Hans Luther.

I told them what was up. The stooge practiced a little on his accent and until it was heavy enough. Then we went down and met Hoffman.

## Meet Me in St. Louis

I introduced him to Hans Luther, who acknowledged in English, with a heavy German accent that was quite convincing.

"Yah, I think I would like that house," he replied, when I had explained the proposition to him in Hoffman's presence. "Could I see it maybe?"

"Certainly," said Hoffman.

"Fine," I cut in. "You go ahead, Mr. Hoffman. We'll drive out later and take a look at the house."

This was agreed. Hoffman drove off and the three of us went to dinner.

Now it seemed reasonable that Hoffman should have asked about the deal for the iron works since Hans Luther was the man we were waiting for to close it. But Hoffman was like all the others who fell for my stock scheme. The fever of speculation had hit him so hard he seemed to have forgotten all about the original deal.

Later that evening we drove out to Alton and I took Buck and the stooge to see the house. Then we called on Hoffman. Hans Luther agreed to pay $25,000 for the house, but demanded that the title be free of encumbrance.

"I can fix that up all right," Hoffman promised, his eyes shining.

"Good," I told him. "You get that done as early as you can in the morning. Then meet us at the Jefferson in St. Louis."

"It may take all day to get it," said Hoffman. "But I can meet you the next day."

"That will be fine. Make it ten o'clock."

"I'll be there," he agreed.

He was there. He had a court title to the house. This was possible because eighteen months had elapsed since the mortgage was due.

Hans Luther was there, too, and so was a very good lawyer. He is now a federal judge in Missouri. He represented Mrs. Gibbons, but Hoffman didn't know that.

Luther had a draft on a New York bank to pay for the property. I volunteered to go to the bank and have it cashed while the lawyer and Hoffman were completing the transaction. This was agreed to by Hoffman.

I got him to one side to prevent the others from hearing.

"Come over to the Boatman's National Bank as soon as you're through," I whispered. "We've got to get to Logansport before that option expires. I'll draw out my money and we'll drive over to Logansport and pick up the stock."

"I understand," he whispered. "I'll be there."

An hour later when he walked into the Boatman's National Bank I was waiting with a bag. I opened it and showed him several neat piles of money.

"There it is," I said. "$175,000 in cash. Have you got your $25,000?"

"Yes." He patted his pocket.

"Good. We'd better be going. We've only a few hours until that option expires."

We set out for Logansport in the Toledo touring car. We arrived there early in the afternoon. As we approached the O'Donnell Transfer Company, Hoffman stopped the car.

"What's the matter?" I asked.

He reached in his pocket. "Here," he said, "you might as well take all the money and put it together." He counted out five $5,000 notes and handed them to me.

I put them in the bag with the rest of the money. Hoffman made a perfunctory inspection of the contents of the bag. The currency was mostly boodle, with good money on the top and bottom. Each bundle was neatly wrapped with money wrappers from the Boatman's National Bank. There was a date on each and the initials of the tellers who supposedly had counted the money. It all looked genuine enough, even to a banker.

We went up to the O'Donnell livery barns and again found Strosnider on hand. He endorsed the stock and turned it over to me and I gave him the bag containing the boodle — and Hoffman's $25,000.

I insisted I was hungry, and we stopped to have a late lunch, thereby delaying our return to St. Louis. Hoffman didn't eat very much. He was elated over the success of our mission and was anxious to get back to St. Louis so we could dispose of the stock and he could collect his $60,000 profit.

When we did get back to St. Louis it was after dark. Bright and

## Meet Me in St. Louis

Company was closed. This had been fully planned. I had purposely delayed our return.

If Hoffman had been a less frugal man he would have stayed in St. Louis overnight, attended a show, and had a good time. He would also have been on hand the next morning to collect his money. But that would have cost him too much, so he returned to Alton, thereby relieving me of the problem of getting rid of him.

"Suppose you take this stock with you for safekeeping," I suggested, though I had no intention of turning it over to him. "I'll meet you here in the morning."

"No," said Hoffman. "It's a lonely road from here to Alton and I might get held up. Can't you have 'em put it in the hotel safe overnight?"

"Why, yes, I can do that."

I arranged to meet him at the hotel the next morning, and Hoffman drove off. That was the last I ever saw of him.

I might add here that I never let a victim keep a single one of the fake stock certificates. That would have been evidence, and I didn't want any evidence outstanding against me.

Buck was waiting at the hotel.

"What luck?" he asked.

"Just as I figured," I replied. "What about you?"

"The lawyer and I went to Alton while you were gone. We transferred ownership of the house to Mrs. Gibbons, and the lawyer had it recorded at the court house. He turned the deed over to the widow. He says that the transaction is airtight. Hoffman won't be able to get the house back from her, no matter what happens."

"Fine. I'm glad to see the good woman get her house back. I am sure she is most deserving of it."

Strosnider came in from Logansport later that evening and turned the boodle and the money over to me. I paid him $1,000 for his services and Buck and I split the balance. Our net profit was less than we had spent, but we had no regrets. We had had a lot of fun, besides doing a good deed on the side.

## 18. The Law Catches Up

ENGLAND WAS AT WAR WITH GERMANY. AMERICA WAS STIILL AT PEACE, but was not neutral. Feeling ran high against the Kaiser and the Germans.

Buckminster and I took full advantage of that. We selected our victims with care. They were men who would not be swayed by any feeling of patriotism. The fact that the country was on the brink of war with Germany would not stop them from dealing with agents of the Kaiser.

We continued to pose as representatives of the Central Powers. Our story that we were seeking factory and industrial buildings where the Germans could manufacture munitions was logical enough, and all the victims fell for it. Apparently none of them gave a thought to the possibility that the munitions might be used against their own country.

After making several good scores from which we never had any beefs, Buck and I lined up a man who was the president of a bank in Fort Wayne, Indiana. His name was Hamilton. He was wealthy, but one of the most avaricious men I've ever seen.

"The Germans are fine people," he declared when we told him we represented the Central Powers. "I have no sympathy for the British and I hope they are defeated."

His eyes burned greedily when we agreed without quibbling to pay the exorbitant price he asked for his factory building, which was run down and hadn't been used for years.

As in other deals of this character, there was the inevitable delay while we "communicated" with Berlin and awaited the final okay before we completed our negotiations.

## The Law Catches Up

Meanwhile, we switched Mr. Hamilton's attention to the stock deal. He went into this with vigor. We kept him dangling and bought up small blocks of stock for ourselves, but did not permit him to participate. Finally he became impatient and insisted that he be allowed to buy some of the stock.

We yielded when it came to buying the big stock. That was when Mr. Hamilton parted with his $50,000. Shortly after that we took leave of him and expected that he would be like most of our other victims. We thought he would not care to have all his friends know that he had been swindled by a couple of sharp con men.

But we soon found out differently. Money meant more than anything else to him — even more than his reputation. He had made a careful note of every place we had visited to buy the stock and was able to lead the police to all these places.

What is more, he was able to give them an accurate description of both Buckminster and me. The police recognized us and picked us up.

At the trial in the Criminal Court in Chicago, Hamilton testified that we were German spies. He also denied that he had ever said that the Germans were fine people or that he had ever considered making a deal with representatives of the Kaiser.

By that time war had been declared on Germany. I think that this aspect of the case influenced the jury as much as the fact that Hamilton had been swindled. Anyhow, we were convicted and sentenced to eighteen months in Joliet.

Prison life was not as horrible as I had pictured it. The Warden was not tough. Instead he was fatherly and often offered us good advice, particularly about rehabilitating ourselves and going straight when our time had been served.

I had no desire to remain in prison any longer than necessary. For that reason, I was a model prisoner and earned the maximum amount of time off for good behavior.

I knew how to use a typewriter — an accomplishment that was not too common at that time, especially among convicts — and the Warden made me secretary to the prison physician. This had many advantages and made my stay more pleasant.

For one thing, I was allowed to dress in white, including a white shirt, instead of the usual attire of a convict. Most of my work was in the prison hospital, and I had comparative freedom. My funds had not been depleted and I was able to buy anything I needed from the outside.

Moreover I constantly associated with the doctor, and absorbed a great deal about medicine, diagnosis, and medical terms. Before my term was up, the inmates in the hospital were calling me "Doctor."

When we came out the war was over, but money still flowed freely. We paid scant attention to the Warden's admonition to go straight.

But one thing we had learned. It was not a good idea to conduct any of our operations close to Chicago, where we were known to the police. We decided that hereafter all our swindles would be outside the jurisdiction of the Chicago police, preferably in another state. By sticking to that rule, we always had Chicago as a refuge.

When we needed to take a victim to a large city to complete a deal, we usually selected Indianapolis, Cincinnati, Columbus, Akron, Toledo, Cleveland, Harrisburg, or some other community several hundred miles away. We never even mentioned Chicago to our victims.

This worked out well, for though we were known as con men to the Chicago police, they never had anything on us. There were many times when we were picked up on suspicion, but we were soon released.

We continued to work our stock swindle with amazing success and used Chicago as a refuge while the heat was on.

## 19. Magic Money

THE OLD DILL PICKLE CLUB IN CHICAGO WAS DIFFERENT FROM ANY other institution that ever existed. I think I am in a position to judge, for I visited Bohemian resorts in all the capitals of the world.

Many attempts have been made to imitate or recapture the atmosphere of the Dill Pickle, but none has succeeded. The late Jack Jones founded and operated the club, and it was his liberal policy that made it a success. To Jones it didn't make much difference who you were or what you were. If you had an idea, you were welcome to the club. If you had no ideas at all you were still welcome.

Perhaps it was this lack of organized planning that gave the Dill Pickle its extremely informal, unplanned, you-never-know-what's-going-to-happen-next atmosphere. It was not at all unusual for a recognized crook to appear on the rostrum the same night two learned scientists carried on an erudite debate.

Atomic energy, about which we hear so much today, was discussed in a heated debate by University of Chicago scientists on the platform of the Dill Pickle. Juvenile delinquency, another current topic, was also a favorite subject. I recall that I discussed this subject myself in a debate with a safe-cracker!

Making something appear what it isn't is a con man's stock in trade. When Fred "The Deacon" Buckminster and I were working together we were frequent visitors at the Dill Pickle Club. Many of the visitors knew who we were. By that time we had an international reputation.

We often appeared on the platform on any subject that suited our fancy. We debated anyone who wanted to take the opposing side. In nearly every case we used our right names.

## "Yellow Kid" Weil

But I remember one occasion when we decided to have some fun. We framed it beforehand with Jack Jones. Our props were all set when we made our appearance. Jones introduced us:

"And now, ladies and gentlemen, those two eminent scientists, Dr. Reuel and Dr. Buckner, will give a demonstration of their latest invention."

Some of the audience howled, for they knew quite well who we were. Others who applauded us expected to see a new marvel of science and regarded us with awe. In this connection I might mention that people not only are easily fooled but often fool themselves. Take any gathering, announce that the next speaker is "eminent" or "famous," and you will convince two-thirds of them, even though the speaker is unknown. Some will take your word for it, but others will actually convince themselves that they have heard of the "famous" man.

"Tonight," I said, "our demonstration is a very simple one. But it will be welcomed by all the housewives of America. We are going to show you how, through our marvelous invention, you can have roast chicken in thirty seconds. Bring on the chicken!"

Buckminster went to the edge of the stage and a boy handed him a chicken — dressed but not cooked. He held the chicken up so that everybody could see it.

"Now," I continued, "your attention is called to the invention. We have here our patented electric roaster." It was a roasting pan all right, placed in an elaborate looking case that might have contained electric wiring equipment. "Now, please time me. I place the chicken in the roaster, cover it with the lid, then close the case."

I went through these operations as I talked. The audience watched me closely.

"Now I press this button and wait thirty seconds."

Actually what happened during those thirty seconds was this: a man under the platform removed the chicken from the roaster and substituted one that was freshly roasted. Any but the most gullible should have realized what was going on.

"Time's up!" I said, consulting my watch. "Dr. Buckner, please remove the chicken."

## Magic Money

Buckminster opened up the case and removed the lid from the roaster. The first thing the audience saw was steam rising from it. Then Buck lifted the roaster from the case and proudly displayed the chicken.

"There you are, ladies and gentlemen," I said, with a triumphant flourish. "Roast chicken in thirty seconds. Step right up, ladies and gentlemen. A slice of roast chicken for everybody in the house as long as it lasts!"

People crowded around the stage. Buck carved the chicken and handed out slices to the interested spectators. To us it was just a pleasant prank. But we had momentarily forgotten how gullible people are.

As soon as the act was finished we left the rostrum to make way for the next speakers. We were immediately approached by a University of Chicago professor.

"Most marvelous thing I ever saw!" he cried enthusiastically. "When are you putting them on the market?"

"I beg your pardon?" That was Buck.

"When are you starting to manufacture your chicken roasters?" the professor continued.

"We hadn't given it much thought," Buck admitted.

The professor turned to me.

"What about you, Dr. Reuel?"

"I hadn't thought much about it, either," I replied.

"Surely you're not going to let somebody else have your invention?"

"We have no facilities for making it," I said.

"Do you have something to suggest?" Buck asked.

"Yes," replied the professor. "Organize a corporation. Sell stock in it if you don't have enough money. I'd like to invest a little money in it myself."

Apparently the professor was very fond of roast chicken.

"We're inventors, professor," I said gravely, "not manufacturers. We don't know much about business."

"But we'll keep your proposal in mind," Buckminster promised. "We'll certainly remember you if we decide to form a company."

The professor was reluctant to let it go at that, but we succeeded in

213

## "Yellow Kid" Weil

brushing him off. We went into Jack Jones' office and had a good laugh. Later in the evening we mingled with the crowd, and before the night was over we had another offer to put money into the scheme.

Ordinarily we would have been glad to accommodate these gentlemen and relieve them of their money. But the scheme was so patently silly that we couldn't regard it seriously.

This unbelievable episode actually happened. No other incident in my entire career so convinced me of the gullibility of man. In other cases I had always put on a plausible show before taking a man's money. No project of mine was so obviously impossible as this one.

During this time Buck and I were going easy on the stock scheme until the heat from one of our recent deals cooled off. We hit upon the money-making machine as a good substitute for the interlude.

One night at the Dill Pickle I met a man whom I shall call Joseph Swartz. He was the type of fellow who knew all the answers and didn't mind telling you right out that he did.

He didn't know my true identity, but thought that I was the scientist, Dr. Reuel. In the company of two young women he came to me and suggested I take one of them out. We started on a tour of cabarets. It did not take me long to probe Swartz's character and to discover that he was stingy.

"Doc," he said to me in an aside. "Do you have change for a ten?"

"Of course." I reached into a pocket and withdrew a wallet I had been saving for just such an occasion. I counted out ten singles.

"Funny smell to these bills," he said.

"Yes," I replied. "Must have got near some chemicals during one of my experiments."

Actually the bills had been dipped in creolin, a strong disinfectant. It was my intention that he should notice the odor. We continued our round of the cabarets and took the girls home.

The next night I saw Swartz at the Dill Pickle. Taking his arm I led him to a secluded corner. "Did you spend all those bills I gave you last night?"

"Yes. Why?"

"Did anybody question them?"

"Of course not. What are you driving at?"

## Magic Money

"I had just made those bills last night!" I whispered.

"You what?"

"I said I made those bills. I finished them just before I came over here. That's why they smelled so strongly of chemicals."

"Are you kidding, Doc?"

"Certainly not."

"Can you make more like 'em?"

"Of course."

"Say —"

"Not so loud." I put a finger to my lips. "Let's get out of here before we talk about it any more."

Just to give him time to think about it and to build up the suspense, I lingered around the club. Several times in the course of the evening he came up to me and urged that we leave.

"What's your hurry?" I said.

"I want to talk to you about that proposition."

"Oh, that can keep," I told him. "We'll talk it over later."

This served only to whet his appetite, as I knew it would. He could hardly contain himself when finally we left.

"How about it, Doc? Can you make some of those for me?" He was like a small boy who can hardly wait for Santa Claus.

"Why should I?"

"Aren't we pals?"

"Well, yes, in a way. But you must swear to keep secret anything I tell you or show you."

"Doc, I swear I won't tell a soul."

"All right. I did make those bills. And I can make some for you. But I'll have to show you how it's done first. Early tomorrow morning go to the bank and get a brand-new one dollar bill. Then meet me at this address."

"Can't you show me tonight?"

"No, because the bill must be brand new."

The address I had given him was an office over a drug store on the North Side. I doubt if he slept much that night. At ten minutes past nine he met me in front of the drug store. He carried a crisp, new dollar bill.

215

## "Yellow Kid" Weil

We went up to the office where Buck was waiting. He was surrounded by tables on which were numerous pans and dozens of bottles containing strange-looking liquids. All had labels that few chemists had ever heard of.

"Mr. Swartz," I said, "this is Dr. Buckner, the well-known chemist."

They shook hands. The Deacon looked the part. He was coatless and wore an apron. There was an irritated expression on his face. He seemed displeased that I had brought Mr. Swartz with me.

"Mr. Swartz is a good friend of mine," I explained. "Do you suppose you could run off a bill for him?"

Buck did not reply for a few moments.

"You weren't followed here, were you?" he asked Swartz sourly.

"No. Why should anyone follow me?"

"I just want to be sure," Buck replied. "You understand that reproducing money is illegal?"

"Yes. But I'm sure nobody followed me."

"Very well. Do you have a new bill?"

"Yes." Swartz handed him the bill.

Buck examined it, then handed it back to Swartz. Or at least Swartz thought he did. Actually Buck handed him a bill that he had palmed.

"What is the serial number?" he asked.

Swartz examined the bill. "A 8978638," Swartz replied.

"Make a note of that, both of you, will you?"

We wrote the number down on slips of paper from a pad.

"Very well," said Buck. "Now we may proceed."

He took the bill from Swartz and laid it flat on a board on the table. Then he picked up a bottle containing a dark liquid. "This is a special formula," he said, "and is the product of years of research. Of course, the formula is secret."

"Yes, sir," said Swartz. He was awed by the mysterious and interesting-looking chemicals and gadgets.

Buck picked up a swab of cotton, tilted the bottle, and soaked it with the chemical. It had the same odor that Swartz remembered from the ten bills I had given him. Very carefully, Buck swabbed both sides of the bill. Leaving it flat on the board to dry, he brought

216

## Magic Money

two pieces of paper. This paper was actually absorbent, though Buck said:

"This is highest quality bond paper made from a secret formula. It must be the exact size of the bill."

He then carefully placed the bill between the two pieces of paper. Then he rolled it up on a pencil into a very compact roll. This was rolled back and forth on the board for about twenty times. Then he put the roll down.

"More chemicals are needed now," he said and reached for a couple of pans. One of them contained plain water. The other was empty.

From the array of bottles, he picked up a large one that contained a purple liquid. He poured this into the empty pan. Then he reached for another bottle containing white crystals. This he poured into the purple liquid, which began to effervesce. As soon as the bubbling had subsided, he poured some liquid from another bottle. This produced a flash and smoke. It was all very impressive.

While the liquid was still smoking, he picked up the roll and dipped it in the pan. Then he quickly submerged it in the basin of plain water.

"Now, we have our impression," he said, and unrolled the paper. "Here is your money back."

He handed the bill back to Swartz, who was now so impressed that he could hardly talk.

"Just put it aside until it dries," I said. "It's yours. We won't need it any more."

Swartz laid the bill down on the table.

Buckminster continued with the demonstration. He placed the two pieces of paper, face up, on the table and invited Swartz to examine the impressions. There were in fact exact impressions of both sides of the bill.

"Now, from these impressions, we make your bill," Buck said.

He placed a piece of bond paper, the exact size of a dollar bill, between the two pieces of paper on which he had made the impressions. Then he brought out the machine.

This was no more than two pieces of plate glass in between which were several thicknesses of blotting paper. Thumbscrews in each end screwed to a bolt held the glass together. What Swartz didn't notice, however, was that there were similar thumbscrews on the bottom. No matter which end you turned or whether you viewed it from top or bottom, the machine looked the same.

Buck didn't give Swartz the opportunity to view it from every direction. He merely removed the top thumbscrews, lifted the glass and inserted the paper with the impressions. Then he replaced the glass and screwed it down.

"There's nothing more to do but wait."

"How long will it take?" Swartz asked eagerly.

"Oh, about twenty minutes. Have you ever been in a chemist's office before? You might be interested in seeing mine."

Buck led Swartz to another part of the room. The purpose of this was to get him away from the table and get his back turned. As soon as it was, I quickly turned the machine over.

We conversed for about twenty minutes. Buck showed Swartz vials, bottles, test tubes, and tanks. He seemed in no hurry to continue with the money experiment, but Swartz couldn't wait. As soon as twenty minutes had elapsed he asked eagerly: "Can't we open it now?"

"Yes, I think it ought to be ready now," Buck replied.

He removed the thumbscrews and lifted the glass. Underneath it were two pieces of paper. Between them was a dollar bill. Buck handed the bill to Swartz. It still reeked with chemicals.

"Doctor," he said to me, "will you read the number you both jotted down so that Mr. Swartz can compare it?"

"A 8978638," I read from my slip. That was the number Swartz read on his slip and bill.

"That's it!" he said jubilantly. Then he reached for the bill Buck had returned to him. He compared them carefully. Both bore the same number.

"Creepers!" he exclaimed. "You really can make money, can't you?"

"Of course," Buckminster replied. "Did you doubt it?"

"Well, I wasn't so sure."

"Just to be sure," I said. "We'll take those bills over to the bank and see if we can pass both of them."

Swartz and I went to the bank a block away, where I approached

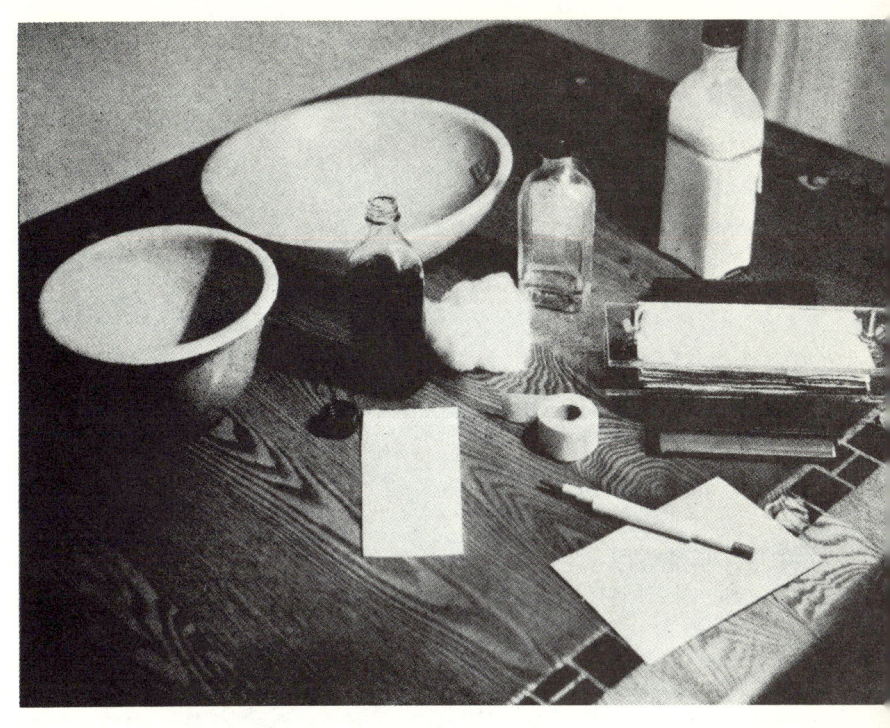

*Commonplace materials used in the money-machine scheme.*

*The first operation: bill is well soaked with creolin.*

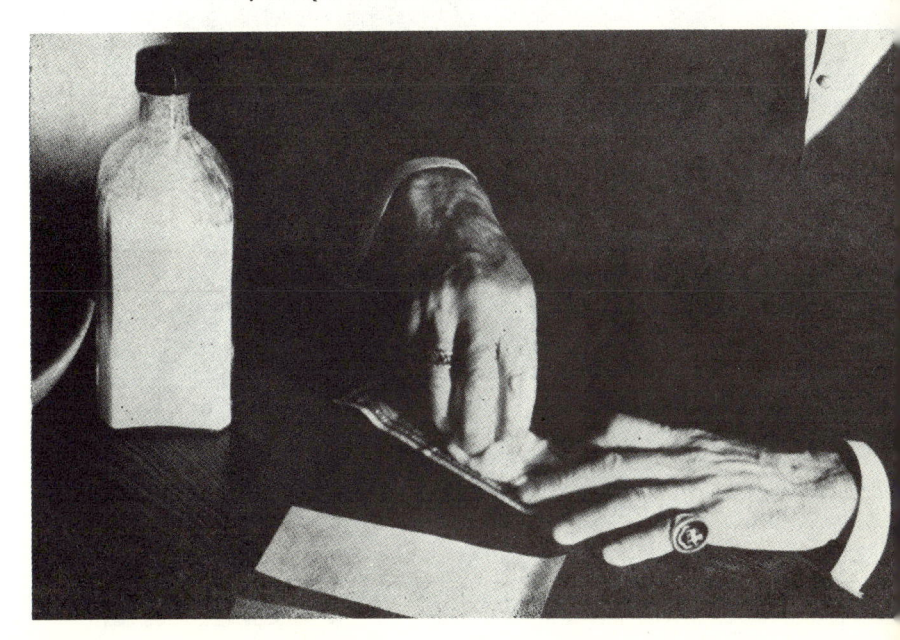

*Bill is then inserted between two pieces of paper and rolled tightly on a pencil.*

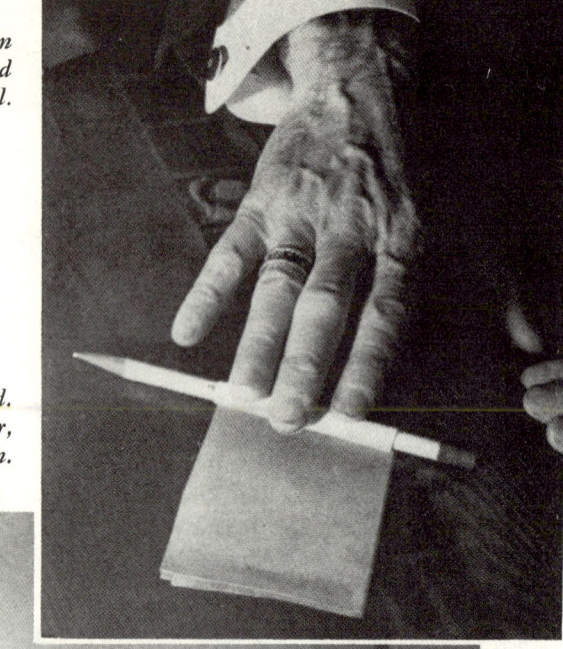

*The ingredients are mixed. W. T. Brannon, co-author, poses as the credulous victim.*

*Roll containing the bill is dipped into the mixture and saturated.*

*Impression is put into the machine and the thumbscrews tightened.*

*As a final flourish, the machine is carefully sealed with adhesive tape.*

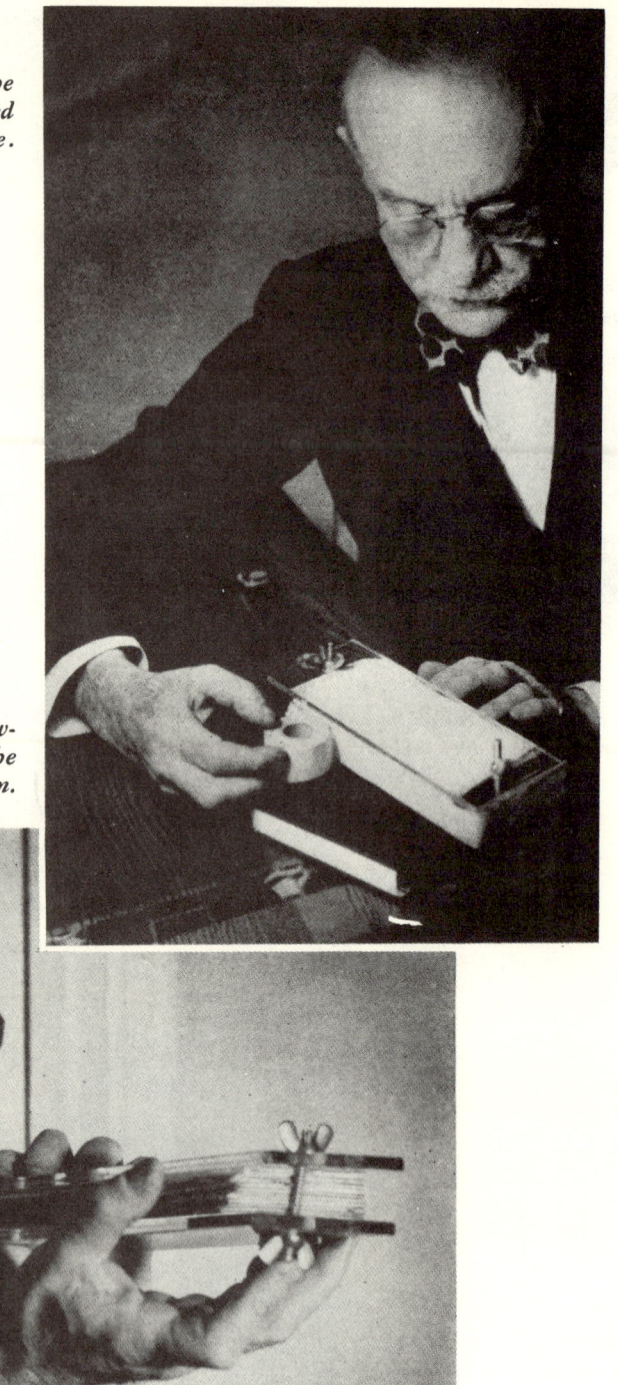

*Machine is held up showing that it is exactly the same on top and bottom.*

## Magic Money

the teller and said: "Would you give me quarters for these bills? I want them for my daughter's piggy bank."

"Of course," the teller replied and handed me eight quarters.

"Those bills are good, aren't they?" I asked.

"Sure," he said, making a close examination. "Why?"

"I just had them made," I replied, smiling.

The teller laughed. "They do smell funny," he remarked, "but I'd be glad to have a bushel like 'em."

Swartz, now convinced beyond a doubt, accompanied me back to Buck's place.

"Can we make some more of those bills?" he wanted to know.

"You can make as many as you like," Buck replied. "But for every one you make, you must have a new bill. It must be new — otherwise it won't reproduce. It can only be duplicated once. As soon as the gloss of a new bill is worn off it won't make an impression."

"Can you make larger bills just as easy?"

"Just as easy."

"Well, I've got $1,900," Swartz said. "Can we make $1,900 just like it?"

"Yes. The best way to do that is to make it in $100 denominations. That means you'll have to get nineteen new $100 bills from the bank."

"When can we do it?"

"When can you get the money?"

"As soon as I go to the Loop and back."

"Very well," said Buckminster. "I'll help you this afternoon."

In great jubilation, Swartz left for the bank. I went along with him. I wanted to be sure that he really did go to the bank rather than to the police. While he trusted us, I didn't trust him. While we were gone Buck got the wheels in motion for the next act. Everything was set when we got back from the bank.

"It would be a rather tedious process to make these impressions one at a time," Buck said. "The best way is to make all nineteen at the same time."

He took the nineteen new $100 bills and swabbed them all with the chemical. Then he placed each between two sheets of paper and put the whole thing in the machine. He had just finished putting the glass on and was about to insert the thumbscrews when there was a commotion at the door.

The door burst open and in walked two men in blue uniforms. They looked like policemen. They drew guns.

"So!" one boomed, a note of triumph in his voice. "At last we've caught you with the goods! Up with your hands, all of you."

"What's the meaning of this?" I demanded.

"I don't know who you are, sir, but this blackguard you're here with"—he motioned to Buckminster—"is a criminal that we've hunted from coast to coast. Wherever he goes a trail of new money follows. Are you two his accomplices?"

"No, no," I protested. "We're his innocent victims."

"Who are you?" one of the policemen asked Swartz.

"I'm a business man," he said, "and I haven't done anything wrong."

"That's your story. I think all three of you had better come along. We'll soon find out if you're in league with this crook."

"But officer," I protested, "we had nothing to do with this man's criminal activities. I am Dr. Henri Reuel. Maybe you have heard of me—mining engineer and scientist. I was just here to watch this man make an experiment."

One of the bluecoats lifted the glass top of the machine and flipped out some of the bills. "Looks to me like you were going to do some counterfeiting," he said.

I appeared amazed. "Why, officer, we know nothing about that money," I insisted. "Isn't that correct?"

"Absolutely," Swartz fervently agreed. "We never saw that money before."

"Well, in that case—"

"I'm sure you won't want to hold us, Officer," I put in.

"Okay. You two seem to be honest. But leave me your names and addresses. I'll want you for witnesses."

"Don't give your right name and address," I whispered to Swartz.

He gave them a phony name and address. I told them again that I was Dr. Henri Reuel and that they could reach me at the Palmer House. After they had jotted down this information, one of them said: "Alright, you can go. But be on hand when we need you."

## Magic Money

Swartz and I hurried out. I know he hated to leave his money, but he was so frightened that he made no fuss about it. We took a cab for about six blocks then changed to another.

"See that car back there?" said Swartz.

"What about it?"

"It's following us. They won't let us out of their sight."

"Forget about it," I advised. "Quick, get in this cab and we'll throw them off the trail."

We rode a great distance, but Swartz was still uneasy and convinced we were being followed. Finally I got him safely home. "I'd advise you to keep under cover for a couple of days."

"Don't worry," he responded. "I will!"

I have never seen a man so frightened. Perhaps he was involved in something else that was illegal and had a double fear of the law. I left him after promising that I wouldn't mention his name to anybody who questioned me.

I have told this episode as it appeared to Swartz. Now I will explain what really happened.

We didn't make a bill from the impressions we took. We just made it appear to Swartz that we did. Actually it is impossible as far as I know to print anything from the impressions.

The ten bills with which I had first snared Swartz's interest were dipped in creolin so there would be an odor to them. Creolin dries almost immediately after it is applied to currency, but the odor lingers. The ten bills, of course, were good.

The demonstration we gave was for the express purpose of convincing the victim we could duplicate money. Before we started we had two brand-new one dollar bills. Both had the same serial number except that one ended in a 3 and the other ended in 8. With a few deft strokes of a pen, the 3 had been changed to look like 8. So we apparently had two bills with the same number.

One of these was placed in the machine between two pieces of paper. The other Buckminster had in the palm of his hand. When Swartz handed him a new note, Buck examined it and apparently handed it back. Actually he performed some sleight-of-hand and gave Swartz the bill he was already holding. Swartz hadn't checked the serial number on his bill and, since one looks like another, he thought Buck gave him the same bill back.

Not only was he given an opportunity to check the serial number before we made the impression but the bill was given back to him and he was allowed to hold it while we apparently duplicated it. When he compared the two bills they looked exactly alike, including the serial numbers.

The impression we made was no trick. There is a glaze on all new bills. When a bill is swabbed with creolin an exact impression will come off and will be transferred to any absorbent paper — newsprint, preferably. But this can be done only once. As soon as that one impression is made, the chemical glaze is gone from the bill. The next time it wouldn't work.

To make the impression, the bill and paper have to be rolled on a board. Then before they are unrolled, they must be dipped in water. That was the reason for the basin of plain water.

The pan containing the "secret" chemicals was pure hocus-pocus. Its only purpose was to impress the victim. The first chemical poured into the pan was a solution of water and potassium permanganate. A half-dozen tablets dissolved in a bottle of water will create a dark-purple liquid.

The second chemical poured into the basin was bromo-seltzer. This made the liquid effervesce — a magic effect at any time. The final bottle contained spitfire, which flared and smoked and gave an even more magical effect. Swartz was not familiar with chemicals and was easily fooled. The con men dressed as cops fooled him too.

The success of this, like all the other schemes we executed, was in the build-up. Nothing is more important to a good con man. It was in the build-up that we convinced our victims we could actually reproduce money. Once we had done that the rest was easy.

We went through an elaborate build-up to get to James Hogan, an official of a bank in Indianapolis. He was also receiver for a number of banks that had failed. From our many stock deals we had learned that bankers at that time were nearly always the greatest dupes of easy money schemes.

We decided to get to Hogan through a man I will call Joe Danford,

## Magic Money

a former player for the Chicago White Sox, who operated the Hotel Chestnut in Fort Wayne, Indiana. The plan required a great deal of background work, and we started in Dubuque, Iowa.

Joe Danford was the heir to the Danford Wagon Works, which had lost business steadily after the advent of the automobile and had folded completely during the depression. But the name was still well known in Dubuque.

Buckminster and I went to Dubuque and in time became acquainted with one James Patch. Patch owned an iron mine and was one of the leading citizens of Dubuque. I introduced myself as Dr. Henri Reuel, the mining engineer and Buckminster as Mr. Kimball, my confidential secretary.

Patch was very friendly and took us down into the mine. We lunched and dined with him on several occasions before telling him that we were going to Washington to look up some data in the patent office.

"Washington?" he said. "Why, I have two daughters living in Washington."

"Is that so?" I replied, although we already knew about the daughters, that being our reason for cultivating him.

"Yes. Why don't you look them up while you're there? They will be glad to see someone who has just visited their old dad," he said proudly.

"We'll be glad to do that," I replied.

He supplied their address and said he would write them about our coming. Soon afterwards we left for the capital. Our business was not the patent office but to look up the Patch sisters, who proved to be two very attractive young women employed in government offices. We wined and dined them several evenings, thereby combining business and pleasure.

Two weeks later we left Washington and went back to Fort Wayne, where we registered at the Hotel Chestnut. We had been at the hotel for two days when I first became acquainted with Joe Danford, the owner. Our reconnaissance had already told us that Danford had purchased the hotel with money lent him by Hogan, the Indianapolis banker.

223

## "Yellow Kid" Weil

I made it a point to cultivate Danford's acquaintance. He was an amiable fellow and it was not hard to draw him into a conversation about the hotel business, which was his big interest in life. Our conversations together eventually became more personal.

"Are you a native of Fort Wayne?" I asked.

"No. I'm from Dubuque, Iowa. Did you ever hear of the Danford Wagon Works?"

"Of course. Were you ever connected with that?"

"I owned it until the automobile and the depression forced me out of business. Have you ever been in Dubuque?"

"Yes, for a short time. But we came here from Washington. And by the way, speaking of Dubuque, we were entertained by two charming young ladies from there who are now living in Washington. Maybe you know them?"

"I probably do," said Danford. "I know just about everybody from Dubuque."

"They were the Patch sisters," I said. "Their father owns an iron mine in Dubuque."

"The Patch sisters!" he exclaimed, "Why, I went to school with them."

"We enjoyed their company so much," I remarked. "They were most kind to Mr. Kimball and me."

"Mr. Kimball? Who is he?" Danford asked.

"He is my associate now. But for many years he was connected with the Bureau of Printing and Engraving. He's known as the 'Chemical Wizard.'"

"I'd like to meet him."

"I'll arrange it as soon as possible," I promised.

So in this manner we established our identity. We didn't want our authenticity questioned. Our having been friendly with the Patch sisters clinched that. Joe Danford was quite convinced we were the eminent men we claimed to be.

A couple of days later he was showing me about the hotel, proudly pointing out some refurbishing he had done, including the hanging of some oil paintings.

"I suppose those are prints?" I asked.

## Magic Money

"Yes, they're copies, but they're pretty good don't you think?"

"Excellent," I agreed. "But my associate, Mr. Kimball, could duplicate those by a special chemical process so you wouldn't be able to tell them from the originals."

"He must be good," said Danford. "Can he duplicate other things?"

"He can duplicate anything," I replied. "He has duplicated Liberty Bonds so even an expert couldn't tell which was the original and which was the duplicate."

"That's very interesting," muttered Danford. He was silent for a few moments, and I had a pretty good idea what he was thinking. He laughed and in an offhand manner said, "I suppose he can duplicate money, too?"

"Of course. That's very easy."

"Could he make duplicates that would pass a banker's inspection?" he persisted.

"He could," I replied, "but I doubt very much if he would."

"Do you suppose he'd let me see him do it?" Danford was eager now.

"I'm not making any promises," I replied. "But I'll talk to him. He has a great humility and is rather reticent about any display of his chemical genius. But I might get him to put on a demonstration for you, if I ask it as a special favor."

"I certainly would be interested in seeing it," Danford said enthusiastically.

"I'll do my best to persuade him to show you the trick," I told him. "However, you mustn't tell anybody else about it."

Buckminster knew what was going on, but we decided to give Danford a couple of days to become impatient. Finally I informed him that "Mr. Kimball" had reluctantly agreed.

We went through the same routine as with Swartz. When it was completed Danford appeared to have two bills with the same serial number.

"It sure does look good," he glowed. "How can you tell that it will pass?"

"For the fun of it take it to the bank," I suggested, "and have it examined."

"I've got to run up to Indianapolis," he said. "Suppose I take it to one of the banks there?"

"That's all right," Buckminster replied. "It would pass if you took it to the Treasury."

Hardly able to conceal his elation, Danford took his bill and left. We knew that he was going to Indianapolis to see Hogan. That's what we had expected and wanted him to do.

He returned the following morning, and Hogan was with him. He brought the banker up to our rooms.

After introductions, the banker said: "Joe showed me the bill you made."

Buck acted startled and looked accusingly at Danford. "I thought you understood that my little experiment was confidential and only done as a personal favor," he said with exasperation.

"Oh, don't worry," said Hogan. "I haven't told anybody."

"Perhaps not," Buckminster said. "But I wouldn't want it talked around that I am counterfeiting money, which is not the case. I merely conducted a private experiment."

"Your secret is safe with me," Hogan assured him.

"That's a relief," Buck sighed.

"Just as a matter of interest, would you mind answering some questions?" the banker asked.

"I'll try to answer them."

"Could you duplicate a bill of higher denomination as easily as you did a one dollar bill?"

"Of course."

"Could you duplicate more than one at a time?"

"Yes," Buck replied. "I could duplicate as many as I could get in the machine."

"How many would that be?" Hogan persisted.

"Oh, fifty or sixty, I suppose. As I told you, I have done this only as an experiment and I never counted the number of bills the machine would hold. But I imagine it would hold sixty easily enough."

"Let us suppose," said Hogan, "That I had sixty one thousand dollar bills. Could they all be duplicated so they wouldn't be detected?"

"Yes, I think so."

## Magic Money

"What about the serial numbers?"

"They would be the same as on the original notes."

"And that's where you would run into trouble," said Hogan. "Thousand dollar bills are not very common. Banks keep records of them. If two sets with the same numbers turned up, the bank would know that one of them was counterfeit and the Treasury would be notified. How would you get around that?"

"Oh, in the case of one thousand dollar bills that would be comparatively simple, since you ask me," Buck replied with a smile. "You remember that ocean liner that was sunk not long ago?"

"Yes."

"Well, it carried $200,000 in currency, all in thousand dollar bills. It so happens that I am the only person who knows those numbers. I was working in the Bureau of Printing and Engraving at the time."

"But how could you get those numbers on bills you duplicated?"

"That would be easy enough. I could put the numbers on a strip of paper and paste the strip over the number on the bill to be duplicated. Thus when the duplicate was made it would have another number. The strip of paper could be removed from the original bill and you would have two identical bills, but with different numbers."

"Excellent!" crowed Hogan, rubbing his hands.

"I beg your pardon," put in Buckminster. "Just what are you leading up to?"

"I'll put my cards on the table," said Hogan. "You aren't a wealthy man, are you?"

"No."

"But you'd like to have enough money to put up your own laboratory, wouldn't you?"

"Yes," Buck admitted, "more than anything else in the world."

"I need money, too. I lost a considerable sum in the stock market crash of 1929. I have several notes at the bank that I must pay. Suppose I furnish the $1,000 bills and you duplicate them, using the numbers that you alone have. I'll dispose of the duplicates through my bank. We'll split fifty-fifty. You will get your laboratory and I pay off my notes."

"Oh, I couldn't go into a scheme like that," Buck protested. "Why, that would be counterfeiting."

"In a way, yes," Hogan replied. "But actually you'd just be restoring to circulation the $200,000 that was lost on that boat."

"I can't do it," Buck said firmly. "As you know, all employees of the Bureau of Printing and Engraving are under constant surveillance, even after they quit the Bureau. They would be sure to catch me."

Up to this time I had been silent, as had Danford.

"I'll tell you what," I proposed. "I'll help Mr. Hogan. You can remain in the background. When we have the money duplicated I'll turn over your share to you. I'd like very much to see you get that laboratory."

Deacon Buckminster got up and began pacing the floor. Occasionally he paused to rub his hand on the back of his neck.

"Dr. Reuel," he said, "I don't know what to say. You know that I have been honest all my life."

"Yes, I know," I replied. "Too honest for your own good. Look at you now. You have your heart set on a fine laboratory. But you can't have it simply because you have given so much of your life to the government at starvation wages."

"At least I sleep well at night. I have nothing on my conscience, which means a great deal."

"You'll sleep even better with your own laboratory," I said.

"My own laboratory!" The Deacon paused in his pacing. There was a dreamy, faraway look in his eyes. A smile played on his lips. He stood thus for several moments. "My own laboratory!" he repeated, and it was as if his own words had snapped him back into the land of reality. He resumed his pacing, his face stern. "I must have time to think it over," he said finally. "I haven't much, but what I have has been earned by honest toil. I can't make such a move on the spur of the moment."

"When are you planning to leave?" I asked the banker.

"I'm driving back to Indianapolis this evening," Hogan replied.

"Maybe you can decide before Mr. Hogan leaves," I suggested to Buckminster.

"Maybe," he replied.

Hogan and Danford left. I ordered lunch sent up because "Mr.

## Magic Money

Kimball desires seclusion." We spent the afternoon playing cards while Buck was supposedly making his big decision.

At five o'clock I called Hogan and told him that Mr. Kimball had finally yielded, but that he declined to do the work himself. He would furnish all the equipment and I would do it. This was satisfactory to Hogan, and I arranged to meet him at his home in Indianapolis the following Tuesday.

Buck and I registered at the Claypool in Indianapolis, and on Tuesday evening I went out to Hogan's house. I had a kit in which I carried the bottles and the machine. I also had a series of numbers. These had actually been clipped from good currency though they were supposed to be the numbers of the bills that had been lost on the boat.

Hogan led me into his private den, and I set out my paraphernalia on the table. I showed him the numbers I had.

"They're perfect," he said. "They look just like the numbers on good money. How did he do it?"

"Oh, Mr. Kimball has the right kind of paper and he used a numbering machine. He said they must look exactly like the Treasury's numbers."

"Fine, fine," said Hogan, rubbing his hands.

He gave me the money he had brought from the bank — fifty-seven crisp, new $1,000 bills. I pasted a different number on each one. Then I swabbed each with creolin and dipped each bill in the hocus-pocus solution. But I said nothing about making impressions.

Instead I placed each bill between two sheets of paper the exact size of currency and put them all in the machine. Then I tightened the thumbscrews and sealed the sides and ends of the machine with adhesive tape.

"We'd better leave it here overnight," I said, leaving the machine on the table. "I'll come back in the morning and we'll take out the old bills and a complete set of new ones."

Hogan agreed to this and ushered me out. I might say here that a strange thing about the money-making scheme is that the victims seem to forget how it was done the first time. In the demonstration we always completed a bill in twenty minutes. Yet when we repeated the performance it was to take all night. Anyhow Hogan didn't question it.

The following morning when I returned Buckminster was with me. In his overcoat pocket he carried another machine. It looked just like the one I had left in Hogan's den.

As soon as Hogan admitted us, we went straight to the den. I looked at the machine, and even before I had touched it I said, accusingly: "You've tampered with this machine!"

That, I knew, was a pretty safe guess. The victim is always tempted to open it up and see if his money is still there and if the duplication is taking place.

Hogan said nothing but watched me while I removed the adhesive tape and loosened the thumbscrews. The money was all there but of course there was no new money. I looked sharply at the banker.

"I did peek into it last night," he admitted.

"And spoiled the whole thing," I grunted. "Now we'll have to start all over again."

"I'll do it myself," Buckminster offered. "This time no tampering. Perhaps you didn't know it but this process works the same as a time exposure on a film. When you opened it up last night and exposed it to the light you ruined the sensitivity of the chemicals."

This was a lot of hokum, but it sounded plausible enough. Buck removed all the money from the machine, swabbed all the bills again, dipped them in the solution, and placed each between fresh sheets of paper. Then he put them in the machine and started to adjust the thumbscrews.

"Take this pan and get me some fresh water," he told me.

I picked up the pan and looked questioningly at the banker.

"Get it from the bathroom," he said. "It's over there. I'll show you."

He went to the door and pointed out the bathroom. His back was turned away from Buckminster for only a few moments. But that gave him time to switch machines. When Hogan turned around Buck was still adjusting thumbscrews. What Hogan didn't know was that they were on a different machine — one that contained only blank paper and no money at all.

## Magic Money

I brought the pan of water, and Buck submerged the whole machine. He sealed the ends and sides with adhesive tape and put the machine down on the table.

"Don't touch it for at least eight hours," he instructed the banker. "We'll be back this evening and your money will be made by then.'

We knew that Hogan wouldn't open the machine this time. We left — and with us went the machine containing the fifty-seven thousand dollar bills. By the time the banker began wondering what had happened to us we were several hundred miles from Indianapolis.

If Hogan ever reported us to the authorities we never heard about it. But we did hear more about Hogan. His defalcations ran into big figures and he was eventually indicted by the government for embezzling more than $300,000, not only from his own bank but from those for which he was receiver. He died before he was ever tried.

## 20. The Hotel Martinique

BUCKMINSTER AND I HAD ACCUMULATED CONSIDERABLE CASH AND property. I had real estate, and securities amounting to more than a million dollars. As I had done on numerous other occasions, I began to consider the advisability of going into a legitimate business. My wife seconded this with great enthusiasm.

Among the things I had always wanted to do was to operate a fine hotel. Now seemed an excellent opportunity. My record in Chicago was clean. The police had no complaints against me and could not stop me if I tried something legitimate.

My wife and I looked around and decided to buy a hostelry on the North Side. It was the Hotel Huntington, a six-story modern building with 215 rooms. I sold much of my property at a loss in order to swing the purchase. I decided to change the name to the Shenandoah.

The next day I was in the Loop when I noticed a big headline: SHENANDOAH BLOWN UP. I thought it was my hotel, but after I had bought the paper I learned it was the famous dirigible that had blown up.

Perhaps I should have known then that my hotel venture was jinxed. I did change the name again, this time to the Hotel Martinique. One of my early projects was a landscaped roof garden. I had big plans, but perhaps I didn't know enough about the hotel business.

In connection with it, I operated a restaurant and a laundry. One of my big attractions was a large stock of imported liquors. This was during prohibition and many entertainers — now celebrities whom I shall not embarrass by mentioning names — reserved rooms where they could stage parties without having to register. I furnished the liquor.

## *The Hotel Martinique*

The news spread rapidly that Joe Weil was running a hotel. Soon swarms of con men, swindlers and other criminals were checking in. Some were quiet enough and would have been good tenants in any hotel. But most were small fry who had no conception of honor or decency.

They made plenty of trouble and gave the hotel a bad name. When my income began to drop I learned that many of them were taking all their meals in the restaurant and signing the checks rather than paying cash. Most of the others were having their laundry done and not paying for it. I soon discovered that the manager was allowing some of the guests to "lay stiffs" — that is, to cash worthless checks — at the desk. I myself was responsible for one such case.

A man I did not know had checked in. About three days later a girl moved in with him. That evening two men from the Detective Bureau came in and asked if I had such a guest. I was not inclined to be cooperative and denied it. They left.

I went upstairs and called the man into the hall, not wishing to embarrass him in front of the girl. "A couple of detectives are looking for you," I told him. "They said you laid $300 worth of stiffs at the Edgewater Beach Hotel. You'd better pack up and get out."

"That's darned decent of you." He thanked me and promptly moved out. You can imagine my consternation when the manager told me the next day that this guest had cashed $100 worth of bad checks at the desk!

The hoodlums often staged parties and became noisy. The permanent guests, who paid their bills on time, eyed them distastefully and began to move out. As these people vacated rooms, more criminals moved in; thugs of various descriptions, safe-crackers, and robbers. Some I knew by sight and many I did not know at all.

Before I realized what was happening the underworld was regarding the Martinique as a hide-out. I soon learned I was expected to cover up for criminals whose only relation to me was that we had both operated outside the law.

The police heard about my guests. Though I had started out with the intention of running a legitimate business I was soon hounded by them. No charges were pending against me and I had nothing to fear, but the police were not convinced that I had not launched the whole thing as a hide-out for criminals.

My natural reaction was to cover up for some of my former friends who had moved in. They repaid my generosity by regaling me with hard luck stories and by refusing to pay their bills. They also refused to move out. Even if I had wanted to, I wasn't in a position to seek the help of the police. I was stuck with them.

But the expenses of operating the hotel went on while the income dwindled steadily. To keep my head above water, I sold all my remaining property.

In a few months, I had put $750,000 into the venture. Naturally I had no desire to lose this, and I looked desperately for some means of salvaging it. I still hoped I would be able to get rid of the worst elements and make the Martinique a paying proposition.

That eventually led to my downfall. I met a man who operated a gang of bank thieves. In these robberies he often acquired gold coins and negotiable securities such as Liberty Bonds. My first deal with him was for a sack of twenty-dollar gold pieces. He offered them to me for so much per pound. I bought them on the weight basis, then deposited them in my bank at the face value of twenty dollars each. He had stolen them from a bank in downstate Illinois, and was willing to sell them at a bargain price. But nobody could identify them, and I had no trouble. I made $980 on the deal.

Then he offered me some negotiable bonds. I bought them and turned them over through a third party for a profit of $35,000. I did a thriving business as a bond broker, selling through a third man named Hanson. He had connections with a legitimate broker and was always able to sell the bonds I brought him. From these deals I made good profits and was able to keep my hotel going.

Then I bought $750,000 worth of bonds, which I later learned, had come from the Rondout mail robbery. I still had these in my possession when Hanson was questioned by the police and postal authorities. He told them that all the bonds he had sold had come from me.

They came to my hotel and found the bonds in my room. I was

## *The Hotel Martinique*

arrested, charged with participating in the mail robbery, and was convicted. I lost the hotel and, with it, my last real opportunity to get into a legitimate business.

## 21. The Leavenworth Country Club

More than $2,000,000 in cash and negotiable securities were taken in the mail robbery at Rondout, Illinois. I had no idea who had committed this robbery. It was well known among con-men that I never participated in any sort of banditry.

Nevertheless, the possession of the $750,000 in bonds stolen at Rondout implicated me, and I was tried with the others who had been corralled. I was sentenced to five years in the federal penitentiary at Leavenworth. I entered that institution in 1926.

I soon learned that in Leavenworth, as in any other place you can name, money talks. With little difficulty I managed to be assigned to the prison hospital as secretary to the prison physician.

The doctor was an inmate who had been sent up for a ten-year stretch on a charge of using the mails to defraud. He was a tall, kind-faced, mild-mannered man who was friendly to everybody and who exercised the utmost tolerance towards the prisoners. His name was Dr. Frederick A. Cook. He was, of course, the noted Arctic explorer.

Though Dr. Cook offered no alibi, I learned the circumstances of his conviction. He had permitted his name to be used by a group of promoters who were selling Texas oil lands. After a considerable amount of the land had been sold, the charge was made that there was no oil, and that the land was practically worthless.

Instead of being held as an accessory, Dr. Cook was charged with being the leader of this group and with using the mails to defraud. Sentenced to ten years in Leavenworth, he tried to make the best of it.

## The Leavenworth Country Club

It was a pleasure to serve Dr. Cook, and I became one of his staunch supporters. There are still thousands who believe in him. I became interested enough to make my own investigation. It was enough to satisfy me that Dr. Cook was all he claimed.

Dr. Cook had been the toast of the civilized world for a few days after he arrived in Copenhagen and announced that he had discovered the North Pole. His fame was short-lived, however. For he was followed by Commodore Robert A. Peary, who claimed to be the first to reach the Pole and who branded as false every one of Dr. Cook's claims. That started a controversy which raged for months; but Peary was backed by a powerful group in the United States and Cook had no support except for a few private individuals.

In time Peary and his friends succeeded in discrediting Dr. Cook. The latter became regarded as an imposter and a charlatan. He returned home disheartened and disgraced. He tried to present his case, but the opposition was too strong. He wrote a few books in which he described his experiences in detail. These were widely read and increased the number of his supporters, but his account of the discovery of the Pole was never officially accepted. Only one of his accomplishments has remained unchallenged, even by his opponents: he was the first man to discover a preventive for scurvy, perhaps the most dreaded disease of the far north.

My own research convinced me Dr. Cook actually did discover the Pole. My association with him convinced me there was nothing about him that was faked. I became his friend, just as everybody else in Leavenworth was his friend.

Dr. Cook had no knowledge of the things I am about to relate and no part in them.

There was one physician — I shall call him Dr. Lowe — who was in charge of the medical records. Every inmate who was eligible had an application on file with the Parole Board. Before the Board considered an applicant it required a physical examination, the most important part of which was a Wassermann test. No convict with syphilis was eligible for parole.

Dr. Lowe received the records of these tests, and in each he inserted an entry indicating that the inmate's test had been positive.

## "Yellow Kid" Weil

Then before the record went to the Parole Board he contacted the inmate and told him what the record showed. For a consideration he was ready to alter the entry to show that the test had been *negative!*

His price was scaled to the ability of the inmate to pay, from ten dollars up. A certain brewer from Milwaukee had been sent up for violation of the Prohibition laws. When Dr. Lowe learned he was eligible for parole he made an entry indicating that the man's Wassermann test had been 4-plus. The brewer had to pay him $10,000 to change it. A similar fee was extracted from a St. Paul banker.

Dr. Lowe stayed at Leavenworth only long enough to get a good stake. When he pulled out he had saved $100,000 from his "practice."

A guard named Barnum also had a lucrative racket, although it did not pay off as well as Dr. Lowe's. He had charge of the parole rooms. These were not in official use most of the time and Barnum rented them out to convicts who could pay.

He also operated a messenger service to the outside, and a man with money could have almost anything he desired brought to him in the parole room. Actually, for the wealthy convicts — and there were many, such as bootleggers, racketeers, and gangsters — Leavenworth was more like a gentleman's club.

Once a week a Christian Science worker called at Leavenworth with free cigarettes for the inmates. At first he had only a few cartons, but as time went on he brought in larger quantities. These cigarettes were contributed to the Christian Science worker, for this purpose. One Good Samaritan donated large numbers every week with specific instructions that they be given to the inmates of Leavenworth.

A man named Rubin was in charge of the distribution of the cigarettes, which were all turned over to him. As it later developed, these were all loaded with morphine. The Good Samaritan was a dope peddler employed by Rubin, who sold the cigarettes to addicts in the prison. The Christian Science worker acted quite innocently and in good faith.

One day Barnum disappeared and another man took his place. The new guard was a very pleasant young man. He offered all of Barnum's services and with a smile. It was not long before he learned the secrets of the different rackets I have described.

## The Leavenworth Country Club

Then the lid was clamped on. There was a far-reaching investigation, and the whole prison was cleaned up. The new man was an agent of the Federal Bureau of Investigation and he didn't miss a thing. Life in Leavenworth was much tougher after that.

For my part, my time was up and I was let out.

Dr. Cook was released from Leavenworth in 1931 when it was discovered that the supposedly fraudulent oil lands he had helped to sell were far more valuable than the price they had been sold for.

Ted Leitzell, Chicago author, one of Dr. Cook's most ardent supporters, began a campaign to clear his name shortly after he was released from Leavenworth. Through documentary evidence Leitzell established that Dr. Cook had been the first to reach the North Pole. But his efforts to make this official were fruitless. A presidential pardon for Dr. Cook on the mail-fraud charge was sought and was denied. But Leitzel, who had been an Arctic explorer as well as an author, never stopped trying.

The presidential pardon was granted to Dr. Cook by Franklin D. Roosevelt just before Dr. Cook died in 1939.

## 22. The Comtesse and The Kid

THOUGH THE POLICE WERE WATCHING ME MORE THAN USUAL after my release from Leavenworth, Buckminster and I teamed up again and worked the stock swindle. It was shortly after we had netted a particularly good score that we decided to take an ocean voyage. I had posed as Dr. Henri Reuel and Buck as Mr. Kimball. When we heard that our victims were looking for these two men, both of whom were very real people, we decided the climate of Europe might be healthier for a while.

"Let's go to London," Buckminster suggested. "Jimmy Regan ought to have something lined up."

Jimmy Regan operated a café which catered to American tourists. His real business, however, was to act as an international clearing house for con men. Regan always had information about wealthy Americans who were touring Europe — how much money they had, where they were stopping, their hobbies, and so on.

This sounded good. After having our passports validated in Washington, we proceeded to New York, where we booked passage to Liverpool on the *Columbus*.

As soon as we boarded ship and even before she had weighed anchor, I went to our stateroom and went to bed, for I was feeling ill. The Deacon, who had a sturdy constitution, felt fine. He took his meals regularly at the captain's table, a privilege to which our accommodations entitled us.

For me the first twenty-four hours passed miserably. On the second day Buck, who was enjoying the voyage, brought the ship's doctor to see me. After an examination he advised me to drink three bot-

## The Comtesse and The Kid

tles of Pilsener beer. This seemed strange advice, but I followed it and soon began to feel better. I ordered some food sent to the cabin.

That night Buck was gay. "You don't know what you're missing," he told me. "I've been dining with the most exquisite woman —"

"The Queen, no doubt," I broke in with heavy sarcasm.

"No, but she is a member of the English nobility — Lady Agatha Stebbins."

"How did you find that out?"

"The captain told me. He later introduced me to her, and she was my companion at dinner."

"I suppose you've dated her for breakfast?"

"I certainly have."

"Is this business or pleasure?"

"Maybe both," said Buck. "She certainly looks like a million dollars."

"You and your romances!" I still wasn't feeling very good.

"You might change your mind when I tell you about her companion," said Buck good-naturedly.

"What about her?"

"I don't know very much," he admitted, "except that she is petite and gorgeous. She spends most of her time in her cabin and there is something mysterious about her."

I still wasn't interested. After breakfast the next morning the Deacon was more enthusiastic than ever. "Lady Agatha asked about you and why you remained in your cabin. I told her you were a renowned engineer who had acquired a large fortune and that you were occupied with matters of business. She seemed very anxious to meet you and told me to invite you to dinner."

"Did you find out any more about her?"

"Yes. She's the widow of an officer in the Coldstream Guards."

"What about the girl?"

"She's more mysterious than ever. She is traveling under the name of Miss Viola Martin, but I'm sure that's a phony."

"Maybe she's a con woman," I suggested.

"Don't be silly," Buck scoffed. "She's an aristocrat if I ever saw one."

"I'd like to meet this mysterious girl."

"You will," said Buck. "Lady Agatha said she would bring her to dinner this evening if you would come."

That evening Buck and I dressed in dinner jackets and went to the salon. At the captain's table two women were waiting for us. One was a very attractive woman of about forty. She had brown eyes and auburn hair and was dressed in excellent taste. Though she was not slender, she carried herself with dignity and her slight plumpness was not unbecoming.

The young woman with her was, as Buck had said, beautiful. She had black eyes, long lashes, and coal black hair. She was just over five feet and slender. But she was dressed very plainly. She wore a heavy black veil and a fine tailored suit. My guess was she was about twenty-five.

After the Deacon had introduced us we sat down to dinner. Lady Agatha talked with animation and so did Buck. But the girl, who became my companion at the table, had very little to say. At the older woman's suggestion I related some of my experiences as a mining engineer in remote corners of the world. This was easy, since I was posing as Dr. Reuel. I merely appropriated some of Dr. Reuel's adventures and told them as my own.

"Doctor, you must have had a fascinating career," said Lady Stebbins. "Don't you think so, Viola?"

The girl nodded briefly, but said nothing. Dinner had been completed and we were drinking champagne.

"Let's go up on deck and promenade," the Englishwoman suggested.

"An excellent idea," agreed the Deacon, who was obviously infatuated with the woman.

For my part I was attracted to the girl, and this seemed a good way to get better acquainted. She went along, rather unenthusiastically.

On deck Lady Agatha paused. "Mr. Kimball, suppose you and I go this way, and let the Doctor and Viola go the other way. We'll meet later."

The Deacon acquiesced with a broad grin. Nothing could have suited him better. It pleased me, too.

The girl and I strolled slowly down the port promenade. It was a moonlit night, made for romance. But the girl's response was re-

## The Comtesse and The Kid

served and monosyllabic. Finally we paused at the railing and gazed out over the shimmering water. Miss Viola Martin raised her veil over her hat. She was softening.

"Doctor," she said, "are you still active as a mining engineer?"

That wasn't very romantic. But it was the most she had said all evening.

"No," I replied. "I've retired from active work."

"But you do retain an interest in your mines?"

"Yes, I have large holdings in several copper mines in Arizona. And I act in an advisory capacity for Standard Oil and Anaconda."

"How interesting. Do tell me about it, Doctor."

Encouraged, I told her the highlights in my supposed career — actually the career of Dr. Henri Reuel. I concluded by mentioning the books Dr. Reuel had written — in which my own photograph had been bound as frontispiece to make it appear I was the author.

"I am very much interested in mining," she said. "Would you mind if I read your books?"

"I should be delighted," I replied. "I'd be very happy if you would accept an autographed copy of each as a gift."

"That would be splendid," she smiled at last. "You must be very wealthy, Doctor."

I admitted that I had acquired a considerable fortune and told her some of the details, all fictitious but quite convincing. She listened attentively for an hour. When I had told her all about myself I tried again to draw her out, but with no success.

She spoke perfect English, but there was a trace of a French accent and occasionally a French word or phrase slipped into her conversation. I was quite convinced Viola Martin was not her right name, but my efforts to find out anything were futile. She talked again in monosyllables and pulled the veil down over her face.

We resumed our stroll and met the Deacon and Lady Agatha. I proposed a nightcap in the salon, but the girl declined, pleading fatigue. We saw them to their stateroom, bidding them good night after inviting them to breakfast with us the next morning.

"Well, what do you think?" asked the Deacon, after we had retired to our stateroom.

243

## "Yellow Kid" Weil

"That girl is beautiful," I admitted. "But she's as cold as a marble statue. And I still think that name, Viola Martin, is a phony."

"Leave it to me," said Buck. "I'll find out. Lady Agatha likes me."

"Looks to me like it's mutual," I said. "You fawned over her like an eighteen-year-old."

Buck grinned good-naturedly. "I do sort of like her," he admitted.

My belief that the girl was French was partially confirmed the following morning. As they approached the table where we waited the girl was talking volubly to the other woman in French — in which I too am versed. However, as soon as they saw us the girl quickly returned to English.

She was more friendly now. I gave her copies of the books and she thanked me profusely. We strolled several times on the promenade deck and conversed in generalities. I tried to steer the conversation into personal channels, but when I did I got nowhere. Meanwhile Buck got along well with the older woman.

Sometimes an ocean voyage can be tedious, but this one seemed very short. Both Buck and I were sorry to see it end. However, the two women were going to London also and agreed to permit us to keep in touch with them. We went to the Savoy, while they registered at the Grosvenor House.

The next day the Deacon lunched with Her Ladyship at Romano's. The Deacon's infatuation had increased, and she seemed very fond of him. He felt they were close enough now to ask her about the girl.

After some hesitation she finally said: "This is confidential and I haven't told anybody else. I rely on you to tell nobody but the Doctor. Viola Martin is not her right name and she is traveling incognito. Actually she is the Comtesse de Paris."

"That doesn't surprise me," Buck replied. "But why must she travel incognito? Is she afraid of swindlers?"

"Oh, no," said Lady Stebbins. "Her brother, the Duke d'Orleans, is the last of the Bourbons and the rightful heir to the French throne. He and a group of his supporters became very active in a secret movement to revive the throne and restore the Bourbons. But political intrigue in France is dangerous, particularly since this is a plot to overthrow the government.

## The Comtesse and The Kid

"Through some traitor, details of the movement became known to the authorities. The Duke and his supporters were arrested and convicted of trying to overthrow the government. He was sentenced to spend the rest of his life on Devil's Island. But he took an appeal to the high court and is now free on bail pending their decision.

"We have no hope that the high court will act in favor of the Duke. That's why Jeanne — the Comtesse — made a trip to America. There she saw certain influential people who, she hopes, will intercede for her brother. She has enlisted the support of some very powerful people in the United States. Now she is trying to do the same in London. But she must go about it quietly and without publicity."

The Deacon reported this to me in the afternoon. I had been emotionally intrigued by the girl, partly because of her beauty and partly because of the aura of mystery that surrounded her. I was even more so now.

That evening I called at the Grosvenor House where she was registered as Miss Viola Martin. But she wasn't in. The next morning I was more successful. After some hesitation, she accepted my invitation to luncheon.

I took her to a Hungarian restaurant near Grosvenor Square. Though she had on a different outfit, her clothes were as conservative as before. There was just one difference — the exciting fragrance of French perfume.

As I held a chair for her at the table, I said, "Comtesse, allow me."

She looked up quickly.

"Then — you know?"

"Yes. I know."

She sighed. It was a weary sigh as of one who is very tired. When she looked across the table at me there was pleading in her eyes.

"I should have known I couldn't deceive a man who knows so much about the ways of the world," she murmured. "Have you told anybody else?"

"Of course not."

"I hope I can rely on you not to," she said, again with that pleading look.

I assured her that her secret was safe with me.

"It's a relief to have you know," she sighed. "Now I won't have to keep up the pretense of being shy and reserved. By nature I am vivacious and gay. It's just that I have to be very careful of strangers."

"I understand perfectly, my dear," I said. Suddenly the waiter was there. I gave him our orders. "Please feel free to tell me anything you want to. I assure you it will go no further."

"I'm sure it won't," she replied, smiling. Her voice was somehow different. There was more animation in it, less restraint. Her whole manner implied that she had been relieved of a great burden. "It will be nice," she continued, "to have someone I can trust, someone I can turn to for advice. I hope you won't mind if I cry on your shoulder occasionally."

I assured her that would be a pleasure for me — as indeed it would. Then she told me the whole story. Her brother, the Duke d'Orleans, had no strong desire to be enthroned in France. But he had been swayed by his supporters, a group of noblemen who longed for the glory of the court. He had finally agreed to lead the revolution. The plot had been nipped when an informer had turned over details and names to the authorities.

"Poor Ric was tried as the leader and was sentenced to banishment on Devil's Island. Most of the agitators were either acquitted or given light fines."

She told of the appeal to the high court and her despair that the duke would be freed. "Of course," she said, "he's at liberty now on bail. But he's under constant surveillance. If it were not for that, he might have a chance of escaping France."

Then she told me of her trip to America, where she had contacted high officials of the United States, many of whom readily promised to do what they could do to aid the duke.

"The British government is plebeian and conservative," she said. "There isn't much chance of help from the politicians. But there are some very influential men in the nobility. After talking to some of them I have decided to change my plans. I think it is better if Richard can escape and come to England. From here he can go to America. He can start a new life or at least remain there until it is safe to return to France."

## The Comtesse and The Kid

"Do you think that will succeed?"

"I am very hopeful. A very powerful British peer — I hope you will forgive me if I don't tell you his name — has agreed to arrange it. The gendarmes who are constantly watching Richard will allow him to escape to Belgium. He will make his way to the Channel coast where a plane will be waiting to transport him to England."

"I hope you'll let me assist in any way I can," I offered.

"Your advice will be very valuable," she said, "and I shan't hesitate to ask it." She smiled at me across the table, extended her hand. "Some day, Doctor — perhaps soon — I can laugh and be gay again. Until that day comes I must be circumspect."

I assured her I understood. Thereafter we were together often. We dined many times at the Hungarian restaurant. On other occasions the four of us, Lady Agatha and the Deacon, the Comtesse and I, were together.

One night after we had attended the theatre we were at Romano's for supper. We were drinking champagne and Buck had just toasted Lady Stebbins' health when the Comtesse stood up and clutched at her bosom.

"Oh, bother!" she exclaimed. "My necklace has broken!" She caught the necklace in her hands, but some of the pearls scattered on the table. We retrieved them as quickly as we could and handed them to the Comtesse.

She held them in her cupped hands and looked at me rather helplessly. "I don't know what to do now," she said. "Do you suppose you could have them restrung for me, Doctor?"

"Yes, I know a good jeweler," I replied. "But are you willing to entrust them to me?"

"Of course."

"Then I shall be happy to attend to it." She handed me the pearls and I put them away in a special compartment of my wallet.

The following morning Buck and I went to the shop of a jeweler located near our tailor's in Old Bond Street. He took them for restringing and said they would be ready by midafternoon. When we went back for them I paid the bill and Buck asked the jeweler how much the necklace was worth.

## "Yellow Kid" Weil

"About 8,000 pounds," the jeweler said. "That would be $40,000 in American money."

I returned the necklace to the Comtesse that evening when I called for her at the Grosvenor House.

At dinner she told me her negotiations with the British peer were proceeding satisfactorily and that she expected her brother to make his escape within the next two weeks.

About a week later Buck, Lady Agatha, and I took an excursion to Ostend, Belgium, for the races. We urged the Comtesse to go, but she declined.

"I am too well known on the continent," she said. "In spite of my plain clothes and my heavy veil I am afraid I would be recognized." Then she added: "Besides I have a very important engagement. Our plans are almost complete. I expect Richard will be free and be with me in London in another week."

We went to the races without her. I enjoyed the outing. Buck was so enraptured by his feminine companion that he hardly knew what was going on. I placed a small bet on each race but didn't win. That didn't bother me though, for I had long ago learned that you can't beat the horses by betting on them. We returned to London after a very interesting excursion.

A few days later when we called at the Grosvenor House for the two women we found them very excited. The Comtesse had finally arranged her brother's escape from France.

"If all goes well, he will be here tomorrow night," glowed the Comtesse.

"That's wonderful," I said. "Certainly this calls for a celebration."

But the Comtesse seemed far from happy. Instead she was weeping quietly.

"What's the matter?" I asked. "Aren't you happy that your long quest is about at an end."

"Oh I am," she said tearfully. She lifted her long lashes and looked up at me with those big eyes that pleaded for understanding. But I wasn't quite sure what they asked me to understand.

"You might as well tell them, Jeanne," said Lady Stebbins. "After all, they are our dearest friends."

## The Comtesse and The Kid

"Well," the Comtesse said hesitantly, dabbing at her eyes with a dainty handkerchief. "I suppose I might as well tell you. The cost of preparing Richard's escape has been enormous. The bribes to the gendarmes, the Belgian officials, and the man who will pilot the plane, cost much more than I had anticipated. Agatha — Lady Stebbins — very generously gave me all the money she will have until she receives the income from her investments. I had to use it all."

She hesitated and Lady Stebbins urged her to continue.

"Oh, all right. I might as well get right to the point. We are temporarily but quite definitely financially embarrassed. We haven't a shilling between us." Then, as I started to speak: "Oh, we're not paupers. My brother and I have a large fortune in France. Richard will bring ample funds with him. But unfortunately I have some obligations to meet tomorrow morning. I have nothing to meet them with." She dabbed at her eyes and smiled feebly. "But I don't see why I should bore you with my troubles — "

The Deacon and I were both on our feet. We spoke almost in unison: "You must permit us to help you."

"But I couldn't think of such a thing," the Comtesse quickly protested.

"We insist," I said. "After all, it would be only a temporary loan."

"Yes," the Comtesse agreed. "Richard will be here tomorrow night and I can repay you then."

"Will ten thousand dollars — two thousand pounds — be of any use to you?" I asked.

"It will be a life saver," the Comtesse blushed. "But — "

"But what?"

"I will accept the loan on one condition. You must take my necklace as security."

Buck protested: "We don't need any security. Your word is enough for us."

"Of course," I agreed.

"No," the Comtesse insisted. "I won't take it unless you take some security."

"Oh, very well," I agreed reluctantly.

I went to my bank and withdrew two thousand pounds which I

249

turned over to the Comtesse. She gave me the necklace and I dropped it carelessly into my pocket.

That evening we dined at Romano's. The Comtesse, feeling it no longer necessary to be circumspect, was dressed in a low-cut, shimmering evening gown. She was gayer than I had ever known her. We enjoyed a marvelous evening. When we parted we arranged to see them for lunch.

"I want you to meet Richard as soon as he gets here," the Comtesse said as I bade her good night.

The following day at noon we called at the Grosvenor House. At the desk we were told that Lady Stebbins and Miss Viola Martin had checked out.

"You must be mistaken," frowned the Deacon.

"No, I'm not," said the clerk. "They left early this morning. They seemed in a great hurry."

"Did either of them leave a message?"

"No. But you might telephone later. Perhaps we will hear from them."

Greatly disappointed, we turned and walked out. We went to see Jimmy Regan. We didn't tell him what had happened. After a few minutes he called: "You fellows make yourselves at home in the lounge. I've an appointment, but I'll see you later."

We discussed this latest turn of events.

"Maybe the escape plan didn't go through," I ventured.

"That must be it," agreed the Deacon. "Maybe the Sureté or Scotland Yard intervened."

"They'll probably call and leave a message for us."

I went to the telephone and called the Grosvenor House. No message had come.

We sat there for three hours, speculating on what had happened. Every half hour I telephoned the Grosvenor House. I always got a negative answer.

"Maybe we should go to Paris," Buck suggested.

"What good will that do?"

"We might be able to help them. At least, we might find out what happened."

## The Comtesse and The Kid

"Wait a while. I think they'll get in touch with us. After all, we have the Comtesse's necklace."

"That's right," Buck agreed. Then: "Let me have the necklace a moment, will you, Joe?"

"Sure, but don't lose it." I handed it over and he looked at it.

As I started to the telephone again, Buck said: "I'm going out for a little air, Joe. Be back in a few minutes."

I scarcely noticed him as he went out the door. I called and again I was told that there was no message. I rang for a waiter and ordered a drink. I sipped it slowly, contemplating the room without interest.

A few minutes later the Deacon came in and sat down beside me. He was as forlorn as I. He ordered a drink and gulped it.

"Joe," he said, "did you ever know how it feels to be taken in a con game?"

"No. Why?"

"Well, you're about to find out." He threw the necklace in my lap. "Paste," he said. "Our two lady friends worked a switch on us. We've been taken."

"How do you know?"

"I walked over to Old Bond Street. I showed it to the jeweler. He said it was a very clever imitation, worth about twenty-five dollars."

Until that moment the thought that the two women were swindlers had never entered my mind. Even then I found it hard to believe. I didn't want to believe it.

But as my mind went back swiftly over my acquaintance with the girl, it all tied in. She had been mysterious to pique my interest. I recalled how she had questioned me about my career and fortune. She had left it to her companion to reveal the part about the Comtesse. It had all been a very clever build-up.

It was particularly ironical for one reason: back in 1908 I had worked the switch on dozens of gullible buffet owners. I had used virtually the same tactics in the build-up. It had been one of my rainy day schemes. I had fallen back on it at various times through the years when I was in need of ready money. And at last I had become a victim of the same scheme!

## 23. The Case of the Refugee

I ALWAYS MADE IT A RULE TO KEEP ABREAST OF THE TIMES. NEARLY ALL of my schemes were geared to the latest news in national or international affairs.

Early one morning I was driving into Indianapolis. At a tourist camp outside of Lafayette I stopped at a little restaurant and had some of their specialty — homemade chili.

After eating I asked the owner of the place to fill up my gas tank. He pulled the car over to the gasoline pumps. In so doing he noticed my bags, which were covered with stamps from various foreign countries. These were not spurious, having been affixed at various times on my trips abroad.

"Do you do a lot of traveling?"

"Yes. I've spent considerable time in Europe."

"My one ambition has been to see Europe," he shook his head. "What did you do over there?"

"I represented European capital. But there isn't much to represent now."

"Do you know many people over there?"

"Yes. I was in Germany for a long time and I have a very good friend in the Reichsbank."

"How much do you think it would cost to take a trip to Berlin?"

"About $5,000."

"Oh, I could afford it," he assured me. He had finished with the car and continued: "Won't you come in and have a glass of wine with me?"

"Thank you."

## The Case of the Refugee

I followed him into the cottage he occupied. He brought glasses and poured wine for both of us.

"I've retired from active business," he said and I noted he was apparently past sixty. "I run this little place just to have something to do. I used to own a big dairy in Ohio, but I sold it out."

I was beginning to see light. I lingered about an hour, telling him of my European travels. I didn't have to add much fiction because I really had been in all parts of Europe and every big city on the continent was familiar to me. I had only to be careful in telling of my business dealings. None was legitimate, but I always had a good story to cover each trip.

It was easy to see he had not been far from his native Ohio. My tales of Europe intrigued him. He was very friendly and invited me to drop in to see him on my way back from Indianapolis.

I went on into Indianapolis and registered at the Claypool as John Bauer. I fixed up a letter from Mexico, properly stamped and postmarked. The letter read:

DEAR FRIEND:

Now that I've arrived in Mexico, I want to write and thank you for the great risk you took in helping me to get out of the fatherland. I suppose it will be a very difficult task to get into the United States. If I can't get there now, maybe you can dispose of some of my holdings in American corporations. Perhaps you can raise sufficient money to get me into your great country. I shall remain most anxious until you write to me with some hope of the future. Shall I send you some of the stocks and bonds and have you dispose of them or shall I hold them in abeyance? Please let me hear from you.

Faithfully yours,
HENRIETTA

The letter was written in a dainty feminine hand and the envelope was addressed to John Bauer at the Claypool Hotel in Indianapolis.

With this letter and some photographs I returned to the tourist camp. The photos were of my father's relatives in Paris — my aunt and two uncles.

I dropped in to see my new-found friend whose name I had learned was Andrew Lamont. We had coffee and chatted awhile and I departed, purposely leaving the letter and photographs on a table.

I drove on into Lafayette and telephoned Lamont.

"I lost a very valuable letter," I told him. "I prize it highly and will give a reward for its return."

"From Mexico?" he asked.

"Yes, that's it."

"You left it here."

"What a relief!" I sighed so heavily I'm sure he could hear it over the phone. "Would you be good enough to mail it to me?"

"I'll be glad to. You left some pictures, too."

"I wondered what happened to those pictures. They are some of my European relatives. Please mail them with the letter."

He mailed the letter and pictures to me in Indianapolis. I knew he had read the letter. I waited a couple of days and dropped in to see him again.

He was quite chummy and asked how things were going in Indianapolis. Then he maneuvered the conversation to the possibilities of my making a trip to Mexico.

"I have an opportunity to get a lot of money," I told him, "if I can find a man I can confide in — a man with a bank account."

"I have a bank account," he said. "I also have a car. If you want to go to Mexico I'll take you."

"No, let me tell you the story. There was a wealthy Jewish family with vast holdings in Germany and France. All their possessions in Germany were confiscated by Hitler and the family was thrown into a concentration camp. Only one member escaped — the daughter, Henrietta. Through my friend in the Reichsbank I arranged passage for her to Mexico aboard a tramp steamer. The captain was bribed and she was smuggled into his cabin. She had a trunk with a secret compartment in the bottom. This secret compartment held jewels and holdings of American stocks and bonds — Standard Oil, American Telephone and Telegraph, Allied Chemicals, and many others. About a million dollars worth in all.

"In spite of this wealth Henrietta is stranded in Mexico. She would like to get into this country and convert the stocks into cash, with the hope of rescuing her family from the Nazis. But she needs help. I

## The Case of the Refugee

promised to help her as soon as I returned to this country.

"I had some trouble getting out of Germany myself. I went to the American embassy and they arranged my passage. But it cost a lot of money.

"Mr. Lamont, I'd like to go to Mexico and help Henrietta, but I don't have any money. I think I can have her smuggled into this country. She has agreed to turn all her holdings over to me and give me half of what I get out of them. Suppose you tell your banker and ask him to advance me the money to help her?"

"I'll advance the money myself," he replied, a greedy light in his eyes. "But how do you expect to get her out of Mexico?"

"Sailors can be bribed. I hope to find a man with a tramp steamer who will bring her in — for a consideration, of course."

"Suppose you fail?"

"Then I'll bring the stocks back and sell them for her."

"What if you can't get them across the border?" he pressed.

"Then I'll sell the stock in Mexico. Maybe I can get 30 per cent of its value. In that case, I'll buy a small cruiser and smuggle Henrietta into the country myself."

"How much do I get out of it?"

"I'll give you a third of the proceeds. The amount you make will depend on whether I have to sell the stock in Mexico or can get it into this country. But you ought to get from $100,000 to $300,000 out of the deal."

Mention of these figures made Lamont rub his hands. "I'll help you," he said. "How much do you want to start?"

"Five hundred to a thousand dollars."

"I haven't got that much cash here. I'll have to go to the bank. But you can put up here overnight."

I spent the night in one of his cabins. The next morning he went to Lafayette and returned with $500. I took the money and started for Mexico by automobile.

At Dallas I called Lamont.

"I've just heard from Henrietta," I told him. "She needs $1,000 at once. The captain who brought her over demands more money."

"That's a lot of money," he protested.

## "Yellow Kid" Weil

"Yes, I know," I agreed. "But now that we've gone this far we can't afford to let this man upset the whole thing."

"How do you know he won't be demanding more money?"

"Because he's sailing in a few days. As soon as he's out of the way we know he won't be able to talk."

"All right," Lamont yielded. "How'll I send it to you?"

"Wire it care Western Union at Laredo. Use the code word Oscar for identification."

"I'll send it," he promised.

I drove on to Laredo and checked in at a hotel. After I had eaten and relaxed a bit I called at Western Union.

"Do you have a money order for John Bauer?" I inquired.

"John Bauer?" said the clerk. "I'll see." He returned in a short time and asked: "Do you have a dog?"

"Yes."

"What's his name?"

"Oscar."

"Yes, we have a money order for you. Sign here."

I signed the receipt and received the money. From Laredo I drove to Monterey and on into Mexico City. It was really a lark for me. The scenery was interesting and I was in no hurry. There was naturally no Henrietta in Mexico City to distract my attention from the city's night life, which I enjoyed for several days before I called Lamont again.

"Everything is going fine," I told him enthusiastically. "Henrietta is comfortable and nobody is molesting her. I haven't been able to find a boat to smuggle her in though. It may require a few weeks to do that. I'll stay and try to arrange it if you can send me some more money."

"I've already given you $1,500," he objected. "Why can't you get some of the stock and raise some money?"

"I can do that," I replied. "I'll bring some of the stock back and sell it in the United States. See you in a few days."

About a week later I returned to Indiana and checked in at a hotel in Lafayette. Later I drove out to see Lamont. I took with me stock certificates of the Standard Oil Company, American Telephone and

## The Case of the Refugee

Telegraph, and Allied Chemicals, with a total face value of $15,000. They were all phonies but looked so genuine they'd fool almost anybody.

Lamont was enthusiastic when I showed him the certificates.

"Suppose we get your banker to dispose of these?" I suggested.

"Good. I'll let Jim run the place and we'll go into Lafayette now."

He drove into Lafayette and I followed in my car. We went to his bank and he introduced me to the president, a man I will call John Parker.

He looked over the certificates and there was no indication of doubt on his face. "Where did you get these?" he inquired.

I told him of having acquired them from the refugee. "Why," I asked, "they're good, aren't they?"

"Gilt-edged," he replied. "I'd be glad to sell them for you, but they are not endorsed."

"Do they have to be?" I asked, appearing crestfallen.

"Yes. They have to be authenticated."

"Well, I guess there isn't anything else I can do." I got up, disappointment written in every move, and Lamont and I started for the door.

Lamont was already out the door and I was about to leave when the banker said: "Just a moment." He beckoned to me and I returned to his desk.

"Where are you stopping?" he asked in an undertone.

I named my hotel.

"I'll telephone you later," he said quickly. "I have something in mind."

I knew pretty well what was in his mind, but I had no intention of telling Lamont. When I rejoined him he wanted to know why Parker had called me back.

"He just wanted to tell me to be sure to have the certificates notarized," I replied. "They have to be endorsed and notarized."

"What are your plans now?" Lamont asked.

"As soon as I've rested up I'm going back to Mexico and get the certificates signed," I told him.

We chatted for half an hour. Then I parted from Lamont, with the

257

## "Yellow Kid" Weil

promise that I would get in touch with him the next day.

I had been back at my hotel only a few minutes when the phone rang. It was Parker. "Would you come over to my law offices?" he asked. I told him I would and he gave me the address.

Parker's office was in a spacious suite in the best building in town. I later learned he had a number of young lawyers working for him and that he spent a few hours there after the bank closed, supervising their activities and ironing out problems.

Parker himself was in his middle forties, a stocky man with a jutting chin and long, unruly brown hair. He wore horn-rimmed glasses and was a tireless worker. I was soon to learn he also was a tireless schemer and that his main interest in life was the acquisition of money, of which he already had a considerable amount.

He greeted me cordially and offered me a comfortable chair and cigar. Clearly this was a build-up.

"How much does Lamont know about this woman who owns the stock?" he asked.

"Very little," I replied. "Why?"

"Don't tell him any more. I think I'm in a better position than he is to help you. How much are her holdings?"

"About two million dollars."

"Why don't you bring her in?"

I showed him the correspondence and told him the story about her narrow escape from Hitler and her inability to get into the United States.

"I can smuggle her in," I explained. "But I will have to buy a small cruiser, equip it, hire a crew, and bribe a few officials. All that costs money and I don't have any."

"How much are you getting out of it if you do succeed in smuggling her in?" he asked, getting right to the point.

"I think she will give me 50 per cent."

"I might help you finance it," he proposed. "How much of your share will you pay for help?"

"I'd be willing to pay 30 per cent of my share."

"Not enough," he said quickly. "If I do go in with you, it will have to be half."

## The Case of the Refugee

I considered this for a moment, finally shrugged. "There isn't anything else I can do," I said. "I can't buy a boat without money so I'll have to accept your proposal."

"What had you planned to do next?"

"Return to Mexico."

"How soon?"

"Probably in two weeks."

"Why do you have to put it off so long?" he asked. I could see from the look of avarice in his eyes and the way he rubbed his hands that he was very anxious.

"I haven't any money to make the trip," I replied. "I hope to have enough by that time."

"I'll furnish the money," the banker said impatiently. "Meet me here tomorrow morning at nine forty-five. I'll slip away from the bank for a few minutes. Meanwhile you better shake Lamont."

Shaking Lamont was no trouble at all. I called him the next morning and told him I was on my way back to Mexico and that I would get in touch with him as soon as I could.

I met Parker as arranged. He had the look of a well-fed cat who is preparing to gorge himself on a juicy mouse.

"When are you leaving?"

"Right away."

"Fine. The sooner you start the better."

"I still don't have any money," I reminded him.

"Stop worrying about the money," he said. "Here's $500. If you need any more call me at my home." He handed me a card with his home address and phone number.

"This ought to be enough," I assured him, pocketing the money. "I'll keep you informed of my progress."

I drove back to Mexico City and after waiting a couple of days called Parker.

"Henrietta's in hiding," I told him. "She saw the former ambassador to Germany on the street and is fearful of being recognized."

"What are you going to do?"

"Make arrangements to get her out of the country just as fast as I can."

259

## "Yellow Kid" Weil

I waited a couple more days, than drove back to Lafayette. I avoided Lamont but went at once to see the banker.

"The trip only cost me $300," I told him. "Here's the balance of the money you gave me." I returned $200 to Parker and it had a tremendous psychological effect on him.

"What progress did you make?" he asked anxiously.

"I found a tramp steamer that is sailing in a few days. The Captain is willing to smuggle her into the United States for $7,500."

"How do I know that you are telling me the truth?"

"I don't understand."

"How do I know this woman has all that stock?"

"I asked her to give me some sort of evidence. She gave me this letter."

The letter was on the stationery of the Chase National Bank of New York. It was signed "Winthrop W. Aldrich." It looked as genuine as if Aldrich really had written it. The letterhead was an exact replica and the expensive bond paper had a watermark.

According to the letter Mr. Aldrich was glad Henrietta had successfully eluded the Nazis with her vast holdings of stocks and precious jewels. He expressed a desire to serve her and hoped she would permit the Chase National Bank to handle her affairs if she succeeded in getting to New York.

This letter readily convinced Parker. He put aside all doubts and got down to business.

"Does she have the stocks in a safe place?" he asked.

"Yes, she still has them in the trunk," I replied. "Of course, nobody knows that it has a secret compartment. Even the man who is going to smuggle her in doesn't know that she is carrying a valuable cargo. He thinks she's just a poor refugee whose friends are anxious to save her from the Nazis."

"Good. There's no use wasting time."

He made out two documents. One was a note for $7,500 payable on demand. I signed it and, as president of the bank, he approved it. The other was an agreement that, in consideration of his financial help, I would give him fifty per cent of my share. I signed that, too, using the name, John Bauer.

## The Case of the Refugee

With the money I started back for Mexico right away. At Laredo I stopped and called Lamont.

"I've been wondering what happened to you," he said.

"Well, I've been very busy trying to get Henrietta into the United States," I told him. "I've finally located the captain of a freighter who is willing to smuggle her in for $1,500."

"What are you going to do now?"

"I have to raise the money. Can you send it to me?"

"Yes, but that's all I can send you."

"You won't need to send any more. Once she gets to the United States we'll have all the money we want."

"All right, where do you want it sent?"

"The Western Union at Laredo. Use the same code word."

I waited around several hours and the wire didn't come. It was a dangerous game I was playing. If Lamont and Parker had got together and compared notes I was a dead duck. After the second time I had inquired at Western Union I became jittery. I thought of a dozen things that might be happening.

It was nearly dark when I decided to ask once more. But to be sure no trap had been laid I hired a boy to go to Western Union for me. I watched him from across the street while he asked. He returned and told me the wire was there.

I went in, gave the code word, and received the $1,500. As it developed, my fears had been groundless. But I didn't hang around Laredo any longer. I got in my car and drove on to Mexico City.

There I telephoned Parker and told him I needed an additional $1,500 to bribe consular officials who had got wind of the proposed smuggling. He protested but wired the money to me.

I went back to the United States after arranging with a man in Mexico City to send a couple of wires for me. One of them, addressed to me in care of the banker, was signed "Henrietta" and stated:

EVERYTHING ARRANGED. WAITING FOR CLEARANCE PAPERS.

The other was addressed to me in care of Lamont. It read:

## "Yellow Kid" Weil

DIFFICULTY IN ARRANGING CLEARANCE PAPERS. SHOULD BE IN NEW YORK IN TWO WEEKS.

I went out to see Lamont and he handed me the telegram.

"Well, it won't be long now," I told him. "I'll go to New York and meet her and I'll be back here as soon as I can."

This seemed reasonable enough to him. I put up at his camp overnight and told him in detail — quite fictitious — of the trouble I'd encountered in arranging Henrietta's passage. I left the following morning and told him I was on my way to New York.

I drove on into Lafayette and the banker had the other telegram.

"How long do you think she'll be held up?" he asked anxiously.

"Not long," I assured him. "I arranged everything with the consular officials before I left."

"Guess we will just have to wait," he said impatiently.

I went on over to the hotel and registered. That afternoon I returned to the bank. I had a faked airmail letter that read:

> We are about to sail. We expect to be in New York next Saturday. I hope that you will be there to meet me.
>
> Hurriedly,
> Henrietta

In a state of great excitement I went into the banker's office and showed him the letter. He read it with great satisfaction.

"I'm going to drive to New York to meet her," I told Parker. "The poor woman will need help. She has some clothing, but it definitely stamps her as a foreigner. I think she'd better be dressed properly to protect us."

Parker readily agreed.

"I'll need more cash to do that," I pointed out. "Can I increase the note?"

"You're already in about $10,000."

"No, it's $9,000. Suppose you make it $10,000 even."

"But $500 ought to be enough."

"I don't think so. Henrietta is an aristocrat. If she is to be dressed in a manner that befits her I think I'll need a great deal more than that. Suppose you make the note for $12,000."

## The Case of the Refugee

We haggled for some time over this point. He finally compromised by giving me $1,500. I then departed for New York to meet poor Henrietta.

I did actually go to New York. I was there when the boat was supposed to arrive. But I was busy with other activities. I went to a bowery passport photographer's and got a fake photograph of Henrietta. Then I bought a New York paper and had the front page reprinted. The headline read:

CAPTAIN ARRESTED FOR
SMUGGLING WEALTHY ALIEN

The story under the headline stated that the captain of a freighter had been arrested for trying to smuggle into New York a wealthy German refugee. It related how the woman had been put aboard the freighter with a trunk found to contain some two millions in securities and jewels as the result of a plot initiated by one John Bauer, who was being sought by police. The picture of Henrietta was prominently displayed.

With this I hurried back to Indiana and laid the paper in front of the banker. Parker was furious, but he didn't doubt the authenticity of the paper or the story.

"What are you going to do now?" he demanded.

"I'm going back to Mexico. Just as fast as I can."

"Don't be a fool. That's the first place they'll look. You had better go up to the north woods."

"All right," I agreed, "but I'll need more money."

"What!" The banker jumped from his chair and shook an angry fist in my face. "Why should I give you more money?"

"Don't forget," I reminded him coolly, "that if I'm caught, I'll have to involve you."

"I wish I'd never laid eyes on you!" Parker said, fervent hatred in his voice. He was frothing at the mouth, but the threat of exposure was effective. He reached in his pocket.

"Here's $200. Now get out of here and I hope that I never see you again!"

He had his wish. I got out and he has never seen me since. This was one case where I didn't have to worry about documentary evidence. I'm quite sure Parker burned both the note and the agreement I had signed as soon as he could conveniently do it.

This scheme may seem fantastic. But it is no more so than the famous "Spanish prisoner" swindle which is being worked through the mails even today. It is in the same category as the hidden-treasure lure.

There is something about buried treasure that appeals to a wide number of people. If you can produce a yellowed map, presumably made up by a pirate, you can tell a story to fit the circumstances and there will be many people who will believe it. Besides that, there will be many who will invest large sums in expeditions to find the treasure.

My story of Henrietta and her stocks was comparable to that. I used it successfully on others. It was the last big scheme in my fifty years as a confidence man.

## 24. A Proposition for A. Hitler

I DIDN'T GO TO THE NORTH WOODS AFTER I LEFT PARKER. I CAME BACK to Chicago, feeling pretty sure it would never occur to him that he had been swindled. I assume he eventually did find it out, but he never complained.

In Chicago I met a wealthy woman whom I shall call Mrs. O'Keefe. She owned some copper-mining property in Arizona and I persuaded her she needed a famous mining engineer to manage it. She hired me and I made a trip to Arizona at her expense. I engaged Buckminster as my assistant and put him on the expense account.

We visited the mine and learned it was valuable, though not being worked. We lingered in Arizona and enjoyed a nice vacation before returning to Chicago.

Mrs. O'Keefe was not interested in opening the mine, but she did want to sell it. I suggested that foreign interests probably would give her a much better price than she could get in this country.

Germany was not actually at war, though Hitler had begun his bloodless conquests. I proposed to Mrs. O'Keefe that I go to Berlin where I had connections in the Reichsbank and try to make a deal for her mining property.

It was logical that Mrs. O'Keefe should fall for this story. Hitler, on the verge of war, would need all the copper he could get. I persuaded Mrs. O'Keefe he would pay a much higher price than she could get at home. Another case where greed overruled patriotism.

I sailed for Berlin on what was to be my last trip abroad. I had a handsome expense account and full authority to sell the mine to Hitler if we could come to terms.

## "Yellow Kid" Weil

I had no desire to meet the Fuehrer or to sell him the mine. But I made a good pretense. Shortly after my arrival I cabled Mrs. O'Keefe that negotiations were under way. Berlin was not the gay city it had been on my last previous visit.

At the Chancellery I made a formal request in writing for an interview with Adolph Hitler. This was denied, also in writing — and on the stationery of the German government. At the Reichsbank I made an inquiry and received a reply on Reichsbank stationery.

That was all I wanted. I now had samples of Hitler's stationery and that of the Reichsbank. I would need these when I got back to the United States.

Then I went to London, where war clouds were also gathering. But the atmosphere was different. It was still possible to be gay. I visited some of my old haunts and spent several weeks in old Bond Street replenishing my wardrobe.

In London there was hopeful talk of peace. However, my visit to Berlin had convinced me it was only a matter of time until war would come. I had no desire to be in Europe when that happened.

Before returning to Chicago I had the two German letterheads copied. On these I forged letters from Hitler and from the Reichsbank. Both professed great interest in the mining property but explained that negotiations had been delayed because of certain legal technicalities.

I showed these to Mrs. O'Keefe and she was satisfied with the progress I had made. But she had not sold the property and insisted I return to Berlin and continue negotiations. I declined to do this, and she cut off my expense account.

I realized there was danger she would discover that the documents had been forged. I decided to get out of Chicago until things had blown over. I went to Washington and registered at the Hotel Mayflower.

At the Mayflower I met John Harris. He asked what I was doing and I told him I was marking time. Harris invited me to New York. He said he knew a woman who was a close friend of a famous cosmetics manufacturer. She held open house every day and there were ample opportunities to meet people of wealth.

*To further his stock schemes, the "Yellow Kid" Weil had his own picture expertly inserted in this book in place of that of its real author.*

Private 4526

## Standard Oil Company
*(An New Jersey Corporation)*
*26 Broadway*

*New York*

Feb. 9, 1935.

Dr. Henri Reuel,
C/o Book-Cadillac Hotel,
Detroit, Michigan.

My dear Doctor:

Please be advised that Mr. J. P. Morgan and I are now in a position to deal direct with the gentleman who is in complete control of the Verde Apex Copper Mining Company. I have no desire to lock horns with you nor do I feel disposed to associate myself with the house of Morgan in defeating your claims. This is final. Either you deliver to me all documents in the subject matter immediately else I shall join forces against you.

Very sincerely,

W. C. Teagle

WCT/HB

*"Yellow Kid" always had on hand forgeries of letters and signatures.*

## A Proposition for A. Hitler

I went to New York and registered at the Barbizon-Plaza. Harris registered at the Clermont. Already waiting at the Clermont was a con man named Dick Hartley. He joined us when we went to call on Mrs. Richards, the lady who held open house.

We met both wealthy people and government officials. Still I decided it was not a good place for me. Mrs. O'Keefe had learned my true identity and had complained to federal authorities, who had a warrant for my arrest. I decided the Barbizon-Plaza was as good a place as any to hide.

One night Harris and Hartley had a little party in their rooms. I thought it was to be a small gathering and accepted their invitation. As it turned out, however, there were many people there, including a high-ranking Army officer. I was introduced as Dr. Henri Reuel.

Harris and Hartley became drunk and so did several of the guests. When the desk called and said there were a number of complaints about the noise I decided it was time to go.

I remained in New York and did not see Harris and Hartley again. Two months later they were arrested for using the mails to defraud after selling some oil lands in Texas. The Army officer remembered me and reported to the authorities. After my identity was established it was immediately assumed I had been in the scheme with Harris and Hartley.

I was arrested by postal inspectors. When I protested my innocence they brought up the O'Keefe matter. They offered to try to quash that indictment if I would plead guilty in the mail fraud case. I accepted this deal with the understanding that my sentence would be light.

But the United States District Attorney asked Judge Clancy in Federal Court to fix my sentence at four years. In my own defense, I pointed out to Judge Clancy that the fact that I had been in that hotel room did not prove I had been a party to the mail-fraud scheme.

Judge Clancy asked me what I thought my sentence ought to be.

"I consider a year quite enough," I told him.

"All right," he mused. "You ask for a year, the government asks for four. I'll make it two."

That was early in 1940. I was sent to Atlanta, which is perhaps the finest of all federal prisons. I was assigned to do book work in the laundry, a job which had definite advantages. I did not have to dress in the usual prison denim, could have a clean white shirt every day, and the use of a private bath.

In Atlanta every inmate had an opportunity to learn a trade and to rehabilitate himself. The men in charge of the various activities were kind and willing to help anyone who had a desire to learn.

Most of those in the laundry took courses in modern laundry methods and in dry cleaning. They had regular examinations, as they would in any school. It was my job to grade the papers. Some were eager to get high marks and even offered bribes. I always rejected these offers.

There was one course, however, where the inmates did not intend to follow the trade when they got out. That was acetylene welding. Nearly every convict who took that training had one object in mind. He expected to become a better safe-cracker when he got out.

Atlanta offered practically every form of recreational activity. Its stadium compared with the best college athletic fields. All sports were available except golf. Every convict who was engaged in one of the rehabilitation activities was given two hours a day to engage in sports or be a spectator.

Lights went out every night at nine, but if there was something special on the radio, such as a championship boxing match, the radio was left on until later.

The cell blocks were four tiers high, but they were not known as cells in Atlanta. Each block had accommodations for eight inmates and each unit was known as "living quarters."

When I was released from Atlanta in 1942 I was taken into custody and returned to Chicago to face charges in the O'Keefe case. Buckminster had already been tried and been acquitted. My appearance was only a formality. The case was dropped and I was released.

Since that time nobody has charged me with a crime. For a very good reason. After my term in Atlanta I resolved that I would never again be involved in anything that might send me to prison.

I have lived in Chicago since then and it has been a great relief to be able to walk the streets freely, to enter any public place I choose, and to look any policeman in the eye.

## 25. Tricks of the Trade

PEDDLING FAKE STOCK WAS BY FAR THE MOST PROFITABLE OF MY schemes. It was easy for me to tell this story with conviction. It had worked well over a period of twenty years.

Other swindles soon became known or were good only in certain localities, but the stock scheme was good anywhere and at any time. And there were a far greater number of people who could be taken in by it. Until the market crash of October, 1929, nearly everybody believed there were big fortunes to be made in stock. Consequently many folks who ordinarily would not have dealt in stocks were easy victims of my schemes.

My stock story was basically the same for more than twenty years and became somewhat trite. However each victim was different, and the situations varied. As the years passed, many improvements were made in the modus operandi. Strangely enough, the victims themselves made suggestions that helped me to improve the scheme.

For example, Bobby Sims, heir to a soap fortune in Cincinnati, called my attention to an article in *McClure's,* then one of the nation's leading monthlies. The article, titled "$100,000 A Year," was written by Edward Mott Woolley and was the success story of a mining engineer named Pope Yateman who had taken over an almost worthless mine in Chile and made it pay, though he had been compelled to pipe water for more than a hundred miles.

I bought as many copies of that magazine as I could find and fetched them to Chicago. At the first opportunity I took them to Jack Jones, operator of the Dill Pickle Club.

Jones was noted principally for his operation of the Dill Pickle, and

## "Yellow Kid" Weil

only a few knew of his real activities. These were carried on in the daytime when the club was closed. Jones had a well-equipped printing and bookbinding plant in the same building.

Jones employed linotype operators, printers, binders, and one engraver. Their specialty was first editions of famous books. They used their various skills in turning out almost perfect copies of such rarities. The engraver, whom I knew only as Hymie, was an old-time hand-engraver who could copy anything from fifteenth century bookplates to Uncle Sam's currency. He had a secret process for giving the books the appearance of age.

Jones put the volumes, with their yellowed pages, into circulation through underworld channels. For books that had cost him about a dollar to produce he received twenty-five dollars. So far as I know this was the only fraud that Jones ever engaged in.

But Hymie was more versatile. In his spare time at night, while Jones was busy at the Dill Pickle Club, Hymie turned his talent to engravings of United States currency. He turned out some pretty good counterfeits. I had heard of this and went to see him.

He agreed to do all my printing and engraving. He made fake letterheads, stock certificates, letters of credit, calling cards, and any other documents I needed.

Now, I had a special job for him. I asked him to remove the entire article from *McClure's,* substitute my picture for Pope Yateman's, reprint the whole thing, and bind it back in the proper place. He took the job. He made a cut that showed me as the famous mining engineer, copied the rest of the article, printed the requisite pages and rebound the magazine. Even an expert would not have known the magazine wasn't exactly as it had been published.

These magazines were destined to play a big part in my future activities. Who could resist the advice of the $100,000-a-year mining wizard who had taken copper from a worthless mine in Chile? It was all down there in black and white in a highly respected magazine. Many a victim was misled by it.

I was never so crude as to call anybody's attention to the magazine. I selected most of my victims from small towns, outside of Chicago. As soon as I had picked out the victim, I sent on a couple of men with

## Tricks of the Trade

a copy of the faked magazine. These men called at the town's public library and asked for the file of *McClure's*.

It was easy enough to borrow the bound volume from the library. They took it to their hotel room, removed the issue containing the Pope Yateman story and substituted the one containing my faked photograph. Then the volume was returned to the library.

Later on I started my negotiations with the victim. Chances were he had never heard of Pope Yateman. After some preliminary talks I would mention that I had other matters to attend to and left the victim in the hands of Deacon Buckminster, who had been introduced as my secretary, Mr. Kimball.

"Did you read the article about Mr. Yateman in *McClure's*?" Buck would ask in a casual manner.

"Why, no, I don't believe I did," the victim usually replied. "Do you have a copy of it?"

"No, I don't," Buck would say. "But I'm sure you can find it in the public library if you're interested."

Naturally the victim was interested. As soon as he had read this success story and had seen my picture in a magazine on file in the library of his own town he had no doubts at all about my identity. More important, he had new respect for my business acumen. From then on he was an easy victim.

As soon as we had made certain he had read the magazine, my stooges called again at the public library and used their sleight-of-hand to remove the faked magazines and return the original. You can imagine the victim's amazement, after being swindled, to go to the library and look up that article only to find that the picture did not resemble me at all!

A variation of this scheme I used later when Franz von Papen became German ambassador to the United States. I purchased 200 copies of a Sunday issue of the Washington *Post*. They were turned over to Hymie with an article I had written, a photograph of von Papen, and photographs of Buckminster and myself. Hymie had to duplicate the first and last sheets of the main news section in order to get the article in.

He killed three columns of news matter on the front page and

## "Yellow Kid" Weil

substituted the article I had written. Prominently displayed was the picture of von Papen, flanked on one side by Buckminster and on the other by me. The article told of the two plenipotentiaries who had accompanied von Papen to America. Their mission was to purchase industrial and mining property for German capitalists and for the German government. It was an impressive story and layout, occupying the best space in the paper.

I always carried a copy of this paper in my bag. If I had a victim in tow, I would always manage, while removing something from the handbag, to let the paper fall out. The victim would see the spread and would be properly impressed.

"May I have a copy of that?" he would ask.

"I'm sorry," I would reply, "but this is the only copy I have with me. But I shall be happy to send you a copy as soon as I get back to Washington."

The reason for this procedure was that I made it a rule never to let any documentary evidence get out of my hands. Though I displayed thousands of fake letters, documents, stock certificates, etc., to prospective victims, I was always careful to recover them.

On one occasion when a copy of *McClure's* was used against me, I had been charged with fleecing a man in Indiana. I paid a lawyer to get the case fixed. He asked me to let him have a copy of the magazine and I did. It later got into the hands of the state's attorney, who used it for the prosecution.

The state brought the librarian from Indiana to testify that the magazine was a fake. When he had examined it, he was asked:

"Is that a genuine copy of *McClure's*?"

"I can't say," he replied.

"Would you say that it had been faked? That it had been altered after leaving the publishers?"

"I can't say about that either," the librarian responded. "I just can't tell whether it is faked or genuine."

If a professional librarian, who was supposed to know books and magazines, couldn't tell the difference, how could a victim be expected to spot it as a fake? None of them did. The magazines were used as props in many swindles and nobody questioned their authenticity.

## Tricks of the Trade

As the years passed and we gained experience in the stock swindle other props were added. These included fake letters from J. P. Morgan, Walter C. Teagle, and numerous other big figures in the financial world.

The stationery we used for these fakes looked genuine. I always saw to that. First I obtained a letterhead, and Hymie copied it. I had little trouble getting these letterheads. I merely wrote to the firm and asked about a man allegedly in their employ. The name I gave was fictitious, but the firm always wrote back to say that there was no record of the person I had inquired about. This gave me both a letterhead and envelope. Envelopes became important, particularly from foreign countries. I solved the problem of making the foreign envelopes look genuine, too.

I bought a supply of postage stamps of various foreign countries at a stamp store in Chicago. By writing letters of inquiry to hotels or firms in large cities all over the world I had a sample not only of their stationery but a specimen postmark as well. I had postmarking outfits made for all the larger cities of the world. They had loose dates that could be changed at will. Any time I wanted a letter from a foreign city all I had to do was write it, put it in the proper envelope, and postmark it.

At various times during the years from 1914 until the end of my career as a con man, I posed as Dr. Henri Reuel, a famous mining engineer and author. In 1931, Dr. Reuel published some excellent books. One of these was *Our Sons*, a behind-the-scenes story of the beginning of the first World War.

Another was *Oil Imperialism*, whose sub-title was "The Causes of the World's War." A third was *The Romantic Lure and Lore of Copper*, which related stories of great copper-mining ventures, particularly those of the Far West. One chapter dealt in detail with the Law of the Apex and related how Augustus Heintz had used the Law of the Apex to squeeze $25,000,000 out of the Morgan–Standard Oil interests.

The contents of these books furnished excellent material for my build-up on the stock scheme. I referred to various portions of these books in conversations with prospective victims, slanting my talk ac-

## "Yellow Kid" Weil

cording to the character of the victim. Many of these were wealthy Germans who were ready to listen to any plausible story about the World War.

I decided that as long as I was using Dr. Reuel's material and name I might as well become the author of his books too. I had a photograph made of myself in formal attire, clean-shaven except for a mustache.

Hymie made a cut of this picture and printed it on heavy enamel paper. He very skillfully inserted it in the front of each book, opposite the title page. This appeared to be the frontispiece and was titled "Dr. Henri Reuel." If the occasion was right I let the victim see a copy of one of the books. He could not tell that the frontispiece was faked, and as a rule no more build-up was needed to convince him.

Nearly all the victims wanted copies of the books. I sidestepped that by saying I had no other copies with me but that I would mail autographed volumes as soon as I returned home.

These are excellent books, well written, well printed, and well bound. They may be found today in many public libraries, though, of course, my picture doesn't appear in those in the libraries. I still have copies in excellent condition. They were among my most valuable props and helped me to sell many thousand dollars worth of fake mining stocks.

Props played a big part in my success in selling fake stocks. For a long time we had a brokerage house. We usually heard of a brokerage house that was moving or going out of business and rented the quarters completely furnished.

With the furnishings in, all we had to do was hire a few girls to look busy. Generally they were students from a business college who needed typing practice so they copied names from the telephone directories. The victims did not know what the girls were doing and were impressed by their activity.

I have already recounted our St. Louis project, but one of the most impressive layouts I ever used was in Muncie, Indiana. I learned that the Merchants National Bank had moved to new quarters. I rented the old building, which was complete with all the necessary furnishings and fixtures for a banking venture.

# Tricks of the Trade

For a week before I was ready to take my victim in, I had my stooges call at the new Merchants Bank. Each time they went in they secretly carried away a small quantity of deposit slips, counter checks, savings withdrawal slips, and other forms used by the bank. In that manner we acquired an ample supply to spread over our counters.

I bought as many money bags as I could find, but couldn't get enough. So I had the name of the bank stenciled on fifty salt bags. The bags were all filled with shiny steel washers about the size of half dollars and tied at the top. The money bags, together with large stacks of boodle and some genuine silver, were stacked in the cages of the paying and receiving tellers. All the cages were manned by stooges.

When I brought the victim in and asked to see the president of the bank we were told we would have to wait. We waited an hour during which the place bustled with activity.

People would come in to patronize the bank. Most of these were girls from the local bawdy houses, interspersed with denizens of the underworld — gamblers, thugs, touts. There was a steady stream, and the bank appeared to be thriving. Occasionally a uniformed messenger came in with a money bag. These messengers were street-car conductors off duty. They wore their regular uniforms but left the badges off their caps.

The victim never suspected a thing. Fully convinced that he was in a big active bank, he went into the stock deal with me and ultimately lost $50,000.

I have often thought about banks and the confidence which people have in the very word. Not so long ago anybody could start a bank. The main things needed were the right props. Perhaps the most important of these was a big sign outside. If it said "B A N K," great numbers of people who knew nothing at all about the operators would entrust their funds to the institution. The big sign and the cages inside quieted any fears they might have had as to the authenticity of the institution.

I have used banks many times to convince victims of the soundness of my schemes.

Leach and Company was a large brokerage house in Youngstown, Ohio. It had a national reputation. I could not hope to take my victim in there and transact business. But I thought of something even better.

Near by was a bank, one of the largest in Ohio. One day I went in and asked to see the president. I was shown into his private office, a spacious room with a high, panelled ceiling and expensive mahogany furnishings. The pile of the rug was so deep you sank into it almost to your ankles.

I told the president I had come to Youngstown to purchase one of the steel mills. (I rather favored the Youngstown Sheet and Tube Company.) I asked his advice, and he said he thought I couldn't go wrong.

"I hope you'll remember this bank when your deal has been completed," he smiled.

"I certainly shall." Of course, a big firm like the Youngstown Sheet and Tube Company has enormous bank dealings. "But," I continued, "there will be considerable negotiations. It may take some time."

"That goes without saying."

"By the way," I said, "do you happen to have a spare office here in the bank where I might carry on our negotiations? Any room not in use will do."

"I have an excellent place," he replied. "My own office. Any time you want to hold a conference, bring your people in here. I'll get out and you can have complete privacy."

"That is very kind of you," I said. "I'll probably take advantage of your offer within the next two or three days."

Two days later, when I had brought my victim to Youngstown, I called the bank president and asked for the use of his office at 10 A. M. He assured me that it would be available and unoccupied.

I told my victim that we were going to see Mr. Leach, the owner of Leach and Company, who was interested in buying the stock. When we entered the big office of Leach and Company, I addressed a man in shirt sleeves who stood near one of the counters. (He was my stooge, planted there for the purpose.)

## Tricks of the Trade

"Can you tell me where we'll find Mr. Leach?" I inquired.

"Well, he owns this place, but you won't find him here," said the stooge. "See that big bank across the street?"

"Yes."

"Well, that's where he spends most of his time. He's the president of that bank."

By this time my victim was pretty much impressed. Mr. Leach, he decided, was indeed a big man. We went across the street and entered the bank. Near the door a well-dressed man without hat or topcoat walked idly about. He was another stooge.

"Do you have a Mr. Leach here?" I asked.

"We certainly do," the stooge replied. "He's president of the bank. That's his office over there." He pointed across the room to the door marked PRESIDENT. "There's Mr. Leach now, going towards his office."

The man walking across the floor was Jimmy Head. He was well dressed and had a dignified bearing. It required no imagination to believe he was a bank president. We hurried across the room and caught up with him just as he reached the office door.

"Mr. Leach?" I asked.

"Yes."

"I'm Dr. Weed — Dr. Walter H. Weed. I've come to talk to you about some mining stock I believe you're interested in."

"Ah, yes, Dr. Weed. I've heard a great deal about you. Won't you step into my office where we can talk in private?"

"Thank you."

He opened the door and we went in. I led the way, followed by the victim. The room was unoccupied.

Jimmy Head had never before seen the inside of this office. But he went and sat down at the broad desk of the bank president as though he had grown up in these surroundings.

We began to discuss the stock deal and remained in the office for about half an hour. Nobody bothered us. By the time we were ready to go, the victim was firmly convinced he was dealing with the biggest banker in Youngstown. Head shook hands with us and saw us to the door. He, too, left as soon as we were out of sight.

## "Yellow Kid" Weil

The success of my schemes was due largely to the build-up. No matter what difficulties we encountered later, the victim's resistance had already been broken down. He was thoroughly convinced of my authenticity at the beginning and did not stop later to check on any questionable developments.

In some cases the build-up was so convincing that nothing could shake the victim's confidence in me. I remember the case of a German watch manufacturer named Schmaltz. Buckminster and I approached him with an offer to buy the watchworks, located outside Chicago, for the German government.

We carried on negotiations for several days. There was the usual delay while we heard from Berlin. Meanwhile we switched Schmaltz's interest to the mining-stock deal. We brought him into Chicago and took him into the large LaSalle Street brokerage house of Hamill and Company.

A stooge in shirt sleeves was waiting for us near one of the counters. When we asked to see Mr. Hamill, he said: "Why, he doesn't come in here. He's got private offices on the sixteenth floor."

So we led Schmaltz to the sixteenth floor of the building. It happened that few offices had been rented on this floor and we had been able to get a large one at the end of the hall. This bore a sign: MR. HAMILL — PRIVATE.

But to make it more impressive we had it appear that Mr. Hamill's office was flanked by many others. On the doors of vacant offices on both sides of the corridor we had hung signs that read: EXPORT DEPARTMENT, FOREIGN EXCHANGE, BOND DEPARTMENT, and so on.

In the office at the end of the hall, Jimmy Head, posing as Mr. Hamill, waited for us. He agreed to buy our stock at a big profit. He paused a couple of times in the conversation to make long distance calls to New York over a dead phone.

Schmaltz not only was impressed; he was enthusiastic and pleaded with us to let him buy some of the stock so that he could get in on the profits. With apparent reluctance, we finally agreed to let him in on the deal if he could raise $50,000 in cash. He readily accepted those terms.

Buckminster accompanied him to his home-town bank while I

## Tricks of the Trade

remained behind. When Schmaltz presented the check for $50,000 at the bank, the teller hesitated and called the cashier.

"This is rather unusual, Mr. Schmaltz," the cashier frowned.

"What is so unusual?"

"Such a large cash withdrawal. May I ask what you intend to use the money for?"

"For investment," Schmaltz returned shortly.

"I hope you're not dealing with confidence men," said the cashier.

"I'm not."

"It is my duty to warn you that a gang of confidence men are operating in the vicinity. A couple of months ago they fleeced a doctor in Kankakee of $25,000." He eyed the German, who was just as stubborn as ever. "But if you insist — "

"I insist!" growled Schmaltz.

The cashier shrugged. "It's your money," he said and ordered the teller to pay the check.

Schmaltz still did not question us. He was furious at the bank and vowed that he would take his account elsewhere. Our build-up had been so powerful that he was willing to take sides with us — strangers — against a banker he had known for years.

After we had fleeced him of his money and quietly disappeared, Schmaltz probably had more respect for the banker's judgment. But he was stubborn enough to take his medicine. He never made a beef to the law.

There was one man though who wasn't willing to take it. He was Willis, the president of a large bank in Fort Wayne, Indiana. Buck and I approached him as "representatives of the German government" and told him that we were interested in buying a factory.

"We've looked at two sites," I said. "One is the wagon works at Auburn and the other the glass works at Hartford. We were told that you are interested in both of these plants."

"That's true," he replied. "But for your purpose, I believe the Hartford glass works would be better."

We discussed the details for some time, letting hints drop that we would not hesitate because of price. This was music to Banker Willis' ears. While we had been talking, his brain had been racing with a

279

plan calculated to give us a real, old-fashioned shellacking.

"I'd like to take you over to Hartford and show you that factory," he said. "But I have to make a trip to New York and I'm afraid I can't put it off. Could you gentlemen come back in a week?"

Buck and I knew that this was a stall, but we readily agreed. "We have some business in Chicago, anyhow," I returned. "We can come back. But I trust you won't sell to anyone else until we've had an opportunity to look into the proposition."

We waited ten days before we went back to Fort Wayne. We wanted to give the banker plenty of time. We had an idea what he was up to. We knew more about the glass works than the banker thought we did; that it hadn't been in operation for a long time, that it was practically abandoned and partly dismantled, that it was considered a lemon.

When we called on the banker again, he was extremely cordial. He drove us to Hartford, meanwhile telling us what a wonderful buy the factory would be.

We let him think that he was making a big impression. We gave him rapt attention. When we reached the plant it was much different from when we had seen it two weeks before. Part of it had been freshly painted. Signs of decay had been removed and smoke belched from its chimneys. He led us inside and showed us a busy aggregation of workers making glass.

We were all set to buy the plant before we returned to Fort Wayne. We agreed to pay $1,500,000 for it, about four times what it was worth. But, of course, there was the usual delay. We must contact Berlin and get the final approval of our principals. This, I explained, might take ten days or two weeks. That was all right with Banker Willis.

Meanwhile we continued to see him every day. One day I broached the subject of mining stocks. He was interested at once. I finally arranged for him to go with me to Chicago, where an expensive suite in the Sherman hotel had been reserved. Jimmy Head had rented a brokerage office on LaSalle Street. I let Willis accompany me on several trips while I cleaned up on mining stocks. He was particulary impressed when I took the stock — which I had purchased for

## Tricks of the Trade

ten cents a share — and collected two dollars a share for it at the brokerage house.

I took him along on several small deals and finally on a Saturday afternoon, decided he was ripe. The block of stock we wanted would cost $200,000. I didn't have that much money and Willis pleaded with me to let him in on the good thing. I finally relented, and he agreed to raise $143,000. Since the banks were all closed and he couldn't get the money transferred, he drove to Fort Wayne to get the cash out of the vault of his own bank.

Later when he discovered that he had been swindled, he made a loud beef to the police. The fact that he had planned to swindle us on the factory deal made no difference. He had a hard time getting evidence, but he left no stone unturned. He found another man who had been a victim, and between their testimonies I was convicted.

In general, though, my "customers" seldom complained. They preferred to take their losses rather than let the world know that they had been so gullible.

## 26. The Little Things Count

DURING THESE YEARS I DISCOVERED MANY THINGS, BUT MOST important I learned about people, their strong points and their weaknesses — especially their weaknesses. All the people I swindled had one thing in common — greed, the desire to acquire money. But that was not always enough. In numerous cases there was some other factor, some small desire that helped me to clinch a deal.

Some of my tales may sound unbelievable. But they are true. I could hardly believe some of them myself, but as time went on I came to look for the little weaknesses. Trivial matters often meant the difference between success and failure for me.

In my most successful con game, the stock swindle, the mechanics were the same in every case. Yet in each one was some little variation.

One of the most amusing occurred in the case of a banker in Decatur, Illinois, Mr. Appleby. He had been around with me while I acquired blocks of stock at ten cents a share and had accompanied me to the brokerage house where I sold the same stock for two dollars a share. He did not seem to suspect anything wrong, but he was apathetic when it came to buying a big block of stock with his money. I had decided that he was good for $30,000.

Just before the big deal he hesitated. "I don't know why I should speculate," he said, as we walked along the street, discussing it. "I make a comfortable living. I'm not rich, but I get along."

I gave him my best arguments, but it seemed that I was about to lose him. Then we happened to pass a furniture store. Hair mattresses were displayed in the window. He stopped and looked.

*Fred "The Deacon" Buckminster as he appeared in 1941.*

*Says "Yellow Kid" today, "I no longer have any of my ill-gotten gains ... nothing more spectacular than walking the dog happens ..."*

## The Little Things Count

"Hair mattresses!" he exclaimed. "Aren't they beauties?"

"Why, yes," I replied, but without his enthusiasm.

"I've always wanted hair mattresses in my home," he continued, "but I never felt that I could afford them." He gazed at them rather wistfully.

I was quick to recognize this as the weakness I'd been looking for.

"Let's go in and see them," I suggested.

"What good will that do?" he asked. "I don't feel I can afford them."

"Well, it won't cost anything to look. Come on."

We went in the store and the clerk showed us an assortment. But when Mr. Appleby learned the prices, he shook his head and we walked out.

"A hundred dollars is a lot of money," he said. "I would need at least five for my home. I can't afford them."

"Mr. Appleby," I said, "you can have those hair mattresses for nothing, if you want them."

"How?"

"I have offered to let you share in buying that block of stock. With the money we will make you can buy a hundred hair mattresses."

"By George," he exclaimed. "That's right." There was a new light in his eyes. I knew he was sunk.

From then on it was easy. He invested $30,000 in a block of my worthless stock — all for the sake of a hair mattress. I might add that in those days hair mattresses were the last word in style and comfort and were found only in the homes of the wealthy.

While this may seem incredible, every word is true. It's the little things that count.

On one occasion, I worked on the president of a large bank in Omaha. The deal involved the purchase of the street railway system of Omaha, including a bridge across the Mississippi River. My principals were supposedly German and I had to negotiate with Berlin. While awaiting word from them I introduced my fake mining-stock proposition. Since this man was very rich, I decided to play for high stakes. After an elaborate build-up, during which the banker took a trip with me to New York, I had the cables to Berlin busy. They were real cables and the answers were sent by a man in Berlin — the purser on a Hamburg-American Line ship.

Meanwhile, I played golf with the banker, visited his home, and went to the theatre with him and his wife. Though he showed some interest in my stock deal, he still wasn't convinced. I had built it up to the point that an investment of $1,250,000 was required. Of this I was to put up $900,000, the banker $350,000. But still he hesitated.

One evening when I was at his home for dinner I wore some perfume — Coty's "April Violets." It was not then considered effeminate for a man to use a dash of perfume.

The banker's wife thought it very lovely. "Where *did* you get it?"

"It is a rare blend," I told her, "especially made for me by a French perfumer. Do you like it?"

"I love it," she replied.

The following day I went through my effects and found two empty bottles. Both had come from France, but were empty. I went to a downtown department store and purchased ten ounces of Coty's "April Violets." I poured this into the two French bottles, carefully sealed them, wrapped them in tissue paper.

That evening I dropped by the banker's home and presented the two bottles to his wife. "They were especially put up for me in Cologne," I told her.

The next day the banker called at my hotel. His wife was enraptured by the perfume. She considered it the most wonderful, the most exotic fragrance she had ever used. I did not tell the banker he could get all he wanted right in Omaha.

"She said," the banker added, "that I was fortunate to be associated with a man like you."

From then on his attitude was changed, for he had complete faith in his wife's judgment. It was only a matter of time until we had "cornered" the big block of stock. He parted with $350,000. This, incidentally, was my biggest score.

Most confidence games are built on human frailties. There was the case of a wealthy spinster who lived on Lake Shore Drive in Chicago. I had some difficulty arranging an introduction, but finally accomplished it through a priest, who acted quite innocently.

## The Little Things Count

Miss Buckley was about forty, owned several million dollars and some Arizona mining property. I posed as a mining engineer and was engaged to look after her property in Arizona. I later brought in Fred "The Deacon" Buckminster as my associate. But we found she was only mildly interested in the mines.

One day Buckminster took me aside. "I've found out how we can get to Miss Buckley."

"How?"

"She wants to get married," he said. "She lives in deadly fear that she's going to be an old maid."

"What can I do about that?"

"You're going to woo her," Buck replied.

"Buck, I can't do that," I objected. "I've got one wife."

"She doesn't have to know that. You can do it gradually. Meanwhile, we can clean up."

Somewhat reluctantly, I agreed. I began making love to the woman and her attitude changed. When it got to a point I considered dangerous, I got a sudden call to go to Arizona to inspect the mining property. She gladly paid our expenses. And when someone else paid the bill, our expenses were tremendous!

From then on, for several months, that was the routine. I wooed her for a while, then Buck and I made a trip to Arizona. Since the love interest had entered her life she was far more interested in her mining property. We saw to it, however, that our presence at the mines was often required.

We made six trips to Arizona, each more expensive than the one before. Altogether we got about $15,000 for our services as mining engineers. Inevitably, the day came when she expected me to marry her. That was when I had to bow out.

Nearly everybody believes the old saying that "It isn't what you know, but whom you know." I had occasion to cash in on that, too.

I had been to the City Hall, where my brother was a Municipal Court bailiff. As I was leaving, a breezy young fellow approached me. He handed me a cigar and offered to buy a drink. I was surprised, but accepted. Then he suggested dinner and some entertainment. As long as it was his idea and he was paying the bills I went along.

I didn't quite understand what was back of it and he didn't tell me, beyond a hint that he was a stranger and wanted companionship. I let it go at that. We had a pleasant evening and he suggested that we get together again.

The next time he told me that he was a salesman for a sign company in Rochester, New York, and that he was trying to interest the Bureau of Streets in complete new metal signs for Chicago street intersections.

"I understand you're a pretty good friend of the Commissioner?"

I knew now that he must have mistaken me for somebody else. But it looked like an opportunity to make a little money.

"That is correct," I told him.

He then told me his proposition. Metal signs for Chicago streets would amount to $129,000. His commission would be $17,000. He would give me $11,000 of this if I would intercede in his behalf.

I agreed to undertake it. He turned the contracts, long detailed documents, over to me. I made frequent trips to the City Hall, while he anxiously waited to hear the outcome. I told him there was much negotiating to be done and carried this on for a week. Finally I came out with the contracts, signed and notarized. He was overjoyed. He forwarded them to his company and we had a celebration. In a few days I received a check for $11,000. My friend went back to Rochester.

I later heard that a big warehouse in Chicago was piled high with metal signs but that the Bureau of Streets would have no part of them. Presumably they were the signs from Rochester. I don't know what happened to them.

The Deacon and I were the first con-men to introduce Chinese stooges. They were Chinese-Americans who lived in Chicago. But for our purpose, we rigged them out in fancy oriental clothing and told the prospects that they spoke no English.

We used them in a deal with a paper manufacturer in Kalamazoo, Michigan, whom I will call Mr. Stimson. He wasn't much interested until we brought in the Chinese. This was a logical move, since the Chinese had manufactured the first paper. We told him of a new

## The Little Things Count

Chinese discovery that would revolutionize papermaking.

After we had taken the Chinese boys in and introduced them as paper experts from China he fell for this line. The purpose of the whole thing was to get him worked up and then switch his interest to the stock scheme. We succeeded in doing this, thanks to the Orientals.

But we had to make several trips to Kalamazoo. On the last trip, when we were to complete the deal, we were about fifty miles out of Chicago when the Chinese who was driving suddenly stopped the car. Buckminster and I were in the back seat with a bag containing $250,000 in boodle. We both thought they had decided to rob us.

"Why are you stopping?" I asked.

"For a showdown," answered the spokesman for the three Chinese.

"What's wrong?"

"You're making a lot of money on this deal?"

"We expect to," I admitted.

"But you only pay us ten dollars a day."

"That's correct," I said. "What do you want?" I was sure now that he wanted a big cut.

"Ten dollars is not enough," he replied. "We get twenty dollars a day or we don't go another foot."

I felt like laughing, but I gravely agreed to raise their pay. They smiled, the driver started the car, and we went on. They placidly went through their paces and we had no more trouble with them. Mr. Stimson came through for us with $15,000 on the stock deal.

One of the most unusual characters I ever met was a young man in Cincinnati. He was heir to a large soap fortune, but he had little time for business. He had two interests in life — beautiful women and Scotch whiskey.

I interested him in one of my stock transactions and took him to Muncie, Indiana. He took along a small satchel that looked like a doctor's bag. It contained numerous vials, also like a physician's case. But each vial contained Scotch whiskey.

"This is something I never travel without," he said. "I never have to worry about companionship as long as I have my bag." All during the trip he sampled the contents of the vials. I was never present when he ate breakfast, but I sometimes wondered if he poured Scotch on his oatmeal.

I took $50,000 of his money, but he never filed a complaint against me.

## 27. Where the Money Went

THE POLICE AND THE DAILY PRESS HAVE ESTIMATED THAT I ACQUIRED a total of about $8,000,000 in my various swindles. They may be right. I never kept books. Much of that money I made before there was an income tax law and a man could keep all the money he got.

People are curious as to how confidence men spend their money, as well as their leisure. Between victims most con men spend their time in dissipation. If one makes a big score, he throws a party for his friends. Even at such parties the con men play different roles.

On one occasion Buckminster completed a deal that had brought him $15,000. He had a lot of friends who knew him as a financier and had no idea that he was a swindler. These included prominent brokers and real estate men. He had a beautiful home on the North Side and decided to give a lavish party. He invited his prominent friends, and also invited John Strosnider and myself.

To these friends, he was Mr. Kimball of the Kimball Piano Company. I was introduced as Dr. Henri Reuel and Strosnider as Mr. Hagenbeck of the Hagenbeck-Wallace Circus. It was a nice party, where wine flowed freely and the food was excellent.

Strosnider was a peculiar fellow. He was exceedingly proud of his accomplishments as a swindler. About halfway through the party, when he had imbibed considerable wine, he began to say: "I'm not Hagenbeck. I'm John Strosnider, the great confidence man." He staggered through the house, telling this to the guests. They began to get their wraps. Within a few minutes most of them had gone. That taught the Deacon not to invite Strosnider to any more of his parties.

## "Yellow Kid" Weil

Buckminster was different. I think he was a little ashamed of his background, for he never liked to talk about it. I think this desire to get away from the con man atmosphere was the reason he often gave parties for people who had no criminal connections.

Other con men do the same. They are different from other criminals in that few ever resort to violence of any sort and most of them are better educated than those in the other categories of crime. They consider themselves smart and like to mingle with a better class than can be found in underworld haunts.

Nearly every con man is a sucker for a pretty face and a neat figure. That often resulted in revelries which ran to considerable sums.

But, even with all this free spending, most big-time con men have plenty of money left. How they lose these fortunes sounds incredible, but I can cite actual experiences.

There is a widespread notion that a clever swindler could be a great success if he turned his talents to legitimate channels. I say nothing is further from the truth, for when a con man invests his money in a legitimate business he loses it.

Buckminster, Strosnider, and I invested $25,000 each in a lease of the Hagenbeck-Wallace Circus. Hagenbeck was a German, widely known as a sportsman and big-game hunter. The animals for the circus were captured by him — or at least, that is how the menagerie was started. Wallace was a wealthy American showman. These two organized the circus but had nothing to do with the running of it, for they leased it out on a yearly basis. In addition to the original investment, the lessee agreed to pay a guaranteed amount for each day of the circus season.

Shortly after we took it over, there were twenty-two consecutive nights of rain, and the losses were terrific. People don't go to the circus in the rain, but the overhead and the daily guarantee to Hagenbeck-Wallace went on. We were actually licked by the time we had some fair weather. We tried to carry on but didn't know enough about running a circus. Before the season was half over we had to surrender the franchise and had lost $375,000.

Buck and I were broke, and so had to find a prospect for a con game. But Strosnider had saved a little money. He fancied himself a

## Where the Money Went

good showman. He spent $6,000 for a dog-and-pony show and tried to operate it. He lasted a few weeks and then lost the little he had salvaged.

I put a great deal of my money into Chicago real estate. There was a time when I had property valued at more than half a million dollars. All of this had to be sold at a loss.

Then there was the yacht. The *Penguin* was really a luxury cruiser. I bought it for pleasure when I had a lot of money and did a great deal of entertaining on it. At that time, too, I had a penchant for expensive imported motor cars. I bought several in the $10,000 class. They cost plenty to operate and more to keep in repair. Between my yacht and my cars, I probably had as much luxury expense as any man in Chicago.

Buckminster was similarly given to luxury living. He too considered Chicago real estate a good investment and bought income property in the Rogers Park district.

But his weakness was women. A woman much younger than he induced him to file the title to his car in her name. I pleaded with him.

"That woman is not in love with you," I told him. "She just wants to get all she can out of you."

He refused to listen and transferred ownership of the car to her. He had already given her a luxurious apartment in one of his buildings. Then, in 1926, when the heat from one of his deals became uncomfortable and he was likely to be sent to prison, she talked him into turning over to her the title to all his real estate. Her argument was that if the property was in her name, nobody could touch it, even if he were sent up.

Again I tried to point out that he was being victimized. But he would not believe it and made over his property to her. He was sent up, and as soon as he had been safely put away she sold it all and deserted him. When he came out he was penniless.

I was lavish in other ways. I had the highest priced tailors in Europe and America and amassed a wardrobe of fine clothes. But this I have never regretted, because these clothes are still presentable.

In the main, though, I lost my money trying to be a legitimate business man. That's the way most other con men lose theirs.

It takes a great deal of boldness, mixed with a vast amount of caution, to acquire a fortune. But it takes ten times as much wit to keep it.

The notion that any swindler would be a great success if he turned to legitimate channels, is indeed erroneous.

Many people have told me they would like to use me in their businesses. But they always add that they don't dare because of my reputation. For that reason I've had to take any sort of job I could get since I gave up the confidence game.

My most successful occupation has been telephone soliciting. I have worked for various charitable organizations, political candidates, and churches. Needless to say, I do not handle any of the funds. I merely solicit contributions and ask that they be sent to the headquarters of the organization I'm working for. When the funds are received I am paid a percentage.

I no longer have any of my ill-gotten gains and depend on this work for a living. But my wants are modest and I manage to maintain a home on Lake Shore Drive. There I can be near my daughter. Though nothing more spectacular than walking the dog happens in my life now, my peace of mind is very satisfying.

## 28. The Last Word

*Joseph Weil Lies Under the Ground;
Don't Jingle Any Money While Walking Around.*

AFTER MY LATE WIFE HAD GIVEN UP ALL HOPE OF EVER REFORMING ME, she suggested, in a jocular vein, that the above jingle would make an excellent epitaph for me. As the years passed and my reputation as a con man spread throughout the world, more and more people came to share the sentiment expressed in those lines.

It has been several years since I have had any but honest dealings with other men. But I still feel as I always did on one subject — that the men I fleeced were basically no more honest than I was.

Analyzing my own actions in retrospect, I don't believe I ever had any basic desire to be dishonest. One of the motivating factors in my actions was, of course, the desire to acquire money. The other motive was a lust for adventure — and this was the only kind of adventure for which I was equipped.

The men I swindled were also motivated by a desire to acquire money, and they didn't care at whose expense they got it. I was particular. I took money only from those who could afford it and were willing to go in with me in schemes they fancied would fleece others.

They wanted money for its own sake. I wanted it for the luxuries and pleasures it would afford me.

They were seldom concerned with human nature. They knew little — and cared less — about their fellow men. If they had been keener students of human nature, if they had given more time to companionship with their fellows and less to the chase of the almighty dollar, they wouldn't have been such easy marks.

Every swindle I ever developed had a hole in it somewhere. But I made everything plausible — to anyone who did not dig too deep or ask questions.

Only one man seemed to profit by the lesson I taught him. He was a Montana banker who had bought some of my worthless stock. He was ready to take his medicine. Though I was arrested, he declined to identify me as the swindler. As a result I was acquitted. Later I heard him remark: "You can fleece a lamb every year, but you only get his hide once."

Lies were the foundation of my schemes. A lie is an allurement, a fabrication, that can be embellished into a fantasy. It can be clothed in the raiments of a mystic conception.

Truth is cold, sober fact, not so comfortable to absorb. A lie is more palatable. The most detested person in the world is the one who always tells the truth, who never romances.

If a lie is told often enough even the teller comes to believe it. It becomes a habit. And habit is like a cable. Each day another strand is added until you have woven a cable that is unbreakable.

It was that way with me. I found it far more interesting and profitable to romance than to tell the truth. It has taken me five years to break that cable. That's why I haven't told this story until this late date.

People say that I am the most successful and the most colorful confidence man that ever lived. I won't deny it. There is good reason why I am regarded as in a class by myself.

The fact is that I have played more roles in real life than the average actor ever dreamed of. The actor has a script carefully prepared for him in advance. I made my own script as I went along, depending upon my wits for any contingency.

Some small gesture that was out of character in the role I was portraying, or the wrong answer to a question might have betrayed me. Fortunately for me, I always had the right answer and carried off convincingly the role I played.

To do this successfully — as I did for about half a century — I had to possess, first of all, a vast store of general information. Besides that, I had to know the rudiments of many professions. If I played the role of a physician, I had to be in a position to use medical terms accurately. As a mining engineer, I had to know geology and mineralogy. As a

## The Last Word

broker or investment banker, I had to be up on the latest and most intricate financial matters.

Perhaps the most important of all my qualifications was a good knowledge of the law. I kept well posted on this subject. Over the years, I have seen many new laws passed — most of them restricting the freedom of the individual. No doubt I was the inspiration for some of these statutes.

It is my hope that I will live to see the enactment of one more law — to mete out equal punishment for all who have larceny in their hearts. For example, a supposedly honest and respectable man is approached by a con man who offers him an opportunity to get rich quick. This man knows that the proposition is not honest and that if it works, he will get rich at the expense of others.

Nevertheless, his avarice prevails and he invests his money. The con man makes his killing and disappears. The would-be fleecer has been fleeced.

Suppose he goes to the police and cries, "I've been cheated!" If the con man is caught and convicted, he is punished for having taken the other's money. But the man who lost, and had entered into the conspiracy to cheat others, goes free. He isn't even tried or censured. He is applauded as a public-spirited citizen.

An excellent example of what I mean is the money-making machine. One of the oldest of the confidence rackets, it is still being done. I read of a case only recently.

The con men locates Mr. Jones, who has money, but is greedy for more and is not too particular how he gets it. In great secrecy, he shows Mr. Jones the wonderful machine he has invented for making hundred-dollar bills out of ten-dollar bills. Mr. Jones watches a demonstration of the wonderful machine. It is all very simple. You feed a ten-dollar bill into one end, turn a crank, and out pops a hundred-dollar bill.

Mr. Jones wants to buy the machine, but the con man is reluctant to sell. Mr. Jones become persuasive and finally induces the con man to sell. He pays anywhere from $500 to $5,000 for it, depending upon how wealthy he is, how greedy, and how gullible. He hurries home with the machine, locks himself in a room, and prepares to crank out a fortune.

## "Yellow Kid" Weil

What a shock it is when Mr. Jones finds that he has been taken! He hurries to the police and reports the swindle. He even admits that he had planned to counterfeit the currency of the United States. But, in the eyes of the law, he is another victim of a con game.

In my opinion, he should be made a party to a conspiracy to obtain money illegally. He should go on trial alongside the con man and be subject to the same punishment. The same should be true of anybody else who enters into a con man's scheme to get money dishonestly.

When such a law is enacted, you will see an end to complaints against swindlers — for two reasons. The number who enter into such schemes will be fewer, because of the fear of being caught. And those who do go in and lose will keep quiet about it because of the fear of punishment.

I am not talking about small swindles, where an honest person loses his money. I have never been a party to such schemes. I have never taken a dime from honest, hard-working people who could not afford to lose. But the victims of confidence games are usually people who are wealthy and can afford to pay the con man's price for the lesson.

I ought to know. I've had dealings with some of the wealthiest men in the country. They had plenty of money, but they fell for my schemes because they were greedy for more. In my time, I devised some ingenious plans to relieve these people of part of their wealth, at the same time teaching them that it does not pay to be too avaricious.

People will tell you that crime does not pay. Perhaps that is right. But it paid me handsomely. I feel that I have lived a thousand years in seventy. Those periods of incarceration — well, they were not always what I would have chosen, but they gave me time to relax, reflect, and catch up on my reading.

The bad part about serving a prison term is not while you are doing the stretch — it's the stigma that forever clings to you after you come out. In England, it is illegal to refer to a person as an ex-convict, but in this country you can never escape the brand, no matter how hard you try.

Some do try. Most prison officials make a conscientious effort at rehabilitation. When they leave these institutions at least half the inmates

## The Last Word

are resolved to lead a straightforward life. But few ever have a chance. It is a rare person who will give them a chance.

I have told in detail most of the swindles in which any reader might be invited to participate. I have offered them at only a fraction of the cost to the original investors — with all the thrills but with none of the risks.

I am now seventy years old and I look back over my career with mingled feelings. I have retired and I want to do what I can to promote harmony among my fellow men. For this reason, I decided to tell the inside story of my long and, I must admit, dishonorable career.

A CATALOGUE OF SELECTED DOVER BOOKS
IN ALL FIELDS OF INTEREST

# A CATALOGUE OF SELECTED DOVER BOOKS
## IN ALL FIELDS OF INTEREST

AMERICA'S OLD MASTERS, James T. Flexner. Four men emerged unexpectedly from provincial 18th century America to leadership in European art: Benjamin West, J. S. Copley, C. R. Peale, Gilbert Stuart. Brilliant coverage of lives and contributions. Revised, 1967 edition. 69 plates. 365pp. of text.
21806-6 Paperbound $3.00

FIRST FLOWERS OF OUR WILDERNESS: AMERICAN PAINTING, THE COLONIAL PERIOD, James T. Flexner. Painters, and regional painting traditions from earliest Colonial times up to the emergence of Copley, West and Peale Sr., Foster, Gustavus Hesselius, Feke, John Smibert and many anonymous painters in the primitive manner. Engaging presentation, with 162 illustrations. xxii + 368pp.
22180-6 Paperbound $3.50

THE LIGHT OF DISTANT SKIES: AMERICAN PAINTING, 1760-1835, James T. Flexner. The great generation of early American painters goes to Europe to learn and to teach: West, Copley, Gilbert Stuart and others. Allston, Trumbull, Morse; also contemporary American painters—primitives, derivatives, academics—who remained in America. 102 illustrations. xiii + 306pp.
22179-2 Paperbound $3.50

A HISTORY OF THE RISE AND PROGRESS OF THE ARTS OF DESIGN IN THE UNITED STATES, William Dunlap. Much the richest mine of information on early American painters, sculptors, architects, engravers, miniaturists, etc. The only source of information for scores of artists, the major primary source for many others. Unabridged reprint of rare original 1834 edition, with new introduction by James T. Flexner, and 394 new illustrations. Edited by Rita Weiss. 6⅝ x 9⅝.
21695-0, 21696-9, 21697-7 Three volumes, Paperbound $13.50

EPOCHS OF CHINESE AND JAPANESE ART, Ernest F. Fenollosa. From primitive Chinese art to the 20th century, thorough history, explanation of every important art period and form, including Japanese woodcuts; main stress on China and Japan, but Tibet, Korea also included. Still unexcelled for its detailed, rich coverage of cultural background, aesthetic elements, diffusion studies, particularly of the historical period. 2nd, 1913 edition. 242 illustrations. lii + 439pp. of text.
20364-6, 20365-4 Two volumes, Paperbound $6.00

THE GENTLE ART OF MAKING ENEMIES, James A. M. Whistler. Greatest wit of his day deflates Oscar Wilde, Ruskin, Swinburne; strikes back at inane critics, exhibitions, art journalism; aesthetics of impressionist revolution in most striking form. Highly readable classic by great painter. Reproduction of edition designed by Whistler. Introduction by Alfred Werner. xxxvi + 334pp.
21875-9 Paperbound $3.00

*CATALOGUE OF DOVER BOOKS*

VISUAL ILLUSIONS: THEIR CAUSES, CHARACTERISTICS, AND APPLICATIONS, Matthew Luckiesh. Thorough description and discussion of optical illusion, geometric and perspective, particularly; size and shape distortions, illusions of color, of motion; natural illusions; use of illusion in art and magic, industry, etc. Most useful today with op art, also for classical art. Scores of effects illustrated. Introduction by William H. Ittleson. 100 illustrations. xxi + 252pp.

21530-X Paperbound $2.00

A HANDBOOK OF ANATOMY FOR ART STUDENTS, Arthur Thomson. Thorough, virtually exhaustive coverage of skeletal structure, musculature, etc. Full text, supplemented by anatomical diagrams and drawings and by photographs of undraped figures. Unique in its comparison of male and female forms, pointing out differences of contour, texture, form. 211 figures, 40 drawings, 86 photographs. xx + 459pp. 5⅜ x 8⅜. 21163-0 Paperbound $3.50

150 MASTERPIECES OF DRAWING, Selected by Anthony Toney. Full page reproductions of drawings from the early 16th to the end of the 18th century, all beautifully reproduced: Rembrandt, Michelangelo, Dürer, Fragonard, Urs, Graf, Wouwerman, many others. First-rate browsing book, model book for artists. xviii + 150pp. 8⅜ x 11¼. 21032-4 Paperbound $2.50

THE LATER WORK OF AUBREY BEARDSLEY, Aubrey Beardsley. Exotic, erotic, ironic masterpieces in full maturity: Comedy Ballet, Venus and Tannhauser, Pierrot, Lysistrata, Rape of the Lock, Savoy material, Ali Baba, Volpone, etc. This material revolutionized the art world, and is still powerful, fresh, brilliant. With *The Early Work,* all Beardsley's finest work. 174 plates, 2 in color. xiv + 176pp. 8⅛ x 11.

21817-1 Paperbound $3.00

DRAWINGS OF REMBRANDT, Rembrandt van Rijn. Complete reproduction of fabulously rare edition by Lippmann and Hofstede de Groot, completely reedited, updated, improved by Prof. Seymour Slive, Fogg Museum. Portraits, Biblical sketches, landscapes, Oriental types, nudes, episodes from classical mythology—All Rembrandt's fertile genius. Also selection of drawings by his pupils and followers. "Stunning volumes," *Saturday Review.* 550 illustrations. lxxviii + 552pp. 9⅛ x 12¼. 21485-0, 21486-9 Two volumes, Paperbound $10.00

THE DISASTERS OF WAR, Francisco Goya. One of the masterpieces of Western civilization—83 etchings that record Goya's shattering, bitter reaction to the Napoleonic war that swept through Spain after the insurrection of 1808 and to war in general. Reprint of the first edition, with three additional plates from Boston's Museum of Fine Arts. All plates facsimile size. Introduction by Philip Hofer, Fogg Museum. v + 97pp. 9⅜ x 8¼. 21872-4 Paperbound $2.00

GRAPHIC WORKS OF ODILON REDON. Largest collection of Redon's graphic works ever assembled: 172 lithographs, 28 etchings and engravings, 9 drawings. These include some of his most famous works. All the plates from *Odilon Redon: oeuvre graphique complet,* plus additional plates. New introduction and caption translations by Alfred Werner. 209 illustrations. xxvii + 209pp. 9⅛ x 12¼.

21966-8 Paperbound $4.50

## CATALOGUE OF DOVER BOOKS

DESIGN BY ACCIDENT; A BOOK OF "ACCIDENTAL EFFECTS" FOR ARTISTS AND DESIGNERS, James F. O'Brien. Create your own unique, striking, imaginative effects by "controlled accident" interaction of materials: paints and lacquers, oil and water based paints, splatter, crackling materials, shatter, similar items. Everything you do will be different; first book on this limitless art, so useful to both fine artist and commercial artist. Full instructions. 192 plates showing "accidents," 8 in color. viii + 215pp. 8 3/8 x 11 1/4. 21942-9 Paperbound $3.50

THE BOOK OF SIGNS, Rudolf Koch. Famed German type designer draws 493 beautiful symbols: religious, mystical, alchemical, imperial, property marks, runes, etc. Remarkable fusion of traditional and modern. Good for suggestions of timelessness, smartness, modernity. Text. vi + 104pp. 6 1/8 x 9 1/4. 20162-7 Paperbound $1.25

HISTORY OF INDIAN AND INDONESIAN ART, Ananda K. Coomaraswamy. An unabridged republication of one of the finest books by a great scholar in Eastern art. Rich in descriptive material, history, social backgrounds; Sunga reliefs, Rajput paintings, Gupta temples, Burmese frescoes, textiles, jewelry, sculpture, etc. 400 photos. viii + 423pp. 6 3/8 x 9 3/4. 21436-2 Paperbound $5.00

PRIMITIVE ART, Franz Boas. America's foremost anthropologist surveys textiles, ceramics, woodcarving, basketry, metalwork, etc.; patterns, technology, creation of symbols, style origins. All areas of world, but very full on Northwest Coast Indians. More than 350 illustrations of baskets, boxes, totem poles, weapons, etc. 378 pp. 20025-6 Paperbound $3.00

THE GENTLEMAN AND CABINET MAKER'S DIRECTOR, Thomas Chippendale. Full reprint (third edition, 1762) of most influential furniture book of all time, by master cabinetmaker. 200 plates, illustrating chairs, sofas, mirrors, tables, cabinets, plus 24 photographs of surviving pieces. Biographical introduction by N. Bienenstock. vi + 249pp. 9 7/8 x 12 3/4. 21601-2 Paperbound $4.00

AMERICAN ANTIQUE FURNITURE, Edgar G. Miller, Jr. The basic coverage of all American furniture before 1840. Individual chapters cover type of furniture—clocks, tables, sideboards, etc.—chronologically, with inexhaustible wealth of data. More than 2100 photographs, all identified, commented on. Essential to all early American collectors. Introduction by H. E. Keyes. vi + 1106pp. 7 7/8 x 10 3/4. 21599-7, 21600-4 Two volumes, Paperbound $11.00

PENNSYLVANIA DUTCH AMERICAN FOLK ART, Henry J. Kauffman. 279 photos, 28 drawings of tulipware, Fraktur script, painted tinware, toys, flowered furniture, quilts, samplers, hex signs, house interiors, etc. Full descriptive text. Excellent for tourist, rewarding for designer, collector. Map. 146pp. 7 7/8 x 10 3/4. 21205-X Paperbound $2.50

EARLY NEW ENGLAND GRAVESTONE RUBBINGS, Edmund V. Gillon, Jr. 43 photographs, 226 carefully reproduced rubbings show heavily symbolic, sometimes macabre early gravestones, up to early 19th century. Remarkable early American primitive art, occasionally strikingly beautiful; always powerful. Text. xxvi + 207pp. 8 3/8 x 11 1/4. 21380-3 Paperbound $3.50

## CATALOGUE OF DOVER BOOKS

ALPHABETS AND ORNAMENTS, Ernst Lehner. Well-known pictorial source for decorative alphabets, script examples, cartouches, frames, decorative title pages, calligraphic initials, borders, similar material. 14th to 19th century, mostly European. Useful in almost any graphic arts designing, varied styles. 750 illustrations. 256pp. 7 x 10. 21905-4 Paperbound $4.00

PAINTING: A CREATIVE APPROACH, Norman Colquhoun. For the beginner simple guide provides an instructive approach to painting: major stumbling blocks for beginner; overcoming them, technical points; paints and pigments; oil painting; watercolor and other media and color. New section on "plastic" paints. Glossary. Formerly *Paint Your Own Pictures.* 221pp. 22000-1 Paperbound $1.75

THE ENJOYMENT AND USE OF COLOR, Walter Sargent. Explanation of the relations between colors themselves and between colors in nature and art, including hundreds of little-known facts about color values, intensities, effects of high and low illumination, complementary colors. Many practical hints for painters, references to great masters. 7 color plates, 29 illustrations. x + 274pp.
20944-X Paperbound $2.75

THE NOTEBOOKS OF LEONARDO DA VINCI, compiled and edited by Jean Paul Richter. 1566 extracts from original manuscripts reveal the full range of Leonardo's versatile genius: all his writings on painting, sculpture, architecture, anatomy, astronomy, geography, topography, physiology, mining, music, etc., in both Italian and English, with 186 plates of manuscript pages and more than 500 additional drawings. Includes studies for the Last Supper, the lost Sforza monument, and other works. Total of xlvii + 866pp. 7⅞ x 10¾.
22572-0, 22573-9 Two volumes, Paperbound $10.00

MONTGOMERY WARD CATALOGUE OF 1895. Tea gowns, yards of flannel and pillow-case lace, stereoscopes, books of gospel hymns, the New Improved Singer Sewing Machine, side saddles, milk skimmers, straight-edged razors, high-button shoes, spittoons, and on and on . . . listing some 25,000 items, practically all illustrated. Essential to the shoppers of the 1890's, it is our truest record of the spirit of the period. Unaltered reprint of Issue No. 57, Spring and Summer 1895. Introduction by Boris Emmet. Innumerable illustrations. xiii + 624pp. 8½ x 11⅝.
22377-9 Paperbound $6.95

THE CRYSTAL PALACE EXHIBITION ILLUSTRATED CATALOGUE (LONDON, 1851). One of the wonders of the modern world—the Crystal Palace Exhibition in which all the nations of the civilized world exhibited their achievements in the arts and sciences—presented in an equally important illustrated catalogue. More than 1700 items pictured with accompanying text—ceramics, textiles, cast-iron work, carpets, pianos, sleds, razors, wall-papers, billiard tables, beehives, silverware and hundreds of other artifacts—represent the focal point of Victorian culture in the Western World. Probably the largest collection of Victorian decorative art ever assembled—indispensable for antiquarians and designers. Unabridged republication of the Art-Journal Catalogue of the Great Exhibition of 1851, with all terminal essays. New introduction by John Gloag, F.S.A. xxxiv + 426pp. 9 x 12.
22503-8 Paperbound $5.00

CATALOGUE OF DOVER BOOKS

A HISTORY OF COSTUME, Carl Köhler. Definitive history, based on surviving pieces of clothing primarily, and paintings, statues, etc. secondarily. Highly readable text, supplemented by 594 illustrations of costumes of the ancient Mediterranean peoples, Greece and Rome, the Teutonic prehistoric period; costumes of the Middle Ages, Renaissance, Baroque, 18th and 19th centuries. Clear, measured patterns are provided for many clothing articles. Approach is practical throughout. Enlarged by Emma von Sichart. 464pp. 21030-8 Paperbound $3.50.

ORIENTAL RUGS, ANTIQUE AND MODERN, Walter A. Hawley. A complete and authoritative treatise on the Oriental rug—where they are made, by whom and how, designs and symbols, characteristics in detail of the six major groups, how to distinguish them and how to buy them. Detailed technical data is provided on periods, weaves, warps, wefts, textures, sides, ends and knots, although no technical background is required for an understanding. 11 color plates, 80 halftones, 4 maps. vi + 320pp. 6⅛ x 9⅛. 22366-3 Paperbound $5.00

TEN BOOKS ON ARCHITECTURE, Vitruvius. By any standards the most important book on architecture ever written. Early Roman discussion of aesthetics of building, construction methods, orders, sites, and every other aspect of architecture has inspired, instructed architecture for about 2,000 years. Stands behind Palladio, Michelangelo, Bramante, Wren, countless others. Definitive Morris H. Morgan translation. 68 illustrations. xii + 331pp. 20645-9 Paperbound $3.00

THE FOUR BOOKS OF ARCHITECTURE, Andrea Palladio. Translated into every major Western European language in the two centuries following its publication in 1570, this has been one of the most influential books in the history of architecture. Complete reprint of the 1738 Isaac Ware edition. New introduction by Adolf Placzek, Columbia Univ. 216 plates. xxii + 110pp. of text. 9½ x 12¾.
21308-0 Clothbound $12.50

STICKS AND STONES: A STUDY OF AMERICAN ARCHITECTURE AND CIVILIZATION, Lewis Mumford. One of the great classics of American cultural history. American architecture from the medieval-inspired earliest forms to the early 20th century; evolution of structure and style, and reciprocal influences on environment. 21 photographic illustrations. 238pp. 20202-X Paperbound $2.00

THE AMERICAN BUILDER'S COMPANION, Asher Benjamin. The most widely used early 19th century architectural style and source book, for colonial up into Greek Revival periods. Extensive development of geometry of carpentering, construction of sashes, frames, doors, stairs; plans and elevations of domestic and other buildings. Hundreds of thousands of houses were built according to this book, now invaluable to historians, architects, restorers, etc. 1827 edition. 59 plates. 114pp. 7⅞ x 10¾.
22236-5 Paperbound $3.50

DUTCH HOUSES IN THE HUDSON VALLEY BEFORE 1776, Helen Wilkinson Reynolds. The standard survey of the Dutch colonial house and outbuildings, with constructional features, decoration, and local history associated with individual homesteads. Introduction by Franklin D. Roosevelt. Map. 150 illustrations. 469pp. 6⅝ x 9¼. 21469-9 Paperbound $5.00

CATALOGUE OF DOVER BOOKS

THE ARCHITECTURE OF COUNTRY HOUSES, Andrew J. Downing. Together with Vaux's *Villas and Cottages* this is the basic book for Hudson River Gothic architecture of the middle Victorian period. Full, sound discussions of general aspects of housing, architecture, style, decoration, furnishing, together with scores of detailed house plans, illustrations of specific buildings, accompanied by full text. Perhaps the most influential single American architectural book. 1850 edition. Introduction by J. Stewart Johnson. 321 figures, 34 architectural designs. xvi + 560pp.
22003-6 Paperbound $4.00

LOST EXAMPLES OF COLONIAL ARCHITECTURE, John Mead Howells. Full-page photographs of buildings that have disappeared or been so altered as to be denatured, including many designed by major early American architects. 245 plates. xvii + 248pp. 7⅞ x 10¾.
21143-6 Paperbound $3.50

DOMESTIC ARCHITECTURE OF THE AMERICAN COLONIES AND OF THE EARLY REPUBLIC, Fiske Kimball. Foremost architect and restorer of Williamsburg and Monticello covers nearly 200 homes between 1620-1825. Architectural details, construction, style features, special fixtures, floor plans, etc. Generally considered finest work in its area. 219 illustrations of houses, doorways, windows, capital mantels. xx + 314pp. 7⅞ x 10¾.
21743-4 Paperbound $4.00

EARLY AMERICAN ROOMS: 1650-1858, edited by Russell Hawes Kettell. Tour of 12 rooms, each representative of a different era in American history and each furnished, decorated, designed and occupied in the style of the era. 72 plans and elevations, 8-page color section, etc., show fabrics, wall papers, arrangements, etc. Full descriptive text. xvii + 200pp. of text. 8⅜ x 11¼.
21633-0 Paperbound $5.00

THE FITZWILLIAM VIRGINAL BOOK, edited by J. Fuller Maitland and W. B. Squire. Full modern printing of famous early 17th-century ms. volume of 300 works by Morley, Byrd, Bull, Gibbons, etc. For piano or other modern keyboard instrument; easy to read format. xxxvi + 938pp. 8⅜ x 11.
21068-5, 21069-3 Two volumes, Paperbound $10.00

KEYBOARD MUSIC, Johann Sebastian Bach. Bach Gesellschaft edition. A rich selection of Bach's masterpieces for the harpsichord: the six English Suites, six French Suites, the six Partitas (Clavierübung part I), the Goldberg Variations (Clavierübung part IV), the fifteen Two-Part Inventions and the fifteen Three-Part Sinfonias. Clearly reproduced on large sheets with ample margins; eminently playable. vi + 312pp. 8⅛ x 11.
22360-4 Paperbound $5.00

THE MUSIC OF BACH: AN INTRODUCTION, Charles Sanford Terry. A fine, non-technical introduction to Bach's music, both instrumental and vocal. Covers organ music, chamber music, passion music, other types. Analyzes themes, developments, innovations. x + 114pp.
21075-8 Paperbound $1.50

BEETHOVEN AND HIS NINE SYMPHONIES, Sir George Grove. Noted British musicologist provides best history, analysis, commentary on symphonies. Very thorough, rigorously accurate; necessary to both advanced student and amateur music lover. 436 musical passages. vii + 407 pp.
20334-4 Paperbound $2.75

## CATALOGUE OF DOVER BOOKS

JOHANN SEBASTIAN BACH, Philipp Spitta. One of the great classics of musicology, this definitive analysis of Bach's music (and life) has never been surpassed. Lucid, nontechnical analyses of hundreds of pieces (30 pages devoted to St. Matthew Passion, 26 to B Minor Mass). Also includes major analysis of 18th-century music. 450 musical examples. 40-page musical supplement. Total of xx + 1799pp.
(EUK) 22278-0, 22279-9 Two volumes, Clothbound $17.50

MOZART AND HIS PIANO CONCERTOS, Cuthbert Girdlestone. The only full-length study of an important area of Mozart's creativity. Provides detailed analyses of all 23 concertos, traces inspirational sources. 417 musical examples. Second edition. 509pp. 21271-8 Paperbound $3.50

THE PERFECT WAGNERITE: A COMMENTARY ON THE NIBLUNG'S RING, George Bernard Shaw. Brilliant and still relevant criticism in remarkable essays on Wagner's Ring cycle, Shaw's ideas on political and social ideology behind the plots, role of Leitmotifs, vocal requisites, etc. Prefaces. xxi + 136pp.
(USO) 21707-8 Paperbound $1.50

DON GIOVANNI, W. A. Mozart. Complete libretto, modern English translation; biographies of composer and librettist; accounts of early performances and critical reaction. Lavishly illustrated. All the material you need to understand and appreciate this great work. Dover Opera Guide and Libretto Series; translated and introduced by Ellen Bleiler. 92 illustrations. 209pp.
21134-7 Paperbound $2.00

BASIC ELECTRICITY, U. S. Bureau of Naval Personel. Originally a training course, best non-technical coverage of basic theory of electricity and its applications. Fundamental concepts, batteries, circuits, conductors and wiring techniques, AC and DC, inductance and capacitance, generators, motors, transformers, magnetic amplifiers, synchros, servomechanisms, etc. Also covers blue-prints, electrical diagrams, etc. Many questions, with answers. 349 illustrations. x + 448pp. 6½ x 9¼.
20973-3 Paperbound $3.50

REPRODUCTION OF SOUND, Edgar Villchur. Thorough coverage for laymen of high fidelity systems, reproducing systems in general, needles, amplifiers, preamps, loudspeakers, feedback, explaining physical background. "A rare talent for making technicalities vividly comprehensible," R. Darrell, *High Fidelity*. 69 figures. iv + 92pp. 21515-6 Paperbound $1.25

HEAR ME TALKIN' TO YA: THE STORY OF JAZZ AS TOLD BY THE MEN WHO MADE IT, Nat Shapiro and Nat Hentoff. Louis Armstrong, Fats Waller, Jo Jones, Clarence Williams, Billy Holiday, Duke Ellington, Jelly Roll Morton and dozens of other jazz greats tell how it was in Chicago's South Side, New Orleans, depression Harlem and the modern West Coast as jazz was born and grew. xvi + 429pp.
21726-4 Paperbound $3.00

FABLES OF AESOP, translated by Sir Roger L'Estrange. A reproduction of the very rare 1931 Paris edition; a selection of the most interesting fables, together with 50 imaginative drawings by Alexander Calder. v + 128pp. 6½x9¼.
21780-9 Paperbound $1.50

CATALOGUE OF DOVER BOOKS

AGAINST THE GRAIN (A REBOURS), Joris K. Huysmans. Filled with weird images, evidences of a bizarre imagination, exotic experiments with hallucinatory drugs, rich tastes and smells and the diversions of its sybarite hero Duc Jean des Esseintes, this classic novel pushed 19th-century literary decadence to its limits. Full unabridged edition. Do not confuse this with abridged editions generally sold. Introduction by Havelock Ellis. xlix + 206pp. 22190-3 Paperbound $2.00

VARIORUM SHAKESPEARE: HAMLET. Edited by Horace H. Furness; a landmark of American scholarship. Exhaustive footnotes and appendices treat all doubtful words and phrases, as well as suggested critical emendations throughout the play's history. First volume contains editor's own text, collated with all Quartos and Folios. Second volume contains full first Quarto, translations of Shakespeare's sources (Belleforest, and Saxo Grammaticus), Der Bestrafte Brudermord, and many essays on critical and historical points of interest by major authorities of past and present. Includes details of staging and costuming over the years. By far the best edition available for serious students of Shakespeare. Total of xx + 905pp.
21004-9, 21005-7, 2 volumes, Paperbound $7.00

A LIFE OF WILLIAM SHAKESPEARE, Sir Sidney Lee. This is the standard life of Shakespeare, summarizing everything known about Shakespeare and his plays. Incredibly rich in material, broad in coverage, clear and judicious, it has served thousands as the best introduction to Shakespeare. 1931 edition. 9 plates. xxix + 792pp. (USO) 21967-4 Paperbound $3.75

MASTERS OF THE DRAMA, John Gassner. Most comprehensive history of the drama in print, covering every tradition from Greeks to modern Europe and America, including India, Far East, etc. Covers more than 800 dramatists, 2000 plays, with biographical material, plot summaries, theatre history, criticism, etc. "Best of its kind in English," *New Republic*. 77 illustrations. xxii + 890pp.
20100-7 Clothbound $8.50

THE EVOLUTION OF THE ENGLISH LANGUAGE, George McKnight. The growth of English, from the 14th century to the present. Unusual, non-technical account presents basic information in very interesting form: sound shifts, change in grammar and syntax, vocabulary growth, similar topics. Abundantly illustrated with quotations. Formerly *Modern English in the Making*. xii + 590pp.
21932-1 Paperbound $3.50

AN ETYMOLOGICAL DICTIONARY OF MODERN ENGLISH, Ernest Weekley. Fullest, richest work of its sort, by foremost British lexicographer. Detailed word histories, including many colloquial and archaic words; extensive quotations. Do not confuse this with the Concise Etymological Dictionary, which is much abridged. Total of xxvii + 830pp. 6½ x 9¼.
21873-2, 21874-0 Two volumes, Paperbound $7.90

FLATLAND: A ROMANCE OF MANY DIMENSIONS, E. A. Abbott. Classic of science-fiction explores ramifications of life in a two-dimensional world, and what happens when a three-dimensional being intrudes. Amusing reading, but also useful as introduction to thought about hyperspace. Introduction by Banesh Hoffmann. 16 illustrations. xx + 103pp. 20001-9 Paperbound $1.00

CATALOGUE OF DOVER BOOKS

POEMS OF ANNE BRADSTREET, edited with an introduction by Robert Hutchinson. A new selection of poems by America's first poet and perhaps the first significant woman poet in the English language. 48 poems display her development in works of considerable variety—love poems, domestic poems, religious meditations, formal elegies, "quaternions," etc. Notes, bibliography. viii + 222pp.
22160-1 Paperbound $2.50

THREE GOTHIC NOVELS: THE CASTLE OF OTRANTO BY HORACE WALPOLE; VATHEK BY WILLIAM BECKFORD; THE VAMPYRE BY JOHN POLIDORI, WITH FRAGMENT OF A NOVEL BY LORD BYRON, edited by E. F. Bleiler. The first Gothic novel, by Walpole; the finest Oriental tale in English, by Beckford; powerful Romantic supernatural story in versions by Polidori and Byron. All extremely important in history of literature; all still exciting, packed with supernatural thrills, ghosts, haunted castles, magic, etc. xl + 291pp.
21232-7 Paperbound $2.50

THE BEST TALES OF HOFFMANN, E. T. A. Hoffmann. 10 of Hoffmann's most important stories, in modern re-editings of standard translations: Nutcracker and the King of Mice, Signor Formica, Automata, The Sandman, Rath Krespel, The Golden Flowerpot, Master Martin the Cooper, The Mines of Falun, The King's Betrothed, A New Year's Eve Adventure. 7 illustrations by Hoffmann. Edited by E. F. Bleiler. xxxix + 419pp. 21793-0 Paperbound $3.00

GHOST AND HORROR STORIES OF AMBROSE BIERCE, Ambrose Bierce. 23 strikingly modern stories of the horrors latent in the human mind: The Eyes of the Panther, The Damned Thing, An Occurrence at Owl Creek Bridge, An Inhabitant of Carcosa, etc., plus the dream-essay, Visions of the Night. Edited by E. F. Bleiler. xxii + 199pp. 20767-6 Paperbound $1.50

BEST GHOST STORIES OF J. S. LEFANU, J. Sheridan LeFanu. Finest stories by Victorian master often considered greatest supernatural writer of all. Carmilla, Green Tea, The Haunted Baronet, The Familiar, and 12 others. Most never before available in the U. S. A. Edited by E. F. Bleiler. 8 illustrations from Victorian publications. xvii + 467pp. 20415-4 Paperbound $3.00

MATHEMATICAL FOUNDATIONS OF INFORMATION THEORY, A. I. Khinchin. Comprehensive introduction to work of Shannon, McMillan, Feinstein and Khinchin, placing these investigations on a rigorous mathematical basis. Covers entropy concept in probability theory, uniqueness theorem, Shannon's inequality, ergodic sources, the E property, martingale concept, noise, Feinstein's fundamental lemma, Shanon's first and second theorems. Translated by R. A. Silverman and M. D. Friedman. iii + 120pp. 60434-9 Paperbound $2.00

SEVEN SCIENCE FICTION NOVELS, H. G. Wells. The standard collection of the great novels. Complete, unabridged. *First Men in the Moon, Island of Dr. Moreau, War of the Worlds, Food of the Gods, Invisible Man, Time Machine, In the Days of the Comet.* Not only science fiction fans, but every educated person owes it to himself to read these novels. 1015pp. (USO) 20264-X Clothbound $6.00

CATALOGUE OF DOVER BOOKS

LAST AND FIRST MEN AND STAR MAKER, TWO SCIENCE FICTION NOVELS, Olaf Stapledon. Greatest future histories in science fiction. In the first, human intelligence is the "hero," through strange paths of evolution, interplanetary invasions, incredible technologies, near extinctions and reemergences. Star Maker describes the quest of a band of star rovers for intelligence itself, through time and space: weird inhuman civilizations, crustacean minds, symbiotic worlds, etc. Complete, unabridged. v + 438pp. (USO) 21962-3 Paperbound $2.50

THREE PROPHETIC NOVELS, H. G. WELLS. Stages of a consistently planned future for mankind. *When the Sleeper Wakes,* and *A Story of the Days to Come,* anticipate *Brave New World* and *1984,* in the 21st Century; *The Time Machine,* only complete version in print, shows farther future and the end of mankind. All show Wells's greatest gifts as storyteller and novelist. Edited by E. F. Bleiler. x + 335pp. (USO) 20605-X Paperbound $2.50

THE DEVIL'S DICTIONARY, Ambrose Bierce. America's own Oscar Wilde—Ambrose Bierce—offers his barbed iconoclastic wisdom in over 1,000 definitions hailed by H. L. Mencken as "some of the most gorgeous witticisms in the English language." 145pp. 20487-1 Paperbound $1.25

MAX AND MORITZ, Wilhelm Busch. Great children's classic, father of comic strip, of two bad boys, Max and Moritz. Also Ker and Plunk (Plisch und Plumm), Cat and Mouse, Deceitful Henry, Ice-Peter, The Boy and the Pipe, and five other pieces. Original German, with English translation. Edited by H. Arthur Klein; translations by various hands and H. Arthur Klein. vi + 216pp.
20181-3 Paperbound $2.00

PIGS IS PIGS AND OTHER FAVORITES, Ellis Parker Butler. The title story is one of the best humor short stories, as Mike Flannery obfuscates biology and English. Also included, That Pup of Murchison's, The Great American Pie Company, and Perkins of Portland. 14 illustrations. v + 109pp. 21532-6 Paperbound $1.25

THE PETERKIN PAPERS, Lucretia P. Hale. It takes genius to be as stupidly mad as the Peterkins, as they decide to become wise, celebrate the "Fourth," keep a cow, and otherwise strain the resources of the Lady from Philadelphia. Basic book of American humor. 153 illustrations. 219pp. 20794-3 Paperbound $1.50

PERRAULT'S FAIRY TALES, translated by A. E. Johnson and S. R. Littlewood, with 34 full-page illustrations by Gustave Doré. All the original Perrault stories—Cinderella, Sleeping Beauty, Bluebeard, Little Red Riding Hood, Puss in Boots, Tom Thumb, etc.—with their witty verse morals and the magnificent illustrations of Doré. One of the five or six great books of European fairy tales. viii + 117pp. 8⅛ x 11. 22311-6 Paperbound $2.00

OLD HUNGARIAN FAIRY TALES, Baroness Orczy. Favorites translated and adapted by author of the *Scarlet Pimpernel.* Eight fairy tales include "The Suitors of Princess Fire-Fly," "The Twin Hunchbacks," "Mr. Cuttlefish's Love Story," and "The Enchanted Cat." This little volume of magic and adventure will captivate children as it has for generations. 90 drawings by Montagu Barstow. 96pp.
22293-4 Paperbound $1.95

CATALOGUE OF DOVER BOOKS

THE RED FAIRY BOOK, Andrew Lang. Lang's color fairy books have long been children's favorites. This volume includes Rapunzel, Jack and the Bean-stalk and 35 other stories, familiar and unfamiliar. 4 plates, 93 illustrations x + 367pp.
21673-X Paperbound $2.50

THE BLUE FAIRY BOOK, Andrew Lang. Lang's tales come from all countries and all times. Here are 37 tales from Grimm, the Arabian Nights, Greek Mythology, and other fascinating sources. 8 plates, 130 illustrations. xi + 390pp.
21437-0 Paperbound $2.50

HOUSEHOLD STORIES BY THE BROTHERS GRIMM. Classic English-language edition of the well-known tales — Rumpelstiltskin, Snow White, Hansel and Gretel, The Twelve Brothers, Faithful John, Rapunzel, Tom Thumb (52 stories in all). Translated into simple, straightforward English by Lucy Crane. Ornamented with headpieces, vignettes, elaborate decorative initials and a dozen full-page illustrations by Walter Crane. x + 269pp.
21080-4 Paperbound **$2.00**

THE MERRY ADVENTURES OF ROBIN HOOD, Howard Pyle. The finest modern versions of the traditional ballads and tales about the great English outlaw. Howard Pyle's complete prose version, with every word, every illustration of the first edition. Do not confuse this facsimile of the original (1883) with modern editions that change text or illustrations. 23 plates plus many page decorations. xxii + 296pp.
22043-5 Paperbound $2.50

THE STORY OF KING ARTHUR AND HIS KNIGHTS, Howard Pyle. The finest children's version of the life of King Arthur; brilliantly retold by Pyle, with 48 of his most imaginative illustrations. xviii + 313pp. 6⅛ x 9¼.
21445-1 Paperbound $2.50

THE WONDERFUL WIZARD OF OZ, L. Frank Baum. America's finest children's book in facsimile of first edition with all Denslow illustrations in full color. The edition a child should have. Introduction by Martin Gardner. 23 color plates, scores of drawings. iv + 267pp.
20691-2 Paperbound $2.50

THE MARVELOUS LAND OF OZ, L. Frank Baum. The second Oz book, every bit as imaginative as the Wizard. The hero is a boy named Tip, but the Scarecrow and the Tin Woodman are back, as is the Oz magic. 16 color plates, 120 drawings by John R. Neill. 287pp.
20692-0 Paperbound $2.50

THE MAGICAL MONARCH OF MO, L. Frank Baum. Remarkable adventures in a land even stranger than Oz. The best of Baum's books not in the Oz series. 15 color plates and dozens of drawings by Frank Verbeck. xviii + 237pp.
21892-9 Paperbound $2.25

THE BAD CHILD'S BOOK OF BEASTS, MORE BEASTS FOR WORSE CHILDREN, A MORAL ALPHABET, Hilaire Belloc. Three complete humor classics in one volume. Be kind to the frog, and do not call him names . . . and 28 other whimsical animals. Familiar favorites and some not so well known. Illustrated by Basil Blackwell. 156pp.
(USO) 20749-8 Paperbound $1.50

## CATALOGUE OF DOVER BOOKS

EAST O' THE SUN AND WEST O' THE MOON, George W. Dasent. Considered the best of all translations of these Norwegian folk tales, this collection has been enjoyed by generations of children (and folklorists too). Includes True and Untrue, Why the Sea is Salt, East O' the Sun and West O' the Moon, Why the Bear is Stumpy-Tailed, Boots and the Troll, The Cock and the Hen, Rich Peter the Pedlar, and 52 more. The only edition with all 59 tales. 77 illustrations by Erik Werenskiold and Theodor Kittelsen. xv + 418pp. 22521-6 Paperbound $3.50

GOOPS AND HOW TO BE THEM, Gelett Burgess. Classic of tongue-in-cheek humor, masquerading as etiquette book. 87 verses, twice as many cartoons, show mischievous Goops as they demonstrate to children virtues of table manners, neatness, courtesy, etc. Favorite for generations. viii + 88pp. 6½ x 9¼.
22233-0 Paperbound $1.25

ALICE'S ADVENTURES UNDER GROUND, Lewis Carroll. The first version, quite different from the final *Alice in Wonderland*, printed out by Carroll himself with his own illustrations. Complete facsimile of the "million dollar" manuscript Carroll gave to Alice Liddell in 1864. Introduction by Martin Gardner. viii + 96pp. Title and dedication pages in color. 21482-6 Paperbound $1.25

THE BROWNIES, THEIR BOOK, Palmer Cox. Small as mice, cunning as foxes, exuberant and full of mischief, the Brownies go to the zoo, toy shop, seashore, circus, etc., in 24 verse adventures and 266 illustrations. Long a favorite, since their first appearance in St. Nicholas Magazine. xi + 144pp. 6⅝ x 9¼.
21265-3 Paperbound $1.75

SONGS OF CHILDHOOD, Walter De La Mare. Published (under the pseudonym Walter Ramal) when De La Mare was only 29, this charming collection has long been a favorite children's book. A facsimile of the first edition in paper, the 47 poems capture the simplicity of the nursery rhyme and the ballad, including such lyrics as I Met Eve, Tartary, The Silver Penny. vii + 106pp. (USO) 21972-0 Paperbound $1.25

THE COMPLETE NONSENSE OF EDWARD LEAR, Edward Lear. The finest 19th-century humorist-cartoonist in full: all nonsense limericks, zany alphabets, Owl and Pussycat, songs, nonsense botany, and more than 500 illustrations by Lear himself. Edited by Holbrook Jackson. xxix + 287pp. (USO) 20167-8 Paperbound $2.00

BILLY WHISKERS: THE AUTOBIOGRAPHY OF A GOAT, Frances Trego Montgomery. A favorite of children since the early 20th century, here are the escapades of that rambunctious, irresistible and mischievous goat—Billy Whiskers. Much in the spirit of *Peck's Bad Boy*, this is a book that children never tire of reading or hearing. All the original familiar illustrations by W. H. Fry are included: 6 color plates, 18 black and white drawings. 159pp. 22345-0 Paperbound $2.00

MOTHER GOOSE MELODIES. Faithful republication of the fabulously rare Munroe and Francis "copyright 1833" Boston edition—the most important Mother Goose collection, usually referred to as the "original." Familiar rhymes plus many rare ones, with wonderful old woodcut illustrations. Edited by E. F. Bleiler. 128pp. 4½ x 6⅜. 22577-1 Paperbound $1.00

## CATALOGUE OF DOVER BOOKS

TWO LITTLE SAVAGES; BEING THE ADVENTURES OF TWO BOYS WHO LIVED AS INDIANS AND WHAT THEY LEARNED, Ernest Thompson Seton. Great classic of nature and boyhood provides a vast range of woodlore in most palatable form, a genuinely entertaining story. Two farm boys build a teepee in woods and live in it for a month, working out Indian solutions to living problems, star lore, birds and animals, plants, etc. 293 illustrations. vii + 286pp.
20985-7 Paperbound $2.50

PETER PIPER'S PRACTICAL PRINCIPLES OF PLAIN & PERFECT PRONUNCIATION. Alliterative jingles and tongue-twisters of surprising charm, that made their first appearance in America about 1830. Republished in full with the spirited woodcut illustrations from this earliest American edition. 32pp. 4½ x 6⅜.
22560-7 Paperbound $1.00

SCIENCE EXPERIMENTS AND AMUSEMENTS FOR CHILDREN, Charles Vivian. 73 easy experiments, requiring only materials found at home or easily available, such as candles, coins, steel wool, etc.; illustrate basic phenomena like vacuum, simple chemical reaction, etc. All safe. Modern, well-planned. Formerly *Science Games for Children*. 102 photos, numerous drawings. 96pp. 6⅛ x 9¼.
21856-2 Paperbound $1.25

AN INTRODUCTION TO CHESS MOVES AND TACTICS SIMPLY EXPLAINED, Leonard Barden. Informal intermediate introduction, quite strong in explaining reasons for moves. Covers basic material, tactics, important openings, traps, positional play in middle game, end game. Attempts to isolate patterns and recurrent configurations. Formerly *Chess*. 58 figures. 102pp. (USO) 21210-6 Paperbound $1.25

LASKER'S MANUAL OF CHESS, Dr. Emanuel Lasker. Lasker was not only one of the five great World Champions, he was also one of the ablest expositors, theorists, and analysts. In many ways, his Manual, permeated with his philosophy of battle, filled with keen insights, is one of the greatest works ever written on chess. Filled with analyzed games by the great players. A single-volume library that will profit almost any chess player, beginner or master. 308 diagrams. xli x 349pp.
20640-8 Paperbound $2.75

THE MASTER BOOK OF MATHEMATICAL RECREATIONS, Fred Schuh. In opinion of many the finest work ever prepared on mathematical puzzles, stunts, recreations; exhaustively thorough explanations of mathematics involved, analysis of effects, citation of puzzles and games. Mathematics involved is elementary. Translated by F. Göbel. 194 figures. xxiv + 430pp. 22134-2 Paperbound $3.50

MATHEMATICS, MAGIC AND MYSTERY, Martin Gardner. Puzzle editor for Scientific American explains mathematics behind various mystifying tricks: card tricks, stage "mind reading," coin and match tricks, counting out games, geometric dissections, etc. Probability sets, theory of numbers clearly explained. Also provides more than 400 tricks, guaranteed to work, that you can do. 135 illustrations. xii + 176pp.
20335-2 Paperbound $1.75

## CATALOGUE OF DOVER BOOKS

MATHEMATICAL PUZZLES FOR BEGINNERS AND ENTHUSIASTS, Geoffrey Mott-Smith. 189 puzzles from easy to difficult—involving arithmetic, logic, algebra, properties of digits, probability, etc.—for enjoyment and mental stimulus. Explanation of mathematical principles behind the puzzles. 135 illustrations. viii + 248pp.
20198-8 Paperbound $1.75

PAPER FOLDING FOR BEGINNERS, William D. Murray and Francis J. Rigney. Easiest book on the market, clearest instructions on making interesting, beautiful origami. Sail boats, cups, roosters, frogs that move legs, bonbon boxes, standing birds, etc. 40 projects; more than 275 diagrams and photographs. 94pp.
20713-7 Paperbound $1.00

TRICKS AND GAMES ON THE POOL TABLE, Fred Herrmann. 79 tricks and games—some solitaires, some for two or more players, some competitive games—to entertain you between formal games. Mystifying shots and throws, unusual caroms, tricks involving such props as cork, coins, a hat, etc. Formerly *Fun on the Pool Table*. 77 figures. 95pp.
21814-7 Paperbound $1.00

HAND SHADOWS TO BE THROWN UPON THE WALL: A SERIES OF NOVEL AND AMUSING FIGURES FORMED BY THE HAND, Henry Bursill. Delightful picturebook from great-grandfather's day shows how to make 18 different hand shadows: a bird that flies, duck that quacks, dog that wags his tail, camel, goose, deer, boy, turtle, etc. Only book of its sort. vi + 33pp. 6½ x 9¼.
21779-5 Paperbound $1.00

WHITTLING AND WOODCARVING, E. J. Tangerman. 18th printing of best book on market. "If you can cut a potato you can carve" toys and puzzles, chains, chessmen, caricatures, masks, frames, woodcut blocks, surface patterns, much more. Information on tools, woods, techniques. Also goes into serious wood sculpture from Middle Ages to present, East and West. 464 photos, figures. x + 293pp.
20965-2 Paperbound $2.00

HISTORY OF PHILOSOPHY, Julián Marias. Possibly the clearest, most easily followed, best planned, most useful one-volume history of philosophy on the market; neither skimpy nor overfull. Full details on system of every major philosopher and dozens of less important thinkers from pre-Socratics up to Existentialism and later. Strong on many European figures usually omitted. Has gone through dozens of editions in Europe. 1966 edition, translated by Stanley Appelbaum and Clarence Strowbridge. xviii + 505pp.
21739-6 Paperbound $3.50

YOGA: A SCIENTIFIC EVALUATION, Kovoor T. Behanan. Scientific but non-technical study of physiological results of yoga exercises; done under auspices of Yale U. Relations to Indian thought, to psychoanalysis, etc. 16 photos. xxiii + 270pp.
20505-3 Paperbound $2.50

*Prices subject to change without notice.*
Available at your book dealer or write for free catalogue to Dept. GI, Dover Publications, Inc., 180 Varick St., N. Y., N. Y. 10014. Dover publishes more than 150 books each year on science, elementary and advanced mathematics, biology, music, art, literary history, social sciences and other areas.